Social Security Law in Turkey

Social Security Law in Turkey

Second Edition

Kübra Doğan-Yenisey

This book was originally published as a monograph in the International Encyclopaedia of Laws/Social Security Law.

Founding Editor: Roger Blanpain
General Editor: Frank Hendrickx
Volume Editor: Willy van Eeckhoutte

Wolters Kluwer

Published by:
Kluwer Law International B.V.
PO Box 316
2400 AH Alphen aan den Rijn
The Netherlands
E-mail: international-sales@wolterskluwer.com
Website: lrus.wolterskluwer.com

Sold and distributed in North, Central and South America by:
Wolters Kluwer Legal & Regulatory U.S.
7201 McKinney Circle
Frederick, MD 21704
United States of America
Email: customer.service@wolterskluwer.com

Sold and distributed in all other countries by:
Air Business Subscriptions
Rockwood House
Haywards Heath
West Sussex
RH16 3DH
United Kingdom
Email: international-customerservice@wolterskluwer.com

Printed on acid-free paper

ISBN 978-94-035-1874-9

e-Book: ISBN 978-94-035-1900-5
web-PDF: ISBN 978-94-035-1912-8

Printed in the United Kingdom.

The Author

Dr Kübra Doğan-Yenisey graduated from the Faculty of Law, the University of Ankara, Turkey, in 1992. In the same year, she joined the Department of Labour and Social Security Law of the Management Faculty, Istanbul Technical University, Turkey. She received her MA from the Faculty of Law, the University of Marmara, Turkey, in 1994. In 1996, she went to Switzerland as a scholarship holder of Swiss Confederation and studied Labour and Social Security Law at the University of Geneva, Switzerland. In 1998, she received her DES, and earned her PhD by her thesis on 'La modification du contrat de travail, Etude de droit suisse et de droit français' (published by Schultess) in 2000.

Since 2008, Dr Doğan-Yenisey is working as Professor at Istanbul Bilgi University, Faculty of Law. Her main interests are labour and social security law issues and comparative law studies. She is a member of the International Society for Labour and Social Security Law.

The Author

Table of Contents

List of Abbreviations

Bağ-Kur	Esnaf ve Sanatkarlar ve Diğer Bağımsız ÇalıŞanlar Sosyal Sigortalar Kurumu (Social Insurance Institution for Tradesmen and Artisans and Other Self-Employed Persons)
Ch.	Chamber
Cons. Court	Constitutional Court
Court of Cass.	Court of Cassation (Yargıtay)
ILO	International Labour Organization
IMF	International Monetary Fund
İş-Kur	Türkiye İş Kurumu (The Turkish Employment Institution)
LA	Labour Act
OJ	Official Journal
OYAK	Ordu Yardımlaşma Kurumu
RGPI	Regulation on Granting Pensions to Persons over 65 and Indigents
RMRSCS	Regulation on Medical Reports issued in case of Sickness of Civil Servants
RSIP	Regulation on Social Insurance Procedures
RUHIP	Regulation on Universal Health Insurance Procedures
RUHIRCB	Regulation on Universal Health Insurance Registration, Confirmation and Benefits Owners
RWGF	Regulation on Wage Guarantee Fund
TCO	Turkish Code of Obligations
US	United States

List of Abbreviations

General Introduction

Chapter 1. Social and Economic Background

1. Turkey is located between Asia and Europe and has 79,814,871 inhabitants (by 2016). Its 779,452 sq. km are located between south-eastern Europe and south-western Asia. The country is surrounded by Greece, Bulgaria, Georgia, Azerbaijan, Armenia, Iran, Iraq, Syria and three different seas: the Black, Mediterranean and Aegean Seas.

2. The Turkish Republic was founded on 29 October 1923. As emphasized in the Constitution, it is a democratic, secular and welfare state. The unitary nature of the state is an important feature of its administrative structure which has been constructed on the French model. Its legal system belongs to the Roman-German family of law.

3. Turkey's economy is a complex mix of modern industry and commerce along with a traditional agriculture sector that employed about 19% of the population in 2016. The largest industrial sector is textiles and clothing. In addition, the automotive and electronics sectors have rising importance in the area of exports. Over the past decade, the Turkish economy has suffered from several important crises in 1994, 1997, 2000 and 2001. These crises affected the unemployment rate to a very important degree. However, the recent unemployment rate is about 11%.[1]

4. The grave amount of informal employment in the country lies at the basis of the deficiencies in the social security system. Including dependants and pensioners, about 65.3 million people, equal to 81.83% of the population are covered by the social security system. The greater part of the population is young. However, age projections indicate that this population profile will rapidly age.[2]

As of 2018, the population subjected to Article 4/I-a of Act No. 5510, mainly wage earners, is about 14,218,231. The number of pensioners is 7,454,358 and dependants' number is 19,750,636. The total population group subjected to Article 4/I-a is 43,243,212, which is about 54.18% of the total population.[3]

1. *See* Unemployment Statistics from Turkish Statistical Institute, www.tuik.gov.tr.
2. Turkish Statistical Institute, Population Projections, 2013–2075, retrieved 1 Mar. 2013 from www.turkstat.gov.tr/PreHaberBultenleri.do?id=15844.
3. www.sgk.gov.tr/wps/portal/sgk/tr/kurumsal/istatistik, retrieved 1 Mar. 2018 from http://www.sgk.gov.tr.

There are a total of 14,824,457 Self-Employed persons subjected to Article 4/I-b – this means 2,908,530 people are actively insured, 2,587,070 are pensioners and the rest dependants. This equals 18.57% of the population.[4]

A total of 2,990,952 contributors and approximately 2,135,582 pensioners and 6,579,481 dependants, in total 14.66% of the population, is subjected to Article 4/I-c, mainly public officers.[5]

A total of 9,865,166 people are universal health insurance holders.[6]

5. The social security system was constructed progressively by different legislative interventions. The legal status of the working relationship has determined the social security regime to which a person is subjected. Before the reform, those who worked under a contract of employment had been receiving social security benefits from the Social Insurance Institution, those who were Self-Employed from Bağ-Kur, and civil servants from the public entities who employed them and when they were retired from the Pension Fund. An extended legislative reform has brought about two-step reform of the system. First, as of 20 May 2005, the three institutions responsible for providing social security services have been unified into one single institution. Second, the conditions and services of these three formerly different systems have been unified to a certain degree.

---

4. www.sgk.gov.tr/wps/portal/sgk/tr/kurumsal/istatistik, retrieved 1Mar. 2018 from http://www.sgk.gov.tr.
5. www.sgk.gov.tr/wps/portal/sgk/tr/kurumsal/istatistik, retrieved 1 Mar. 2018 from http://www.sgk.gov.tr.
6. www.sgk.gov.tr/wps/portal/sgk/tr/kurumsal/istatistik, retrieved 1 Mar. 2018 from http://www.sgk.gov.tr.

Chapter 2. Historical Background

6. The evaluation of a society's social security depends upon a consideration of its social and economic development. Thus, a study of the history of social security law in Turkey may be divided into three different periods.[7]

§1. The Pre-Republican Period

7. Since the Ottoman Empire had not undergone an industrial revolution as Western societies had, the need for a formal system of social security did not arise in society. Thus, dispersed and restricted social security measures were not transformed into an organized social security system. In the Ottoman Empire, social security was provided by family assistance, professional solidarity and foundations.

8. Even today, the family has a central place in social relations. The first institution which comes to mind whenever a person falls in difficulty remains the family. This fact has also prevented the perception of social protection as a social need and slowed down the evaluation of social politics vis-a-vis social risks.

A more organized assistance system had been provided by religious fraternity guilds since the thirteenth century. Mutual assistance funds organized by craftsmen and artisans within the framework of religious fraternities were the first formal social security institutions in the Ottoman period. After the fifteenth century, guilds of a religious nature were replaced by ones established mostly on a professional basis. Their mutual funds were financed by members' contributions, donations, and special fees paid by master workmen on the occasion of apprenticeships completed under their direction. This system of professional solidarity survived until the end of the nineteenth century.

The real distinguishing characteristic of the Ottoman period was the much-diversified number of foundations. Foundations as social, legal and economic institutions played a very significant role in providing social security. Even certain public services, such as education, health, social assistance, urban and municipal services, were furnished by the government through foundations.

9. The earliest known labour legislation in the Ottoman period dates from 1865. A regulation on mines, issued in 1869, was the very first legislation to specify health and safety regulations as well as employers' responsibility in case of an industrial accident. In addition, some special financial funds with a narrow field of application against the risks of old age and sickness are examples of the very restricted social security applications in the Ottoman Empire.

7. K. Tunçomağ, *Sosyal Sigortalar* (Istanbul, Beta, 1990), pp. 39–49; A. Güzel/A.R. Okur/N. Caniklioğlu, *Sosyal Güvenlik Hukuku* (Istanbul, Beta, 2016), pp. 23–31; C. Tuncay/Ö. Ekmekçi, *Sosyal Güvenlik Hukuku Dersleri* (Istanbul, Beta, 2016), pp. 83–93; Y. Alper, *Türk Sosyal Güvenlik Sistemi ve Sosyal Sigortalar Hukuku*(Bursa, Ekin, 2016), pp. 4–19; M. Şakar, *Sosyal Sigortalar Uygulaması* (Istanbul, Beta, 2017), pp. 2842; K. Arıcı, *Türk Sosyal Güvenlik Hukuku*(Ankara, Gazi, 2015), pp. 6592.

§2. THE PRE-REPUBLICAN PERIOD OF THE TURKISH GRAND NATIONAL ASSEMBLY

10. During the Independence War against the Entente powers (1919–1922), Act Nos 151 and 114 were passed with a view to protecting coal miners in the Zonguldak and Ereli regions by regulating their working conditions and providing some social security allowances. By Act No. 114, forced labour and the employment of children under the age of 18 were prohibited. Furthermore, the daily working hours were limited to eight. According to Act No. 151, employers were obliged to provide free health treatment to employees who had suffered an industrial accident or sickness. In order to conform to this obligation, employers were to establish a hospital or clinic near the workplace. In case of injury, the employer was to pay an indemnity to the employee, or in case of the loss of life, to his surviving family. Moreover, due to this Act, funds for reserve funds and mutual assistance had been established.

§3. THE REPUBLICAN PERIOD

I. The Period before the Social Security Reform

11. Act No. 3008, dated 1936, for the very first time after the proclamation of the Republic, established certain fundaments of a social insurance system. However, it was difficult to consider this system as a unified and extended system. Until 1945, only certain statutory regulations with a very narrow field of application with respect to either risks or beneficiaries were enacted.

12. After the Second World War, the importance of social politics was discovered in Turkey. By Act No. 4772 on Industrial Accidents, Occupational Diseases and Maternity passed on 27 September 1945, insurance for industrial accidents and maternity was established. This Act was replaced by Act No. 5502 in 1950, which brought insurance for health and maternity together. With respect to other insurance branches, Act No. 5417 concerning old-age insurance was adopted in 1949 and, with a series of amendments (Acts Nos 5752, 5937, 6931, and 6708), remained in force until 1957. A new act No. 6900, regarding invalidity, old age and survivors' insurance was passed and came into force on 1 June 1957. Only employees were covered by these Acts. On 1 January 1946, the Employee Insurance Institution (Social Insurance Institution) was established. In addition to social security for employees, in 1949, Act No. 5434 concerning Civil Servants' Pensions Fund provided social security to civil servants.

In 1961, social security was far from being a unified system with an expanded scope. Benefits provided by diversified Acts were insufficient. A large number of dependant employees were excluded from social insurance cover. Moreover, Self-Employed workers had no social security.

13. The Political Reform of 27 May 1960 prompted and implemented a new approach to social and economic problems. The new Constitution of 1961, in addition to other economic and social rights, recognized the right to social security as a fundamental right. According to Article 48 of the 1961 Constitution, 'Everybody has a right to social security'. In order to ensure this right, the state was under the duty to establish a social insurance and social assistance organization. The Constitutional Court had emphasized that the rule of law only had a sense within the context of a social welfare state. Thus, the state was under an obligation to bring about substantial equality and social balance by protecting vulnerable groups in society.[8]

However, these duties were to be fulfilled within its economic and financial capacities (Article 53 of Constitution 1961). Nevertheless, it should be underlined that the Constitutional Court refrained from supervising the government with respect to the performance of its duties under the Constitution of 1961.[9]

Through social targets fixed by the Constitution of 1961 and development plans, 1961 and the following years witnessed extended reforms regarding both contributory and Non-contributory regimes. With respect to contributory regimes, Social Insurance Act No. 506 was passed on 17 July 1964 and came into force on 1 March. In 1971, artisans and all self-employed, except those working in agriculture, were covered by a special social security organization (Bağ-Kur). By Act No. 1479, the Self-Employed were provided protection against the risk of disability, old age and death. Furthermore, the scope of risks was extended, and health insurance was covered by Act No. 1479 in 1985.

14. The Constitution of 1982 also recognizes the right to social security as a constitutional right. Besides a general declaration restating that everyone has a right to social security (Article 60 Al. 1), the duty of the state to protect certain vulnerable groups is emphasized. Thus, it states that:

> The State shall protect the widows and orphans of those killed in a war and in the line of duty, together with the disabled and war veterans, and ensure that they enjoy a decent standard of living.
> The state shall take measures to protect the disabled and secure their integration into community life.
> The aged shall be protected by the state. State assistance to the aged, and other rights and benefits shall be regulated by law.
> To achieve these aims, the State shall establish the necessary organizations or facilities, or arrange for their establishment by other bodies.

15. Moreover, the state is required to take the necessary measures to ensure the social security of Turkish nationals working abroad (Article 62 of Constitution 1982).

---

8. Cons. Court., 17 Oct. 1972, 16/49, *AYMKD, 10*, p. 539.
9. B. Tanör, *Anayasa Hukukunda Sosyal Haklar* (Istanbul, 1978), pp. 377–378.

16. The welfare state is under obligation to take necessary measures and establish necessary institutions to comply with its duties. The extent of the economic and social duties of the state is also fixed by the Constitution in Article 65 according to which 'The State shall fulfil its duties as laid down in the Constitution in the economic and social fields within the capacity of its financial resources, taking into consideration the priorities appropriate to the aims of these duties' (Article 65 as amended on 17 October 2001). However, with respect to a case wherein the conformity of certain time restrictions to constitutional health insurance benefits was discussed, the Constitutional Court refused to accept Article 65 as a legal basis providing conformity of restrictions to the Constitution, basing its argument on the clear connection between health insurance benefits and the individual's right to live.[10]

17. Following the adoption of the Constitution, a wave of legislation was enacted in the field of social security. With regard to Non-contributory regimes, Act No. 2828 on Social Services and Infant Protection Institution, which was responsible for the execution of social service and protection of poor infants, aged and the disabled, was adopted in 1983. Act No. 3294 on Incentive for Social Assistance and Solidarity Fund and Act No. 2022 on Granting of Pensions to Persons over 65 and Indigents are the two important acts enacted in the 1980s. In addition, Act No. 3816, passed in 1992, provides medical assistance for persons in need.

Furthermore, with respect to contributory regimes, the coverage of social security has been extended gradually. Those who work in agriculture have acquired social security within a limited scope through Act No. 2925 on the Social Insurance of Employees Working in Agriculture, and by Act No. 2926 on Social Insurance of the Self-Employed in Agriculture. A very important extension with regard to social risks was achieved by Act No. 4447 on Unemployment Insurance, passed on 25 August 1999 which came into effect on 1 June 2000. Thus, employees have received protection against another important social risk, unemployment.

18. Following this Act, as a part of comprehensive organizational reforms, the Turkish Employment Institution replaced the Public Employment Services Organization by a Decree-Law No. 617 to govern unemployment insurance and to undertake activities to protect and develop employment. Another Decree-Law No. 616 had brought structural changes to the Social Insurance Institution. Decree-Law No. 618 proclaimed the establishment of the Social Security Institution and by Decree-Law No. 619, Bağ-Kur, for the social insurance of the self-employed, was amended. Pursuing the annulment of authorization Act No. 4588,[11] Decree-Law Nos 616, 617, 618 and 619 were annulled by the Constitutional Court.[12] New Act Nos 4958,[13]

---

10. Cons. Court, 17.1.1991, 1990/27, 1991/2, OJ, 19.8.1991, No. 20965, Judgment and notes by A. Güzel/Gökçeolu, *İHD*(Nisan-Haziran, 1993), pp. 283–298.
11. Cons. Court, 5 Oct. 2000, 45/27, OJ, 28 Oct. 2000, No. 24214.
12. Cons. Court, 26 Oct. 2000, 61/34; 31 Oct. 2000, 62/35 and 31 Oct. 2000, 63/36, OJ, 8 Nov. 2000, No. 24224 and 31 Oct. 2000, 65/38, OJ, 10 Nov. 2000, No. 24226.
13. OJ, 6 Aug. 2003, No. 25191, for further information, *see* A. Güzel/S. Ocak, '506 Sayılı Sosyal Sigortalar Kanunu'nda 4958 Sayılı Kanun İle Yapılan Değişiklikler', 1, *Legal-İSGHD*(Ocak- Mart, 2004), pp. 121–161; Y. Alper, '4958 Sayılı Kanun Sonrası Dönemde Sosyal Sigorta Uygulamaları',

4904,[14] 4947[15] and 4956[16] were adopted in 2003, enacting the principles which had essentially already been stated by the decrees. The wave of legislation also continued into 2004 with Act Nos 5073,[17] 5198[18] and 5264, [19] which brought further amendments.

II. The Reform Process

19. All these partial modifications infer problems in the system whose fundamentals have been questioned since the beginning of the 1990s.[20] Among criticisms directed at the system, the followings may be enumerated: the change in population structure, the inability of the current system to provide protection against poverty, negative impacts of the financial deficits of the social security institutions on the economy, the inability to protect the whole population and various problems of social security institutions.

20. Shortly after the coming into force of the above-mentioned acts in 2004, the Ministry of Labour and Social Insurance once again introduced a reform project. To resolve the problems of the social security system, on the basis of the model suggested by the International Monetary Fund (IMF) and World Bank, the government had undertaken to reform the social security system, aiming to unify the three institutions responsible for the social security of employees, the Self-Employed and public servants under the same organizational roof, while the fragmented nature of the Turkish social security system was considered an important defect of the system. This model is called the 'single roof' model. The problem was, on the one hand,

---

Mercek(Nisan, 2004), pp. 41–52; A.N. Sözer/C. Saraç, 'Sosyal Sigortalar Hukukunda 4958 Sayılı Kanun İle Gerçekleştirilen Değişiklikler', *Mercek*(Ekim, 2003), pp. 47–64.

14. OJ, 5 Jul. 2003, No. 25159.
15. OJ, 24 Jul. 2003, No. 25178.
16. OJ, 2 Aug. 2003, No. 25187.
17. OJ, 28 Jan. 2004, No. 25360; For further information, see A. Güzel/E. Özkaraca, '506 Sayılı Sosyal Sigortalar Kanunu'nda 4958 ve 5073 sayılı Kanunlar İle Yapılan Deiiklikler', 2, *Legal-İSGHD*(Nisan-Haziran, 2004), pp. 433–473.
18. OJ, 6 Jul. 2004, No. 25514.
19. OJ, 11 Dec. 2004, No. 25667, for further information, *see* A. Güzel/S. Ocak, '506 Sayılı Sosyal Sigortalar Kanununda 5198 ve 5264 Sayılı Kanunlar İle Yapılan DeğiŞiklikler', 5, *Legal-İSGHD*(2005), pp. 147–201.
20. *See, as example,* Y. Alper, '1990 lı Yılların BaŞında Türk Sosyal Güvenlik Sisteminin Karşılaştığı Temel Problemler', *Çimento İşv. Der.*(Kasım, 1990), pp. 3–16; The same author, 'Sosyal Güvenlik Sistemlerinde Yeniden Yapılanma İhtiyacı', in *Prof. Dr. Metin Kutal'a Arma&gbrevel;an* (Ankara, tühis, 1998), pp. 607–614; The same author, Yeni Bir Yüzyıla Girerken Yeniden Yapılanmanın Eşiğinde Sosyal Güvenlik', I, II, *Çimento İşv. Der.*(Mart, Mayıs, 1999), pp. 19–30; T. Centel, *Sosyal Güvenlikte Yapısal De&gbrevel;işim* (Istanbul, MESS, 1997), pp. 106 et seq.; A.C. Tuncay, 'Türk Sosyal Güvenlik Sisteminde Reform İhtiyacı', in *Prof. Dr. Kemal Oğuzman'a Armağan* (Ankara, Kamu-İş, 1997), pp. 349–378; C. Talas, 'Türkiye'de Sosyal Güvenlik Düzeninin Bunalımı', in *Prof. Dr. Metin Kutal'a Arma&gbrevel;an* (Ankara, tühis, 1998), pp. 641–647; A.N. Sözer, 'Bağımsız Çalışanların Sosyal Güvenlik Açısından Yeniden Yapılanmalarına İlişkin Bir Model Önerisi', in *Prof. Dr. Turhan Esener'e Armağan* (Ankara, Kamu-İş, 2000), pp. 639–658; A. Güzel, 'Türk Sosyal Güvenlik Sisteminde Yeniden Yapılandırma: Nedenler ve Amaçlar', in *Sosyal Güvenliğin Yeniden Yapılandırılması Semineri* (Ankara, 2007), pp. 27–39.

one part of society was left with no social security, and on the other hand, the level of services and benefits provided by the three Institutions differed greatly. As a result, Act No. 5502, Social Security Institution, came into force on 20 May 2006.[21] The new Social Security Institution which covers the Social Insurance Institution, Bağ-Kur and the Pension Fund, is responsible for the administration of the system.

21. This organizational reform is accompanied by substantial legal amendments with respect to conditions and kinds of service provided to insured persons. Thus, the Draft on the Reformation of Social Security was proposed on 29 July 2004 and replaced by a new one with very few amendments in April 2005. On the basis of the above-mentioned arguments, different draft acts and bills were issued: a Draft Bill on Retirement Insurance, a Draft Bill on Universal Health Insurance, and a Draft Bill on Non-contributory Regimes. Finally, a Draft Bill on Social Insurance and Universal Health Insurance was sent to Parliament. After being sent to Parliament for renewed consideration by the President, the Act was passed on 31 May 2006.[22]

22. The new Act No. 5510 brings three different regimes under one. This means that the previous legislation, originally composed of about 1034 articles, has been reduced to about 120 articles, which would facilitate the system to a considerable degree. However, the difficulty of achieving such an adaptation is obvious. While envisaging the difficulty of combining and harmonizing the three different systems under one roof, the challenge is not only economic but also juridical, as it means a loss of rights for certain groups. Thus, certain provisions of Act were brought before the Constitutional Court and annulled even before its entry into force.[23] The important part of annulled provisions was about civil servants. The unification had brought loss of rights from many perspectives for civil servants. The main argumentation of the Constitutional Court was based on the principle of equality, the requirements of the welfare state and a special provision of the Constitution, Article 128, which regulates personal rights and status of civil servants. According to the Court, since the status and the service offered by civil servants carry particularities with regard to those of wage earners and Self-Employed persons, the social security of civil servants must also be ruled by different principles than those applied to wage earners and civil servants. Such a regulation would not be in conflict with the principle of equality, while the different status justifies different rules. This annulment resulted with the postponement of Act No. 5510 just before its entry into force.[24] By this annulment, the single roof is cracked.[25] By lots of amendments, including those regarding civil servants[26] and after many postponements,[27] Act No.

21. OJ, 20 Jul. 2006, No. 26173.
22. OJ, 16 Jun. 2006, No. 26200.
23. Cons. Court, 15.12.2006, 111/112, OJ, 30.12.2006, No. 26392 (Mük.).
24. Act No. 5565 of 26 Dec. 2006, OJ, 29 Dec. 2006, No. 26391 (Mük.).
25. C. Tuncay/Ö. Ekmekçi, n. 7, p. 135; F.B. Savaş Kutsal, *Türk Sosyal Sigortalar Hukukunun Temel İlkeleri* (Istanbul, Beta, 2016), pp. 10–13.
26. About evaluation of these amendments, *see* for example A.R. Okur/H. Ergin, '5510 Sayılı Kanunda Değişiklik Öngören 25.10.2007 Tarihli Taslağın Değerlendirilmesi', 16, *Legal-İSGHD*(2007), pp.

5510 on Social Insurance and Universal Health Insurance entered into force mainly on the 1 October 2008, while Act No. 5510 had different dates for entry into force with regard to different provisions.[28]

23. However, whether this Act is able to meet the need for reform is a debatable issue.[29] The reform project has been received sceptically by a majority of the public. The problems such as mass unemployment and early retirement are pressing over the system. Very little has been improved in terms of finding a solution to the problem of non-registered employees, which has an extensive practice. In addition, the third axe of the reform, Draft Bill on Non-contributory Payments, is still pending.

1443–1470; Ş. Ertürk, '5510 Sayılı Sosyal Sigortalar ve Genel Sağlık Sigortası Kanunu'nda Değişiklik Öngören 5754 Sayılı Kanun'dan Sonra Uzun Vadeli Sigorta Kollarına Genel Bir Bakış', 19, *Legal-İSGHD*(2008), pp. 1047–1066; N. Gerek, '5754 Sayılı Sosyal Sigortalar ve Genel Sağlık Sigortası Kanunu (5510) İle Bazı Kanun ve Kanun Hükmünde Kararnamelerde Değişiklik Yapılmasına Dair Kanun İle Getirilen Yenilikler', 21, *TÜHİS Der.*(Ağustos-Kasım, 2008), pp. 1–17.

27. Act No. 5655 of 9 May 2007, OJ, 20 May 2007, No. 26527; Act No. 5724 of 14 Dec. 2007, OJ, 28 Dec. 2007, No. 26740 (Mük.); Act No. 5754 of 17 Apr. 2008, OJ, 8 May 2008, No. 2687; A.N. Sözer, '5510 Sayılı Yasaya İlişkin Değişiklik Tasarısında Genel Sağlık Sigortası, İlgili Anayasa Mahkemesi Kararı Işığında Bir Değerlendirme', *İşveren*(Nisan, 2008).

28. For details, *see* F. Uşan, *Türk Sosyal Güvenlik Hukukunun Temel Esasları* (Ankara, Seçkin, 2009), pp. 45–53; The same author, '5510 Sayılı Sosyal Sigortalar ve Genel Sağlık Sigortası Kanunu'nun Yürürlük ve Uygulama Başlangıcına İlişkin Tespitler', *Sicil Der.*(Haziran, 2009), pp. 239–247; A.R. Okur, 'Hukuk Tarihimizin Yürürlük Özürlüİlk Yasası: 5510 Sayılı Sosyal Sigortalar ve Genel Sağlık Sigortası Kanunu', *İşveren*(Mayıs, 2008).

29. *See, as example,* A. Güzel, 'Türk Sosyal Güvenlik Sisteminde Öngörülen Reform Mevcut Sorunlara Çözüm mü?', 7, *Çalışma ve Toplum*(2005/4), pp. 61–76; The same author, 'Yasa Tasarısının Genel Değerlendirmesi', 8, *Çalışma ve Toplum*(2006/1), pp. 171–178; Y. Alper, n. 7, pp. 46–49; M. Şakar, n. 7, pp. 35–42.

Chapter 3. Sources of Social Security Law

§1. General

24. The sources of social security law refer not only to the form that social security rules take while coming into force but also to organs and authorities which are empowered to lay down binding rules. In this respect, the sources of social security law may be examined under three sub-categories: legislative acts, executive regulations and judicial decisions. Among legal sources, in addition to national ones, international treaties and agreements should also be mentioned.

§2. Legislation

I. Constitution

25. The supremacy of the Constitution is expressed clearly in Article 11 of the Constitution. The provisions of the Constitution shall bind legislative, executive and judicial organs, as well as administrative authorities and individuals. No act shall be in conflict with the Constitution. With respect to social security norms, Article 2 of the Constitution states the welfare state as a fundamental principle of the Turkish Republic. Moreover, under the sub-title of 'social and economic rights and duties', Article 60 recognizes the fundamental nature of the right to social security, and Articles 61–62 lay down principles regarding those needing particular protection. These provisions constitute the guiding principles of the system.

II. Acts (Statutes)

26. The main source of social security law is legislation. The number of acts which regulate the social security system is quite considerable and has been amended several times. The main acts may be listed as follows:

(a) Social Insurance and Universal Health Insurance:
  (1) Act No. 5510 of 31 May 2006 on Social Insurance and Universal Health Insurance.[30]
  (2) Act No. 4447 of 28 August 1999 on Unemployment Insurance.
  (3) Act No. 657 of 17 July 1965 on Civil Servants.
  (4) Act No. 5502 of 16 May 2006 on Some Provisions related to the Social Security Institution (renamed and amended by Article 88/1-a of Decree-Law No. 703).
  (5) Act No. 4632 of 28 March 2001 on Individual Retirement Savings and Investment System.

30. For English version of Act No. 5510, http://www.sgk.gov.tr/wps/wcm/connect/1513fcb9-6954-42f1-9711-1708b08ff3a0/SOCIAL_INSURANCE_AND_UNIVERSAL_HEALTH_INSURNCE_LAW.pdf?MOD=AJPERES.

(b) Social Assistance and Social Services:
   (1) Act No. 2828 of 24 May 1983 on Social Services.
   (2) Act No. 3294 of 29 May 1986 on Incentive for Social Assistance and Solidarity Fund.
   (3) Act No. 2022 of 1 July 1976 on Granting of Pensions to Persons over 65 and Indigents.

27. Although main acts based on the nature of the employment status were abrogated by Act No. 5510, due to difficulties of the transition period, a considerable number of their provisions are still in force. These abrogated acts may be enumerated as follows:

- Act No. 506 of 17 July 1964 on Social Insurance.
- Act No. 2925 of 17 October 1983 on Social Insurance of Employees Working in Agriculture.
- Act No. 1479 of 2 September 1971 on Social Insurance Institution for Tradesmen and Artisans and Other Self-Employed (Bağ-Kur).
- Act No. 2926 of 17 October 1983 on Social Insurance for the Self-Employed in Agriculture.
- Act No. 5434 of 8 June 1949 on Pension Fund for Civil Servants of the Republic of Turkey.
- Act No. 2829 of 24 May 1983 on Aggregation Services Subjected to Different Social Security Institutions.
- Act No. 3201 of 8 May 1985 on Assessment of Services Provided to Abroad by Turkish Citizens living in Abroad with respect to Social Security.

28. Decree-laws were another category of legal sources which had the power and effect of statutes. The Council of Ministers was empowered by an authorization act to issue decree-laws. Article 91 of the Constitution was repealed in 2017. Therefore, decree-laws exist no more as a source of law.

29. International treaties also constitute an important legal source under Turkish law. According to Article 90/end of the Constitution, international agreements duly put into effect have the force of law. No appeal to the Constitutional Court can be made. The Universal Declaration of Human Rights is frequently cited as a reference. As regards the right to social security, the International Labour Organization

(ILO) Convention No. 102 on Minimum Standards of Social Security,[31] the European Social Charter of 1961,[32] the Revised European Social Charter[33] and the European Code of Social Security[34] are among the international treaties ratified by Turkey. These international treaties are taken by the Court of Cassation as the basis for its legal argumentation.

Although approximately 5,000,000 Turkish citizens are living abroad, there are only twenty-eight bilateral agreements between the Turkish Republic and other countries. The absence of bilateral agreements between Turkey and fourteen of the European Union Member States, as well as the United States (US) and Saudi Arabia, where quite a number of the citizens are working, is a considerable deficiency.[35]

§3. Executive Sources

30. The implementation of basic principles is set out by various kinds of executive acts. Presidential decrees and regulations are the ones mostly used.

31. Presidential decrees are issued by the President of the Republic on matters relating to the executive power of the President. No presidential decree shall be issued on matters which have been regulated by an act. The fundamental rights, individual rights and duties in the first and second chapters of the Constitution, as well as political rights and duties, shall not be regulated by presidential decrees. In case of a conflict between an adopted act and presidential decree, the provisions of the act shall prevail (Article 104 of Constitution).

32. Regulations are drafted and issued either by the president or individual ministries or public bodies to implement acts and presidential decrees, which fall into their sphere of authority (Article 124 of Constitution). It is evident that regulations cannot be contrary to either acts or presidential decree-laws. In the social security system, there are numerous regulations issued by the ministries authorized on labour and social security issues, as well as by the Social Insurance Institution.

33. The Social Security Institution is also authorized to take binding measures within their own field of authorization as determined by acts, presidential decree-laws and regulations. These decisions, called 'ordinances' are issued with the aim of implementing acts and other regulations.

---

31. Act No. 1451 of 19 Jul. 1971, OJ, 10 Aug. 1971, No. 13.922; Decree of Council of Ministers for approval of 1 Apr.1974, 7/7964, OJ, 15 Oct. 1974, No. 15037.
32. Act No. 3581 of 16 Jun. 1989, OJ, 4 Jul. 1989, No. 20215; Decree of Council of Ministers for approval of 7 Aug. 1989, 89/14434, OJ, 14 Oct. 1989, No. 20312.
33. Act No. 5547 of 27 Sep. 2006, OJ, 3 Oct. 2006, No. 26308; Decree of Council of Ministers for approval of 22 Mar. 2007, 2007/11907, OJ, 9 Apr. 2007, No. 26488.
34. Act No. 2170 of 21 Oct. 1978, OJ, 29 Sep. 1978, No. 16419; Decree of Council of Ministers for approval of 28 Feb. 1979, 7/17346, OJ, 23 Jul. 1979, No. 16705.
35. *See* A.N. Sözer, 'İkili Anlaşmalarla Sosyal Hukukun Koordinasyonu Türkiye Açısından', 5, *Legal-İSGHD*(2005), pp. 203–221.

34. The main executive sources are listed below:

- Regulation of Social Insurance Procedures.
- Regulation of Universal Health Insurance Registration, Contribution and Benefit Owners.
- Regulation of Universal Health Insurance Implementation.
- Regulation of Granting Pensions to Persons over 65 and Indigents.
- Regulation of Determination Loss Ratio in Earning Capacity and Capacity to Work.
- Regulation of Assessment of Services Provided to Abroad by Turkish Citizens Living in Abroad with respect to Social Security.

§4. Judicial Precedents

35. Judicial precedents play an important role as secondary legal sources in the construction of acts and dealing with their lacks. Since judicial precedents do not have binding effect, they are among the secondary sources of law. Only the precedents set by the General Assembly on the Unification of Judgment are binding all other courts, including the Court of Cassation itself.

In addition, the decisions of the Constitutional Court, the Council of State and, from time to time, the Court of Jurisdictional Disputes are also among important judicial precedents in social security law.

36. Numerous decisions of the Court of Cassation are published in a number of periodicals, the most important of which is the '*Yargıtay Kararları Dergisi*' published by the Court of Cassation (Yargıtay) itself and *Journal of Social Security* published by the Ministry for Labour and Social Security. '*Legal İş ve Sosyal Güvenlik Hukuku Dergisi*' published by a private 'Legal' Publishing House. In addition, employers' associations and trade unions' have systematic reviews, such as '*Çalışma ve Toplum*' (Labour and Society) published by BirleŞik-Metal İŞ Sendikası, '*Sicil*' published by MESS '*İŞveren*' published by TiSK or '*Çimento İŞveren*' published by Çimento Müstahsilleri İşveren Sendikası, wherein actual judicial precedents find place. In addition, many databanks belonging to private companies exist.

Part I. The Institutions

Introduction

37. The contributory regime constitutes the main axis of the Turkish social security system. The non-contributory regime has only a secondary role, which is divided into two: social assistance and social services. Since it is a welfare state, the state is under a duty to provide social assistance to vulnerable groups in society.

38. Up until the reform, the legal nature of the employment relationship has been the distinguishing factor in social security organizational division. The Social Insurance Institution, Bağ-Kur and the Pension Fund were the three important institutions in charge of social security. This fragmented structure results in a diverse assortment of health and old-age benefits. Moreover, the absence of an autonomous administrative structure for these institutions intensified the problem.

Thus, under the framework of organizational reform, three legally established public agencies, the Social Insurance Institution, Bağ-Kur and the Turkish Employment Institution, were brought together under a new central body, the Social Security Institution by Act No. 4947.[36] However, the Pension Fund has been excluded from this merger. In 2006, another organizational change was adopted by Parliament. The Social Insurance Institution, Bağ-Kur, the Pension Fund and the newly established Social Security Institution were transferred with all their assets and obligations to the new Social Security Institution.[37] The unplanned nature of the reform programme may be inferred from the frequency of such fundamental organizational changes.

39. Moreover, the supplementary role of private institutions in the current system is changing towards an essential one since the enactment of Act No. 4632, Individual Retirement Savings and Investment System.[38]

36. Act No. 4947 of 16 Jul. 2003, OJ, 24 Jul. 2003, No. 25178.
37. Act No. 5502 of 16 May 2006, OJ, 20 May 2006, No. 26173.
38. OJ, 7 Apr. 2001, No. 24366.

Chapter 1. Public Institutions

§1. Ministerial Departments

40. The constitutional duty to ensure social security has led the state to regulate the structure of the social security organizations as dependent institutions. Despite all efforts intended to strengthen the financial and organizational autonomy of social security institutions, the various ministries hold the authority to decide on their structure and management. The new Social Security Institution has not been exempted from this deficiency. The status of 'affiliated institution' facilitates the intervention of ministerial bodies.

The Ministry of Labour and Social Security was the most important one under which the Social Security Institution was structured, and the Ministry of Family and Social Services was responsible for the social assistance and social services provided to children, handicapped and old-aged people and children without a family. This Ministry had a considerable role in non-contributive social security services. Decree-Law No. 703 merged these two ministries under the name of the Ministry of Family, Labour and Social Services. Many social services and assistance such as child protection, social assistance and solidarity, services for people with disabilities and elderly are provided under the head of this Ministry.

The Ministry of Finance was the ministry to which the Pension Fund was attached. Under this new system, it is represented by one member on the board of management and one member of the consultancy.

§2. Other Public Institutions

41. Historically, public institutions have played an important role in the social security system. The competent public institutions have their own legal personality with tight links to the concerned Ministry. The administrative and financial autonomy of these institutions has been a major problem.

42. The most important public institutions are listed below:

- The Social Security Institution (Sosyal Güvenlik Kurumu) is the main Institution in charge of the implementation of Act No. 5510 on Social Insurance and Universal Health Insurance. It is the umbrella agency covering the Social Insurance Institution, Bağ-Kur, and the Pension Fund. Before the legal amendment, the Social Insurance Institution (Sosyal Sigortalar Kurumu) was the principal institution in charge of the social security of employees who work under a contract of employment. The Institution of Social Insurance for Craftsmen and Artisans and Other Self-Employed Workers (Esnaf ve Sanatkarlar ve Diğer Bağımsız ÇalıŞanlar Sosyal Sigortalar Kurumu, Bağ-Kur) was the Institution providing social insurance to the self-employed, and the Pension Fund (Emekli Sandığı) was responsible for the social security of civil servants.

- The Turkish Employment Institution (İŞ-Kur) is responsible for the application of unemployment insurance as well as job placement and vocational training services.

43. Many public organizations, different ministries and public bodies, and mayors of the local communities have roles in the administration of social services and social assistance.[39] Act No. 5502 attempts to unify, under one umbrella, not only those institutions responsible for contributory regimes but also those responsible for the administration of social services. However, whether the new Social Security Institution is able to meet the requirements of the non-contributory regime was a matter of discussion.[40]

---

39. A.N. Sözer, 'Yerel Yönetimlerce Yürütülen Sosyal Hizmetler', 2, *Legal-İSGHD*(Nisan-Haziran, 2004), pp. 474–490; L. Akın, 'Sosyal Yardımlar ve Yardımların Organizasyonu', in *Sosyal Güvenliğin Yeniden Yapılandırılması Semineri* (Ankara, 2007), pp. 252–277; K. Arıcı, n. 7, pp. 529–566.
40. K. Arıcı, 'Getirdikleri ve Getirmedikleriyle Sosyal Güvenlik Kurumu Kanunu Tasarısı', *Mercek* (Ocak, 2006), p. 90; L. Akın, 'Sosyal Yardımlar ve Yardımların Organizasyonu', pp. 261–277.

Chapter 2. Position and Competence of the Public Institutions

§1. The Social Security Institution

44. One of the biggest achieved steps of the social security reform is the unification of the institutional structure of the system. The fragmented nature of social security organizations had been considered a source of problems while bringing all institutions under one institutional roof has been regarded as a solution. Since 2000, many legislative regulations had been adopted[41] and finally, by Act No. 5502, adopted on 16 May 2006,[42] the Social Security Institution replaced the other competent authorities. Thus, the Social Security Institution, which was established by Act No. 4947, the Social Insurance Institution, Bağ-Kur, the Pension Fund are the institutions transferred to the new Institution with all their assets and obligations (Trans. Article 1 of Act No. 5502). Act No. 5502 provides that all of these four institutions with all of their central and local organizations, movable and immovable properties are transferred to the Social Security Institution. In addition, all personnel working in these institutions are transferred to the Social Security Institution (Trans. Article 1 of Act No. 5502). Presidential Decree No. 4 gives the actual structure to the Institution.[43] The Social Security Institution is affiliated to the Ministry of Family, Labour and Social Services. The Ministry is competent not only to determine the membership of its board of management but also to approve its budgets and confirm or reject its critical decisions.

Although these three institutions had not been operating anymore, a brief remark on their competency may be helpful. The Pension Fund, founded in 1949, was responsible for the social security of civil servants. The Social Insurance Institution was the competent authority in the social security affairs of wage earners. The last group covered by a compulsory social security system is that of the self-employed. The Institution of Social Insurance for Craftsmen and Artisans and Other Self-Employed Workers was founded in 1971.

45. The aim of the Social Security Institution is to manage a social security system according to modern standards and which is based upon the principles of social insurance, and which is efficient, fair and easily accessible and sustainable economically and from an actuary point of view (Article 405 of Pres. Decree No. 4). As a policy-making institution, it should develop social security policies and carry out preparations for social security agreements, which might be concluded between Turkey and other countries. As a service provider, it should inform the individuals on their rights and obligations, facilitate their access to services and carry out their engagements.

---

41. For legal development *see* A.N. Sözer, 'Sosyal Güvenliğin Organizasyonu', in *Sosyal Güvenliğin Yeniden Yapılandırılması Semineri* (Ankara, 2007), pp. 61–68.
42. OJ, 20 May 2006, No. 26173.
43. OJ, 15 Jul. 2018, No. 30479.

46. The governing organs of the Institution are a general assembly, a board of management and the presidency. The general assembly has only a consulting function. Its meetings are organized on a triennial basis. The Assembly gives its opinion on the budget for the previous years and activity reports, and the balance sheet for income and expenses accounted for by each insurance branch. As a policy-making organ, it should develop social security policies and their applications. Moreover, a certain number of members of the Board of management are elected by the Assembly.

Meetings will be held under the chairmanship of the Ministry of Family, Labour and Social Services, or some other person entrusted by the Minister and consist of representatives of different groups and ministries: nine representatives of the recognized three most representative employees' organizations, nine representatives of the recognized most representative employers' organizations, nine representatives of the most representative public officers' unions, nine representatives of the three most representative organizations founded by beneficiaries of the Institution, nine representatives of different ministries and affiliated organizations, two representatives of University lecturers, nine representatives of the three most representative professional organizations of those who perform an independent agricultural activity and nine representatives of the three most representative professional organizations of those who carry on an independent activity excluding agriculture ones.

The board of management is the highest decision-making and executive body of the Institution. It is composed of a chairperson and eleven members, six of which are elected, six appointed. The Ministry of Family, Labour and Social Services, the Ministry of Treasury and Finance are represented by three members on the Board of Management. Two vice-chairs are also members of the board. Employers, employees, civil servants, Self-Employed persons other than those working in agriculture, Self-Employed persons working in agriculture and beneficiaries of the Institution elect six of its members. The important deficiencies in the new institution, Act No. 5502, as well as the Presidency Decree No. 4 provide for equality between the numbers of elected and appointed members of the Board of management. [44] However, if the votes are equal, the vote of the President is determinant. Therefore, representatives of social partners are outvoted in decision-making and management procedures.

The Presidency of the Institution is composed of the President, three vice-chairs and central and local organization throughout the country. The President of the Institution is a public servant appointed by the President. the General Directorship of Social Insurance, the General Directorship of General Health Insurance, The General Directorship of Service Providing and the General Directorship of Retirement Services are all under the central organization.

47. The Social Security High Consulting Committee is made up of representatives of the different ministries such as the Ministry of Defence, the Ministry of Internal Affairs, the Ministry of Finance, and the Ministry of Health. Different organizations and presidencies, such as the General Director of Turkish Employment

---

44. *See* K. Arıcı, 'Getirdikleri ve Getirmedikleriyle Sosyal Güvenlik Kurumu Kanunu Tasarısı', *Mercek*(Ocak, 2006), pp. 91, 94.

Institution, the General Director of Social Assistance and Solidarity Administration, the President of Administration for Handicapped Persons, etc. and other persons and institutions proposed by the Minister are also represented. The Committee gives its opinion on social security policies and applications.

§2. The Turkish Employment Institution (İş-Kur)

48. The monopoly of job placement belonged to the state under the previous Labour Act (LA) No. 1475. With the adoption of unemployment insurance for the very first time in 1999 (coming into force in 2000), the need for a new organizational model became apparent. Therefore, by Decree-law No. 617, the Turkish Employment Institution was established. However, pursuant to the annulment of Decree-law No. 617, Act No. 4904, Turkish Employment Institution was adopted on 25 June 2003.[45] The current structure of the Institution is given by the Presidential Decree No. 4.[46]

49. The main object of the Turkish Employment Institution is to protect, develop and expand employment, as well as to engage in activities for prevention of unemployment (Article 617 of Pres. Decree No. 4). Furthermore, unlike other social insurance branches, the administration of the unemployment insurance services is under the authority of the Employment Institution itself.

50. According to Presidential Decree No. 4, the Employment Institution has a public law personality with financial and administrative autonomy. Achieving the stated objective of financial and administrative autonomy seems difficult considering its firm attachment to the Ministry of Family, Labour and Social Services.

51. The Employment Institution has four organs: a general board, the board of management, a directorate general and provincial employment boards. The general board has only consultative powers. It convenes under the chairmanship of the Ministry of Family, Labour and Social Services or a person assigned by the Minister. It has a tripartite nature, that is, it is composed of representatives of the state and of the most representative employers and workers confederations.

The administrative and decision-making powers belong to the board of management. It is composed of six members under the chair of the general director. The other six members are a representative of the Ministry of Family, Labour and Social Services, a representative of the Ministry of Treasury and Finance and one representative each from the Turkish Tradesmen and Artisans Confederation, the most representative employers' confederation, and the most representative workers confederation.

As an administrative organ, the directorate general consists of a headquarters and district offices.

45. OJ, 5 Jul. 2003, No. 25159.
46. OJ, 15 Jul. 2018, No. 30479.

§3. SOCIAL SECURITY INSTITUTIONS IN COMPLEMENTARY SYSTEM

52. Besides the compulsory social security system, certain public law institutions provide supplementary benefits to their members. The Workers' Association (Amele Birliği) was the first social security institution established (by Act No. 151) with a view to satisfying the economic and social needs of employees working in the region of Ereğli. By the enactment of Act No. 506, the field of application of Act No. 151 was restricted to the area of health insurance in the region of Zonguldak and Ereğli. By Decree No. 7/10616, issued on 9 September 1975, the reciprocal exclusion of Act Nos 506 and 151 with regard to health insurance was abolished. Henceforth, Act No. 151 provided only for supplementary benefits including temporary incapacity allowances, health and education assistance, and loans in case of funeral and industrial accidents.[47]

53. The Elementary School Teachers' Fund for Health and Social Assistance (İlkokul Öğretmenleri Sağlık ve Sosyal Yardım Sandığı/İLKSAN) was established on 13 January 1943 by Act No. 4357. This Fund functions as a complementary social security institution. The Fund aims to provide its members with social assistance, i.e., award loans to its members to provide assistance in the event of marriage, death, disability and retirement. Elementary school teachers, assistant teachers and trainees are compulsory contributors to, and beneficiaries of, this Fund.[48]

54. The Armed Forces Pension Association (Ordu Yardımlaşma Kurumu/OYAK) was established in 1961 to provide its members with supplementary retirement benefits apart from the compulsory regime. Supplementary retirement, disability and death benefits are granted by the Fund. All regular officers and military employees are compulsory contributors to, and permanent members of, this Association.[49]

47. K. Arıcı, n. 7, pp. 184–189; M. Şakar, n. 7, pp. 72–74.
48. K. Arıcı, n. 7, pp. 189–194.
49. K. Arıcı, n. 7, pp. 194–202; M. Şakar, n. 7, pp. 74–75.

Chapter 3. Private Institutions

55. Historically, the role of private institutions with compulsory regimes is very limited.

§1. Bank and Insurance Company Funds

56. Before the enactment of Act No. 506, certain banks, insurance companies, chambers of commerce and industry and commodity exchanges had set up private social security institutions, which covered those of their personnel who were not considered to be 'employees'.[50]

57. Abrogated Act No. 506 recognized their existence alongside the Social Insurance Institution under certain conditions (Trans. Article 20 of Act No. 506): First, these funds must have covered all the personnel of the bank, insurance and reinsurance company, chambers of commerce, industry and exchanges or of unions formed by them on the date of publication (1 August 1964) of Act No. 506. Second, these private funds should have provided, at a minimum, the benefits relevant to industrial accidents, occupational diseases, sickness, maternity, invalidity, old age and survivors allowances as specified in Act No. 506.[51] Finally, in case of the transfer of these personnel to another of these companies with a private fund, rights acquired in their original fund would have been transferred to either the new fund to which the person had been transferred or to a Common Fund to be set up among such institutions and organizations. These private funds were to be established in the form of 'foundations' or 'associations'.

58. Those who gain old-age benefits from these funds would not receive benefits arising from abrogated Act No. 506.[52] The status of these funds and amendments to them are subject to the approval of the Ministry of Labour and Social Security.

59. Members of these funds are not considered to be 'insured' according to abrogated Act No. 506, also Act No. 5510. Thus, although these funds are recognized as pension funds and are established by statutes, conflicts between their members and the fund shall be resolved according to the statutes of the relevant fund. Therefore, the Court of Cassation first held that civil courts had jurisdiction over such conflicts.[53] However, by the transitional Article 20 of Act No. 506, these funds are considered to be among the statutory social security institutions and all disputes arising

50. *See*, for details, S. Ocak, 'Banka ve Sigorta şirketi Sandıklarının Sosyal Sigortalar Kurumuna Devri Sorunu', in *Prof. Dr. Nuri Çelik'e Armağan II* (Istanbul, Beta, 2001), pp. 1865–1871.
51. About this point T. Centel, 'Özel Sandıklarda Asgari Güvence Standardı', in *Prof. Dr. Nuri Çelik'e Armağan II* (Istanbul, Beta, 2001), pp. 1739 et seq.
52. Court of Cass., Unif. Judg., 9 Mar. 1983, 1/1, OJ, 23 Jun. 1983, No. 18086.
53. Court of Cass., 10th Ch., 5.4.1983, 1175/1759, *YKD*(Eylül, 1983), p. 1329.

between their members and the fund fall under the jurisdiction of the labour courts.[54] Their members could not receive another pension from the Social Security Institution.

60. By Banking Act No. 5411 passed on 19 October 2005,[55] the bank and insurance company funds dealt with would be automatically transferred to the Social Security Institution within three years following the enactment of this Act. Therefore, all their participants and right owners who receive invalidity, old age and survivors insurance pensions and their dependants would be enrolled under cover of abrogated Act No. 506 and they would be considered 'insured'. By Act No. 5502, the Social Security Institution becomes the recipient organization. However, until the accomplishment of this transfer, services were to be provided according to the related Fund's status; in addition, premiums are to be collected in the same manner (Trans. Article 23 of Act No. 5411). Pursuant to the annulment of transitional Article 23 of Act No. 5411 by the Constitutional Court,[56] Act No. 5510 on Social Insurance and Universal Health Insurance re-adopted principles of the transfer process (Trans. Article 20 of Act No. 5510). Finally, the Council of Ministers had extended the transfer period for two years in 2011.[57] Although the Council of Ministers extended transfer period many times, up until now, the transfer process had not been accomplished. In 2015, the Council of Ministers was authorized to set up the transfer date by a legislative amendment.[58] Thus, the legal requirement related to the period extension was removed.

§2. Supplementary Funds of Banks and Insurance Companies

61. Supplementary funds in banks and insurance companies, established with the aim to provide certain supplementary benefits and pensions to their members, also exist. These funds are assistance funds and do not fall under the scope of abovementioned funds. Therefore, they do not have statutory nature. Membership is voluntary and is not regulated under the social security legislation.[59]

62. In the face of financial difficulties faced by some of these funds, Act No. 3995 passed on 1 June 1994 authorized the Council of Ministers to make decisions concerning the transfer of these supplementary funds of banks to the Social Insurance Institution if their financial situation became insufficient to provide social security to their members. According to the Banking Act, under certain conditions, a decision may be made to merge, transfer the assets, or order the cessation of activities of banks. Certain funds belonging to such banks have been transferred to the Social Insurance Institution (the Social Security Institution) by a decision of the Council of Ministers.

54. Court of Cass., 10th Ch., 26.6.1986, 2066/3881, *YKD*(Kasım, 1986), p. 1646.
55. OJ, 1 Nov. 2005, No. 25983 (Mük.).
56. Cons. Court, 22 Mar. 2007, 139/33, OJ, 31 Mar. 2007, No. 26479.
57. OJ, 9 Apr. 2011, No. 27900.
58. Act No. 6645 of 4 Apr. 2015, OJ, 23 Apr. 2015, No. 29395.
59. C. Tuncay/Ö. Ekmekçi, n. 7, p. 127.

§3. PRIVATE INSURANCE COMPANIES

63. After the 1990s, private insurance companies started to acquire growing importance in the complementary system. In addition to the compulsory public social security model, the private individual old-age pension model was introduced into the system by Act No. 4632, dated 28 March 2001.[60] Through individual retirement savings and investment systems, in addition to retirement pensions provided by the Social Insurance Institution, Bağ-Kur or Pension Fund, individual retirement funding systems provide supplementary benefits. This individual system constitutes the second step of social security in Turkey, where, with the exception of the Armed Forces Pension Fund (OYAK), the Workers' Association (Amele Birlidi) and supplementary funds of banks and insurance companies as mentioned above, no second step supplementary social security institution with a general scope of application previously existed.[61] However, although a considerable amount of state contribution is inserted to the system by Act No. 6327,[62] the number of participants in the system was low. The government, with an aim to increase the ratio of savings in the country, passed another legislative amendment [63] which brings an automatic enrolling of all employees in the private pension system that enters into force starting from the 1 January 2017 progressively with respect to the number of employees recruited by the employer.

Under this new system, all Turkish citizens who are below 45 years of age and who work either with an employment contract or as a civil servant will be included in the pension plan determined by employers. Therefore, voluntary participation is replaced by mandatory participation for those who are below the age of 45 years. The employer shall only provide a pension plan offered by a Pension Company that is deemed appropriate by the Treasury. Nevertheless, the employee may withdraw the pension agreement within two months as of the day on which the employee is informed about being included in the plan.

64. The individual retirement model is based on the capitalization of individual funds. Unlike the pre-determined pension model of Continental European countries, the Turkish system is based on the pre-determined premium model as applied in the US.[64] Thus, the company does not guarantee a minimum pension.

After having completed ten years in the system and reached 56 years of age, the contributor may ask for a lump-sum payment or may conclude an annual income agreement.

65. The amount of the contribution is 3% on the daily earnings of the employees' basis for social insurance contribution. The employee may ask the increase in the contribution rate. There also exists a state subsidy for employees at a rate of 25%

60. OJ, 7 Apr. 2001, No. 24366; *see* B. Ergin, 'Bireysel Emeklilik Sistemi Nedir, Ne Değildir?', 1, *Sicil-*(Mart, 2006), pp. 122–137; S. Uğur, 'Hukuki Açıdan Bireysel Emeklilik Sistemi', 2, *Legal-İSGHD*(Nisan-Haziran, 2004), pp. 512–530.
61. A. Güzel/A.R. Okur/N. Caniklioğlu, n. 7, p. 787.
62. OJ, 29 Jun. 2012, No. 28338.
63. Act No. 6740 of 10 Aug. 2016, OJ, 25 Aug. 2016, No. 29812.
64. A. Güzel/A.R. Okur/N. Caniklioğlu, n. 7, p. 788; C. Tuncay/Ö. Ekmekçi, n. 7, p. 704.

of employees' paid contributions to their private pension account. If the employee stays in the plan, another state subsidy of TRY1.000 will be provided for once (Supp. Article 1 of Act No. 4632). The employer is to deduct the employee's contribution rate from his wage and pay it to the pension company on the following working day of the payday (Supp. Article 2 of Act. No. 4632)

Part II. Contribution and Financing of Social Insurance System

Introduction

66. Based on the contributory system, those who work are under the obligation to pay contributions. The previous system, which was characterized by a strongly fragmented nature, was composed of three different social security acts, that participation depended on the nature of the employment relationship. Thus, the previous system had three different contributory systems, one each for wage earners, Self-Employed workers and civil servants, respectively. In addition, regarding wage earners and Self-Employed persons, Act Nos 506 and 1479 did not cover all those whose employment status may have been described as being in an employment relationship or self-employed. In particular, the social security of those who work in agriculture, either as employees or independently, was dealt with by other acts. The work status was the primary determinant of social insurance status. This nature resulted from the historical evaluation of the social security system. Having a strongly Bismarckian nature, different working groups have acquired social security through different acts adopted at different times.

67. In lieu of a system based on the nature of the employment status, Act No. 5510 passed on 31 May 2006 proposed a new system based on the risk, in other words, insurance branch. However, whether such a fundamental change would solve its problems is a debatable issue. As from 2008, the above-mentioned three different systems were unified under one regulation, Act No. 5510 on Social Insurance and Universal Health Insurance. The reform Act No. 5510 brings about two fundamental changes in the structure of the social security regulations: covering all working groups under the same roof both in terms of legislation and institution and detaching social insurance benefits from healthcare services. Therefore, the field of application of social insurances and the field of application of healthcare services differentiate from each other.

68. Although Act No. 5510 seems to have unified different statuses, the differences between different working groups have been maintained. As mentioned above, before the reform, insurance holders were subjected to different legislations according to the nature of their employment relationship. Due to the reform, they are now subjected to the different provisions of the same Act. Therefore, Bismarckian reciprocity is still the central principle within the social insurance programme. The social insurance system is based on the principle of status maintenance.

Chapter 1. Contribution Regulation for Those Who Are Subjected to Article 4/I-a (Mainly Employees)

§1. Field of Application

I. Territorial Field of Application

69. Turkish social security law applies, in principle, within the territories of the Turkish Republic.[65] According to Article 60/I of the Constitution, 'everybody' has social security rights. Therefore, any person, either a national or a non-national, benefits from the social security protections. The principle of equal treatment between nationals and non-nationals are guaranteed by many treaties that Turkey has ratified, such as the International Covenant on Economic, Social and Cultural Rights, the ILO Convention No. 102 on Minimum Standards of Social Security, the ILO Convention No. 118 on Equality of Treatment, European Social Charter and Revised European Social Charter, and the European Convention on Social Security.[66] The first section of exemptions consist of the non-nationals' social security rights in Turkey, and the second section is about the social security of Turkish nationals working abroad.

70. Foreigners who work under a contract of employment in Turkey are compulsorily subjected to all insurance branches, the same as Turkish citizens. Before an amendment was made by Act No. 4958 in 2003,[67] in order to profit from invalidity, old age and survivors' insurance branches, they had to demand this by written request. Such regulation was criticized by many writers since it was against the principle of equality between nationals and non-nationals.[68] Act No. 5510 makes no difference between nationals and non-nationals with regard to social insurance rights unless a bilateral agreement between Turkey and the non-national's home country on the basis of reciprocity provides another solution (Article 4/II, c Act No. 5510). Although the wording of the provision raises doubts, it has been confirmed that if Turkey concluded a bilateral social security agreement with the country of the non-national and if both countries exempted the other non-nationals from the compulsory social security system, then the non-nationals are not obliged to be covered by the social insurance system.[69] However, if a non-national is not covered by any social security in their home country, he/she shall be considered an insurance holder compulsorily. Refugees and stateless persons are also considered among non-nationals.

---

65. A.N. Sözer, 'Uluslararası Sosyal Hukukta Mülkilik ve Şahsilik İlkeleri', in *15. Yıl Armağanı*(Istanbul, 1991), pp. 125–127; F.B. Savaş Kutsal, n. 25, pp. 79–123.
66. *See* H. Dursun, 'Yabancıların Sosyal Güvenlik Hakkına Genel Bir Bakış', *Kamu-İş Der.,* C. 10, S. 4/2009, pp. 209–223.
67. OJ, 6 Aug. 2003, No. 25191.
68. A. Güzel/A.R.Okur/N. Caniklioğlu, n. 7, p. 92; C. Tuncay/Ö. Ekmekçi, n. 7, p. 290; N. Caniklioğlu, 'Sosyal Hukukun Bir Görevi Olarak Ayrımcılıktan Kaçınma ve Mağduriyetin Giderilmesi', *İş Hukuku ve Sosyal Güvenlik Hukuku Türk Milli Komitesi 30. Yıl Armağanı* (Ankara, 2006), pp. 687–688.
69. A. Güzel/A.R. Okur/N. Caniklioğlu, n. 7, p. 92.

71. According to Article 6/I, e of Act No. 5510, employees who have a foreign nationality and who are charged by an employer for a period lasting not more than three months, based abroad with a task that will be performed on his behalf in Turkey, shall not be covered by the social insurance regulations, only if they document to be subjected to social insurance in the foreign country. Therefore, foreign nationals who are sent to Turkey for work to be done on behalf of, and on account of an undertaking whose headquarters are located abroad, shall be subjected to Act No. 5510, only if they are unable to prove their subjection to a social security system in their home country. The task should not continue for more than three months. Therefore, for duties which continue for more than three months, foreign employees must also be notified to the Institution. The Regulation on Social Insurance Procedures (RSIP) provides a period of three months, with or without interruption, for each foreign employee (Article 10/1, d of RSIP). Thus, foreign employees who have a work permit for three months and have worked for two months may have a later task. In that case, whenever the period of three months is completed, they shall be insured. If there exists a bilateral agreement, a foreign national shall be considered an insurance holder at the end of the period fixed by the bilateral agreement; for example, for a French national, it is three years and it may be extended for six years more; for German nationals, it is five years, and it may be extended for three years more, and for British nationals there is no time limitation.[70]

Similarly, both nationals and non-nationals who work in Turkey on their own account are not covered by the compulsory social insurance system if they reside abroad and are subjected to a social insurance system of that country.

72. The social security of employees, having Turkish nationality but who are working for a limited time in a foreign country under a contract of employment concluded with a Turkish employer, constitutes an important problem, as the number of countries with whom a bilateral social security agreement has been signed is not too many. Pursuant to Article 5/1, g of Act No. 5510, if an employee is working in the workplace of a Turkish employer in a foreign country with whom the Turkish Republic has no bilateral agreement, that employee shall be deemed to be an insurance holder according to the same provisions applicable to employees working within the country. However, the cover of their compulsory insurance status is restricted with short-term insurance branches and universal health insurance. Such a restricted compulsory regime can result in employees who have worked abroad for a long time encountering the risk of not benefiting from any protection against the risks of invalidity, death and old age. Therefore, Article 5/1, g enables those employees to be able to benefit from voluntary insurance, with respect to the long-term insurance branches without seeking the condition of legally residing in Turkey. However, they have to pay the total amount of long insurance contributions

70. Ordinance No. 2011/43; *see also* M. Bulut, 'Son Düzenlemeler Işığında Türkiye'de Bağımlı ve Bağımsız Çalışan Yabancıların Sosyal Güvenlikleri', *Sicil Der.*(Eylül, 2011), pp. 208–215; A.N. Sözer, *Türk Sosyal Sigortalar Hukuku* (Istanbul, Beta, 2015), p. 107; F.B. Savaş Kutsal, n. 25, pp. 134–137.

themselves.[71] As regards the length of time passed in the foreign country (détaché), there is no limitation, except in the case of certain countries with which the Turkish Republic has signed a social security agreement.[72] Nevertheless, a temporary duty whilst abroad falls out of the scope of application. Therefore, Turkish employees who are sent abroad on a temporary mission are compulsorily insured.[73]

It should be underlined that in cases wherein the insurance holders are sent by the employer to a foreign country on temporary duty, the rights and obligations of insurance holders and employers shall continue as long as such duties are fulfilled (Article 10 of Act No. 5510).[74]

II. Personal Field of Application

73. As regards the personal field of application, as mentioned above, Act No. 5510 combines three different regulations under one regulation of social insurance for employees, the Self-Employed and civil servants. It gives a definition of an insurance holder in such a way as to combine the personal scope of the three different acts. Nevertheless, traces of the previous system are detectable, as Act No. 5510 divides insurance holders into three categories: Those subjected to Article 4/I-a, consisting mainly of employees, those subjected to Article 4/I-b, consisting of mainly Self-Employed persons, and those subjected to Article 4/I-c, consisting of mainly public officers. The concept of a 'social insurance holder' being divided into these three categories reflects the personal field of application of the three abrogated acts.

74. Act No. 5510 not only covers those who were covered by the abrogated social insurance regulations but also excludes those who were excluded either by Act No. 506 or by Act No. 1479. Therefore, those who fell out of the scope of the previous system, fall out of the scope of the new system too. In particular, self-employed persons whose annual income is under a certain level were left out of the previous system, and so is the case under the current system. This means that the mere condition of employment would not be enough to be covered by the social insurance system. In addition, insured persons are supposed to have an income above the fixed limit.[75] If the aim is to provide all groups in society with a social security guarantee, Act No. 5510 is far from achieving it. In order to make up for this deficit, the new act emphasizes voluntary insurance. In addition, the structure and wording of the related provisions (Articles 4, 5 and 6 of Act No. 5510) have the potential to cause considerable problems during their application.

---

71. A. Güzel/A.R. Okur/N. Caniklioğlu, n. 7, p. 128; A.N. Sözer, n. 70, p. 93; F.B. Savaş Kutsal, n. 25, pp. 125–127.
72. A.N. Sözer, 'Mülkilik ve Şahsilik İlkeleri', p. 127.
73. A. Güzel/A.R. Okur/N. Caniklioğlu, n. 7, pp. 128–129; F. Uşan, n. 28, p. 106; A.N. Sözer, n. 70, p. 94; F.B. Savaş Kutsal, n. 25, p. 129.
74. *See* F.B. Savaş Kutsal, n. 25, pp. 128–134.
75. L. Akın, 'Sosyal Sigortalar ve Genel Sağlık Sigortası Kanun Tasarısının Kişiler Açısından Kapsamında Yeni Gelişmeler', 8, *Çalışma ve Toplum Der.*(2006/1), pp. 26–49.

A. *Insurance Holder*

1. Compulsory Insurance

75. Social insurance holder is a person for whom the payment of contributions in terms of long-term and long-term insurance branches is mandatory or who is under an obligation to pay contributions on his/her own account. According to Article 4/I-a Act No. 5510 on Social Insurance and Universal Health Insurance Act, those who are employed by one or more employers under a contract of employment are deemed to be an 'insurance holder' for the purposes of implementing short-term and long-term insurance branches of Act No. 5510. Employees and their employers are the principal contributors to this group. If the contract of employment is the determinant criteria for the status of being insurance holders of 4/I-a, certain other groups who do not work under a contract of employment are also mentioned in Article 4/I-a of Act No. 5510.

76. In order to determine whether an employee receives social insurance coverage, he/she must be employed under a contract of employment. The Court of Cassation introduces an additional condition that work should be performed in the workplace of the employee. Additionally, he/she must not be in a condition of employment listed in Articles 5 and 6, which determine those excluded from the Act's field of application.[76]

77. A contract of employment is that type of contract whereby the employee undertakes to perform a service in a subordinate way in return for a certain wage (Article 393 of TCO, Article 8 of LA). This definition also includes craftsmen and journalists whose labour relations are regulated by specific acts such as the Maritime Labour Act and the Act concerning Labour-Management Relations in the Press. Before the entry into force of Act No. 5510, social insurance of agricultural workers was regulated by a special Act No. 2925 on Social Insurance for Workers in Agriculture. This Act is abrogated by Act No. 5510; therefore, social security of workers in agriculture is also set up like the other employees.

78. The invalidity of the contractual relationship does not affect the insured status of the employee. The invalidity of the contract has an *ex tunc* effect (Article 394/3 of TCO); therefore, the status of being insured keeps its validity until the invalidity is revealed.[77]

79. Although not stated directly in the Social Insurance and Universal Health Insurance Act, the interpretation of Articles 4 and 11 has led to a further condition

---

76. Court of Cass., General Council, 2 Feb. 2005, 2004/10-737, 2005/26, 5, *Çalışma ve Toplum Der.*(2005/2), pp. 159–164.
77. A. Güzel/A.R. Okur/N. Caniklioğlu, n. 7, pp. 85–86; F. Uşan, n. 28, p. 80; A.N. Sözer, n. 70, p. 28; Y. Alper, n. 7, p. 93; M. Şakar, n. 7, p. 96; R. Korkusuz/S. Uğur, *Sosyal Güvenlik Hukuku*(Bursa, Ekin, 2015), p. 212, as example *see* Court of Cass., 10. Ch., 20 May 1997, 3965/3791, cited and noted by K. Arıcı, 'Sosyal Sigortalar', *Yargıtayın İş Hukukuna İlişkin Kararlarının Değerlendirilmesi 1997* (Istanbul, 1999), pp. 283–284.

that the insured employee must work in the workplace of the employer.[78] The Court of Cassation held in the same way that in order to be covered by the social insurance system, the work must be performed at the workplace of the employer.[79] Therefore, if the employee performs his work in a place out of the workplace of the employer, he/she shall not be deemed as an insurance holder. However, there also exist opposite decisions, which may indicate a change in jurisprudence.[80]

Due to technological and economic developments, in place of the classic workplace concept, the organization of work or services has become of primary importance. Thus, the LA No. 4857 describes the workplace as an 'organizational ensemble' composed of all premises used, and as such these premises must be treated as part of the workplace because they are used by reason of the nature and execution of the work. In addition, workplace includes both facilities and vehicles. Therefore, employees who work under the 'work organization' of the employer should be covered by Act No. 5510.[81] Nevertheless, the whole documentation system of the Social Security Institution is based on the workplace number of the employer. That is why it is quite complicated in practice to make those employees registered.

80. In order to be insured, neither the conclusion of a contract of employment nor the notification of the Institution by the employer is sufficient.[82] The founding element of the social insurance relationship is not the conclusion of a contract, but an active work relation.[83] In many parts of the legislation, there exist provisions which attach active work relation to the insurance holder status. The insurance holder status is acquired by starting work. In addition, 'active work relation' is used to prevent false insurance claims of those trying to profit from the benefits provided by the social security system. Particularly, sham employment contracts being set up, which in the absence of any effective employment relationship, are used to obtain old-age pensions. Such persons are registered as insured in a workplace belonging to a family member or a friend. Therefore, unless an active work relationship can be proven, the status of an insured employee is not accepted. In addition to the notification made to the Institution upon commencing employment, certificates, which show the working days and wages of the insured to determine contributions made, will be taken into consideration when determining the 'active work relation' status of the insured.[84]

---

78. K. Tunçomağ, n. 7, p. 117; A. Güzel/A.R. Okur/N. Caniklioğlu, n. 7, pp. 88–89; C. Tuncay/Ö. Ekmekçi, n. 7, pp. 283–284; Y. Alper, n. 7, p. 93.
79. As example *see* Court of Cass., 25.5.1984, 2729/2927 cited in M. Çenberci, *Sosyal Sigortalar Kanunu Şerhi* (Ankara, 1985), p. 44.
80. Court of Cass., 21st Ch., 8 Jun. 2000, 4586/4611, *İşveren Der.*(Şubat, 2001), pp. 17–18.
81. A. Güzel/A.R. Okur/N. Caniklioğlu, n. 7, p. 89; C. Tuncay/Ö. Ekmekçi, n. 7, p. 285; F. Uşan, n. 28, p. 82.
82. A. Güzel/A.R. Okur/N. Caniklioğlu, n. 7, pp. 86–88; F. Uşan, n. 28, p. 83; *see also* A.N. Sözer, n. 70, pp. 27–28; S. Başterzi, *Çalışmanın Kesintiye Uğramasının Sosyal Sigorta İlişkisine Etkisi* (Ankara, 2007), pp. 19–22.
83. S. Başterzi, n. 83, pp. 19–22.
84. *See, as example,* Court of Cass., General Council, 6.7.2005, 21-437/448, 7, *Çalışma ve Toplum Der. Der.*, 2005/4, pp. 109–112; 10th Ch., 3.5.2005, 2383/4891, 7, *Çalışma ve Toplum Der.*, 2005/4, pp. 275–276; 21th Ch., 27.6.2007, 12696/10413, 17, *Legal-İSGHD*(2008), pp. 272–274 cited and noted

81. Besides employees, Act No. 5510 provides social insurance for certain groups under Article 4/I-a, even if no work relationship under a contract of employment exists. There is no doubt that they work under a contractual relation different from a contract of employment. However, Article 82/II of Act No. 5510 also mentions an 'insurance holder working gratuitously'. The employer shall pay their contributions calculated on the basis of the amount of the minimum wage.

82. Act No. 5510 subjects certain groups to Article 4/I-a, although they do not work with an employment contract:

- Those who are elected to the presidency or management boards of trade unions, union branches or confederations are also covered by the Article 4/I-a of Act No. 5510 (Article 4/II, a of Act No. 5510). Before the reform, presidencies and board members of trade unions had an option to benefit from voluntary insurance provisions, and they maintained their insured status by paying contributions, including the employer's share. Although it is evident that the legal relationship between the board members and trade union is the contract of mandate, with an aim to encourage to taking positions in unions' management, Act No. 5510 regulates their social security like those who are employed under a contract of employment.
- All performing artists and musicians as actors/actresses, singers and those engaged in all branches of fine arts including music, painting, sculpture, decorative and the similar arts, thinkers and authors are covered by Article 4/I-a (Article 4/II, b of Act No. 5510). If an artist or musician is recruited with a contract of employment, there is no need to refer to this particular provision. However, even if they work as a freelancer, their social insurance is regulated according to provisions which govern the social insurance of employees, as long as they are economically dependent and work with one or more employers.

  The social security of performing artists and musicians is increasingly becoming a debatable issue. Through an amendment made by Act No. 6111, artists and musicians are enabled to possibly have social security. According to supplementary Article 6 of Act No. 5510, if they work with part-time contracts for one or more than one employers and if their total working days, calculated on the basis of working hours, in a month are less than ten days, they are enabled to pay their own contributions to get insurance benefits. Since the social insurance relation relies on a work relation, such an opportunity constitutes a kind of forced voluntary insurance, while employers are under a duty to inform the Institution when they recruit an artist. Therefore, contribution payments over thirty days are compulsory with respect to artists. The amount of the earnings, among the lower and the upper limits, based for the contribution is fixed by the insurance holder. However, the Act provides a progressive transition, starting from 2011, contribution payments are calculated eighteen times the daily contribution amount, that for each following year, this rate is increased by one point (Trans. Article 29 of Act

---

by N. Caniklioğlu, 'Sosyal Sigortaların Genel Hükümleri ve Türleri', *Yargıtayın İş Hukukuna İlişkin Kararlarının Değerlendirilmesi 2007* (Istanbul, 2009), pp. 305–306.

No. 5510). Therefore, in 2017, all artists recruited with part-time contracts shall pay contributions for twenty-four days to get insurance benefits due for thirty days.[85]

- As explained above, foreigners who are employed with a contract of employment in Turkey shall be deemed as insurance holders, unless a bilateral agreement between Turkey and his home country on the basis of reciprocity provides another solution (Article 4/II, c of Act No. 5510).
- Rural security guards who are employed according to Act No. 4081 dated 10 July 1941, the Protection of Farmer's Properties shall be deemed as insurance holders under Article 4/I-a (Article 4/II, d of Act. No. 5510).
- Prostitutes as defined by Act. No. 1593 and their employers are covered by Article 4/I-a (Article 4/I, e of Act. No. 5510).
- Those who are employed as master teachers in the courses organized by the Ministry of National Education, those who are charged with a duty in public administrations in return for course fees or those who are employed under Article 4-c of the Civil Servants Act No. 657 are also considered as insurance holders like employees (Article 4/II-f of Act No. 5510). The last group consists of those who are recruited in the public sector with an administrative contract for jobs which lasts less than one year or which has a seasonal nature.
- Those who participate in work programmes organized by the Turkish Employment Institution for the benefits of the society are also covered by Article 4/I-a of Act No. 5510 (Article 4/I-g of Act No. 5510).
- Domestic servants and house cleaners comprise an important part of the workforce in the informal economy. The domestic servants and maids who work permanently with an employment contract are compulsorily insured. However, temporary domestic workers were excluded from the coverage of social insurance, while it is not always easy to claim that they are working with an employment contract. By an amendment made by Act No. 6111, entered into force on 1 January of 2015, the legislator inserted a new model which is financially less burdensome. Domestic servants and maids who work for ten days or more in a month in the same household are compulsorily insured. According to supplementary Article 9 of Act No. 5510, if they work with part-time contracts for one or more than one employers and if their total working days, calculated on the basis of working hours, in a month are less than ten days, they are enabled to pay their own contributions to get insurance benefits. Under this new model, if a domestic worker is recruited by a single employer for ten days or more, the employer is under a duty to register the domestic worker and pay all contributions for social insurance. However, if the domestic worker works with a single employer for less than ten days in a month, the employer should only pay contributions against the risk of an industrial accident and occupational disease. Thus, they are insured against the most frequent risks that they are exposed to – an industrial accident and an occupational disease. However, if they wish, they are enabled to pay their own contributions to have other social insurance benefits.[86]

---

85. A.K. Akpulat, 'Sanatçıların Sosyal Sigortalılığı', *Prof. Dr. Fevzi Şahlanan'a Armağan*, C. II, Istanbul Üniversitei Hukuk Fakültesi Mecmuası, C. LXXIV, 2016, pp. 1189–1213.
86. For details, *see* N. Caniklioğlu/E. Özkaraca, 'Ev Hizmelerinde Çalışanların Sigortalılığı', *Prof. Dr.*

83. As mentioned above, working under a contract of employment is not sufficient to be covered by Act No. 5510. Certain groups fall out of the scope of Article 4/I-a. Some of them are mentioned for the sake of clarifying their status; however, others are exempted from the system, despite the fact that they work with a contract of employment in the workplace of an employer.

84. Those who fall out of the scope of short- and long-term insurance branches of Act No. 5510 are listed below (Article 6 of Act No. 5510). Their status of insurance with respect to universal health insurance will be examined in Part V:

- The spouse of the employer who works gratis in the workplace is not covered by social insurance provisions of Act No. 5510. However, if this spouse's activities exceed the limit required by spousal solidarity, a contract of employment between them is considered to exist. In order to recognize the contract of employment, the Court of Cassation looks for the existence of a wage and active work as indices.[87] The spouse is the married partner under the Civil Code. Those living together without a marriage contract do not fall under the coverage of Article 6/I, a of Act No. 5510.
- Those who live together in the same dwelling and are relatives (up to and including the third degree of kinship) performing an activity in the same domicile without the assistance of non-family persons fall out of the scope of provisions of Act No. 5510 relating to short- and long-term social insurance branches. Regarding the nature of the activities performed in the domicile, the Act does not provide any indication. One group of commentators, referring to Article 5/VII of LA which excludes handicrafts from the scope of Act, argues for a restrictive construction so that only handicrafts such as weaving, carpet-making, shoe-making and similar activities are excluded.[88] Others interpret the Act in a broader manner without any restriction on the nature of activities performed in the domicile.[89]
- During compulsory military service, it is evident that there is no work relationship, which could be a basis for social insurance. However, these periods may be indebted to the Social Security Institution (Article 6/I, d of Act No. 5510).
- Foreign nationals who are sent to Turkey for a period lasting no more than three months, and for work to be done on behalf of, and on account of an undertaking whose headquarters are located abroad and who documents their insured status in their own country, fall out of the scope of provisions related to social insurance branches (Article 6/I, e of Act No. 5510).

Fevzi Şahlanan'a Armağan, C. II, Istanbul Üniversitei Hukuk Fakültesi Mecmuası, C. LXXIV, 2016, pp. 1133–1161; F.B. Savaş Kutsal, 'Ev Hizmetlerinde Çalışanların Sİgortalılığı', *Prof. Dr. Turhan Esener'e Armağan, C. I, Istanbul Kültür Üniversitesi Hukuk Fakültesi Dergisi,* C. 15, S. 1(Ocak, 2016), pp. 651–685.

87. Court of Cass., 21th Ch., 5.6.2002, 4887/5996, cited and noted by A.R. Okur, 'Sosyal Sigortaların Genel Hükümleri ve Primler', in *Yargıtayın İş Hukukuna İlişkin Kararlarının Değerlendirilmesi 2002* (Ankara, 2004), p. 280.
88. K. Tunçomağ, n. 7, pp. 110–111; A. Güzel/A.R. Okur, A.R./N. Caniklioğlu, n. 7, p.108; C. Tuncay, Ö. Ekmekçi, n. 7, p. 325; F. Uşan, n. 28, p. 109; A.N. Sözer, n. 70, p. 100.
89. M. Çenberci, n. 80, p. 60.

- Students engaged in the manufacturing and the production of work carried out during active educational terms in high schools are not covered by provisions of Act No. 5510 related to short- and long-term insurance branches, as these activities are not performed under a contract of employment (Article 6/I, f of Act No. 5510). However, professional and technical secondary school students, while following a vocational training programme in an enterprise, are insured for occupation-related illness and industrial accidents and health (Article 25 of Act No. 3308).
- Sick or disabled persons who are undergoing a course of occupational rehabilitation in health institutions are not covered (Article 6/I, g of Act No. 5510).
- Those who work in agricultural or forestry work with a contract of employment for temporary works, if they do not work in public entities, are not covered by compulsory social insurance system (Article 6/I, ı of Act No. 5510). Temporary employment contracts are contracts concluded for works, owing to its nature, that last only up to thirty days (Article 10 of Act No. 4857).[90] If such a contract is concluded with public entities, the employee is covered by Article 4/I-a.
- Those who take charge temporarily in youth or sports activities or camping, training and other preparatory works related to these activities organized by the Ministry of Youth and Sports, the General Directorate of Sports, Turkish Football Federation or other independent sports federations also fall out of the scope of compulsory insurance system (Article 6/I, m of Act No. 5510).

85. Second, certain groups are partly covered by certain short- and long-term branches of insurance. Although they do not work under a contract of employment, they benefit from these provisions in the same way as employees do.

Those who benefit only from certain branches of insurance under Article 5 are listed below:

- Convicts and detainees who are employed in establishments, workshops and similar units structured under penal institutions, such as penitentiaries and jails, receive benefits from the industrial accidents and occupational diseases, and maternity insurance. Although they do not work under a contract of employment, they are deemed as insurance holders under the frame of Article 4/I-a of Act No. 5510. For the long-term insurance branches such as invalidity, old age and survivors, they may benefit from voluntary insurance.
- Apprentices who work under a contract of apprenticeship according to Act No. 3308, Vocational Training, benefit from insurance for industrial accident and occupational diseases and health insurance. These periods cannot be taken into account with respect to long-term insurance branches.[91] Candidate apprentices and vocational training students also receive insurance benefits. Their contributions are paid by the Ministry of National Education at the rate of 50% of the

90. *See* T. Dereli, *Labour Law and Industrial Relations in Turkey* (Kluwer Law International, 2013), para. 149.
91. Court of Cass., 21th Ch., 3.11.2008, 2007/22085, K. 2008/16972, www.legalbank.net, cited and noted by A. Güzel, 'Sosyal Sigortaların Genel Hükümleri ve Türleri', *Yargıtayın İş Hukuku ve Sosyal Güvenlik Hukuku Kararlarının Değerlendirilmesi, 2008* (Ankara, 2010), pp. 301–302.

minimum wage appropriate to their age. They are deemed to be insurance holders under the frame of Article 4/I-a of Act No. 5510. Before this new legislation, members of their families (such as spouses, children and parents) were not entitled to any benefits, neither health insurance nor allowances paid in the event of the death of an insured apprentice. Such restrictions are revealed by Act No. 5510.[92] Nevertheless, such an insurance holdership covers only monetary benefits provided by those insurance branches.[93] With respect to healthcare services, their status is determined according to the provisions of universal health insurance.

- Trainees who do internships during their education at a vocational high school or higher education had previously no social insurance protection against the risks arising from the fact of working in the workplace. Act No. 5510 brings social insurance protection to these trainees. The internship could be mandatory or voluntary. A mandatory internship is an internship which constitutes a mandatory part of the education given in the school or university. In addition, according to Article 5/I, b of Act No. 5510, those who do an internship during their vocational or technical secondary education or higher education and technical or secondary school students who have vocational training or field education benefit from the insurance branch for industrial accidents and occupational diseases.
- Students who work part-time in universities are partly covered by social insurance. According to Article 46 of Act No. 2547 on Higher Education, students who hold a scholarship or who fulfil the necessary conditions to hold a scholarship may be recruited in part-time, temporary jobs in universities. Such a relationship is not considered as an employment relationship.[94] The amount of the hourly wage shall not be more than one-fourth of the gross daily minimum wage. Although they do not work under a contract of employment, those part-time students whose monthly earnings are not more than thirty times of the lower limits of the minimum daily earnings based on the contribution benefit from the industrial accidents and occupational diseases insurance. Therefore, Act No. 5510 makes a difference on the basis of the student's amount of wage. If the monthly wage is less than the amount equal to thirty times of the lower limits of their minimum daily earnings, students are partly covered; however, if their monthly wage is more than this amount, they are fully covered by social insurance branches.[95]
- Scholarship holders who take charge in projects supported by public law entities are also entitled to receive benefits from industrial accidents and occupational diseases insurance branch.
- Medical interns are students who have completed the fifth year of medical school. They are entitled to receive a monthly salary in return for their services during

---

92. A. Güzel/A.R. Okur/N. Caniklioğlu, n. 7, p. 122.
93. For problems *see* Y. Alper, '5510 Sayılı Kanun'da Primlerin Karşılık Olma Özelliği ve Çırakların ve Mesleki Eğitim Gören Öğrencilerin Sosyal Güvenliği', *Sicil Der.* (Haziran, 2010), pp. 175–183.
94. C. Tuncay/Ö. Ekmekçi, n. 7, p. 312; A. Güzel/A.R. Okur/N. Caniklioğlu, n. 7, p. 124; A.N. Sözer, n. 70, p. 84; for opposite view N. Gerek, 'Üniversitelerde Kısmi Zamanlı Olarak Çalıştırılan Öğrencilerin Sosyal Güvenlik Sorunları', *Sicil Der.* (Haziran, 2009), pp. 237–238.
95. A. Güzel/A.R. Okur/N. Caniklioğlu, n. 7, p. 124; F. Uşan, n. 28, p. 102; N. Gerek, 'Kısmi Zamanlı Olarak Çalıştırılan Öğrenciler', pp. 235–236.

their medical education (Supp. Article 29 of Act No. 2457). Medical interns benefit from industrial accidents and occupational diseases and health insurance.

- If war veterans and individuals receiving job invalidity pensions under Act No. 2330 and Article 56 of Act No. 5434 return to work-life under Article 4/I a, band b-c of Act No. 5510, their pensions would not be cut-off. They continue to benefit from pensions. If they work under the frame of Article 4/I c, they shall be subjected to long-term insurance branches. However, if they work under the frame of Article 4/I a and b, they shall be subjected to the provisions of industrial accidents and occupational diseases insurance (Article 5/I, c of Act No. 5510). If they desire to benefit from long-term insurance branches, they should submit a written request to the Social Security Institution. As of the month following the request, they shall also benefit from long-term insurance branches. However, they are not under obligation to pay contributions to universal health insurance.
- Participants to vocational training organized by the Turkish Employment Institution are deemed to be insurance holders with respect to industrial accidents and occupational diseases branch (Article 5/I, e of Act No. 5510).
- As mentioned above, Turkish employees sent by employers, who undertake work in countries with whom the Turkish Republic has no bilateral agreement, are deemed to be insurance holders under Article 4/I a of Act No. 5510 with respect to short-term insurance branches and universal health insurance. If those employers wish to be subjected to long-term insurance branches, they may benefit from voluntary insurance.[96]
- Like performing artists and musicians, the social security of drivers of taxis, minibuses or any other inner-city transport vehicles is an ongoing problem. The Act provides a special provision which enables them to have social insurance benefits under the condition that they pay contributions for thirty days (Supp. Article 6 of Act No. 5510). If they work with part-time employment contracts for one or more than one employer and if the number of days they work in a month is less than ten days, drivers and other personnel working in these vehicles are obliged to pay contributions to get the benefits. The amount of the earnings, between the lower and the upper limits, based for the contribution is fixed by the insurance holder. However, the Act provides a progressive transition; starting from 2011, the contribution payment is calculated eighteen times the daily contribution amount, that for each following year, this rate is increased by one point (Trans. Article 29 of Act No. 5510).
- Those who receive work loss compensation pursuant to Article 21 of Act No. 4046 on Privatization Implementations are deemed to be insurance holders with respect to long-term insurance branches and universal health insurance. They are exempted from long-term insurance branches (Prov. Article 13 of Act No. 5510).

86. The beginning of the insured status starts from the date of beginning work or vocational education or training (Article 7 of Act No. 5510). Employers are to notify the Institution of the insurance holder before his/her recruitment into the workplace. The beginning of the insured status starts with the employment but not

96. *See* S. Ocak, 'Sosyal Güvenlik Sözleşmesi İmzalanmamış Ülkelere Götürülen İşçilerin Sosyal Güvenliği', 19, *Legal-İSGHD*(2008), pp. 1094–1098.

with the submission of notification.[97] For the same reason, the conclusion date of the employment contract has no importance for the acquisition of insurance holder status.

87. The notification may be done either by directly submitting a notification of employment or by forwarding such notification by registered mail, before the date on which the concerned employee starts work (Article 8 of Act No. 5510). Act No. 5510 provides exemptions to that principle: Insurance holders employed in construction, fishing or agricultural workplaces must be notified, at the latest, on the date of the employee starting work (Article 8/I, a of Act No. 5510). Insurance holders, who are recruited to work in transportation vehicles that travel to foreign countries, are to notify the Institution, at the latest, up to the end of one month from the date they start work. In a similar manner, employees who are recruited during the month starting from the first day of employee recruitment in a workplace for which the workplace notification is submitted for the first time, in other words, in newly founded workplaces, the notification of the insurance holder should be submitted at the latest up to the end of one month from the date of starting work.

88. The insurance holder may also notify the Institution of his employment status himself/herself within one month starting from the date of starting work. However, the fact that the insurance holder has not notified himself/herself does not constitute evidence against the insurance holder.

2. Voluntary Insurance

89. The social insurance system has a compulsory nature. Under Article 92 of Act No. 5510, social insurance holdership is mandatory for those who are covered by the personal scope of the application of Act No. 5510. Employees are insured automatically, as soon as they enter into an employment relationship. However, this principle is not applied in an absolute way under Turkish social security law. Voluntary insurance has always existed under Act No. 5510, and the three abrogated acts.[98] However, Act No. 5510 expanded the coverage of social insurances in society by facilitating application conditions for voluntary insurance.[99]

90. Conditions for utilizing voluntary insurance are as follows: First of all, the candidate must reside in Turkey.[100] Turkish nationals residing abroad do not benefit

97. *See, as example,* Court of Cass., 21th Ch., 9.4.2012, 6998/5507, 35, *Çalışma ve Toplum Der.*(2012/4), pp. 469–471.
98. *See* Y. Bostancı, *Sosyal Güvenlik Hukukunda İsteğe Bağlı Sigortalılık* (Istanbul, 2004); L. Akın, 'Tek Çatı Öncesi ve Sonrasında İsteğe Bağlı Sigortalılık', *Mercek*(Temmuz, 2006), pp. 165–181; M. Balcı, '5510 Sayılı Sosyal Sigortalar ve Genel Sağlık Sigortası Kanunu Döneminde İsteğe Bağlı Sigortalılık Uygulaması Hakkında İnceleme', *Sicil Der.*(Haziran, 2009), pp. 249–253.
99. L. Akın, 'İsteğe Bağlı Sigortalılık', p. 174; A. Güzel/A.R. Okur/N. Caniklioğlu, n. 7, p. 175; C. Tuncay/Ö. Ekmekçi, n. 7, p. 346; F. Uşan, n. 28, p. 117.
100. About this issue *see* M. Balcı, 'İsteğe Bağlı Sigortalılık', pp. 250–251; Güzel/A.R. Okur/N. Caniklioğlu, n. 7, pp. 177–178; C. Tuncay/Ö. Ekmekçi, n. 7, pp. 348–349.

from this opportunity unless decided otherwise by bilateral agreements. For example, social security agreements between the Turkish Republic and France, as well as with Sweden, allow Turkish nationals to be voluntarily insured. However, Turkish workers employed in the workplaces of Turkish employers founded in a foreign country with whom the Turkish Republic has no bilateral agreement may benefit from voluntary insurance if they reside in Turkey. Non-nationals may also benefit from this opportunity if they have been residing in Turkey for more than one year.[101]

Second, the candidate must not be insured compulsorily under Act No. 5510. However, the provision has an exemption: Those who work for less than thirty days in a month or who work part-time may benefit from this opportunity. Although part-time workers are compulsorily insured, the number of contribution paid days is counted by dividing the total number of working hours by 7.5 hours, as the daily working hour. Therefore, if, for example, a part-time employee works fifteen hours in a week, eight days of contributions shall be paid. Considering the difficulty to complete 7,200 days to benefit from the old-age pension, the Act gives the opportunity for part-time workers to pay contributions for the rest of the month.[102] Therefore, the insurance holder shall carry compulsory and voluntary insured statuses for the same period, which is quite exceptional. Performing artists and musicians, as well as personnel of commercial taxis and bus drivers, benefit from this opportunity, only if they work for ten days or more in a month. As mentioned above, if they work for less than ten days in a month, they are subjected to supplementary Article 6.

Third, the candidate must not be drawing a pension due to his own work relation (Article 50/II, a of Act No. 5510). Since the Act requires drawing a pension due to his own work relation, those who receive an 'allowance' may benefit from voluntary insurance. In a similar manner, the Act prohibits only those who receive a pension due to their own work. Therefore, if a person receives a pension from survivals' insurance, he/she may still benefit from voluntary insurance.[103]

Fourth, the Act provides that only those who are 18 years or over may benefit from this opportunity (Act. No. 50/II, c of Act No. 5510).

Lastly, it is obligatory to apply to the Institution in writing (Article 50/II, d of Act No. 5510). Voluntary insurance shall start from the beginning of the month, which follows the submission of the application to the Institution.

91. The most important change brought by Act No. 5510 with regard to the application conditions for voluntary insurance is the absence of a minimum contribution payment requirement. According to abrogated Act No. 506 on Social Insurance, the candidate had to pay contributions for at least 1,080 days (Article 85/A of

101. A.N. Sözer, n. 70, p. 15.
102. A. Güzel/A.R. Okur/N. Caniklioğlu, n. 7, p. 178; C. Tuncay/Ö. Ekmekçi, n. 7, p. 350, F. Uşan, n. 28, p. 117; A.N. Sözer, n. 70, p. 16, notes 4–5.
103. A. Güzel/A.R. Okur/N. Caniklioğlu, n. 7, p. 179; C. Tuncay/Ö. Ekmekçi, n. 7, p. 350; A.N. Sözer, n. 70, p. 21.

Act No. 506). Such a long contribution requirement was heavily criticized.[104] However, according to the new regulation, even registration to the Social Security Institution is not required. Therefore, anyone who has never entered into a work relationship, either as an employee, or independent, or public officer, may benefit from voluntary insurance. Such an exemption has an abrogative effect on the compulsory nature of the social insurance system. It is one of the points that the Bismarckian structure has totally ignored.

92. Voluntary insurance holder should pay contributions for long-term insurance branches and universal health insurance over thirty days for each month (Article 52 of Act No. 5510). An income level between lower and upper limits of Act No. 5510 shall be chosen by the insurance holder. The contribution rate is 32% of this income level.

93. Periods for which contributions are paid shall be taken into account while executing invalidity, old-age and survivals insurance branches and universal health insurance. However, in order to get granted pensions from invalidity, old-age and survivals insurances, insurance holders covered by Article 4/I-a (mainly employees), by Article 4/I-b (mainly Self-Employed persons) and by Article 4/I-c (mainly public officers) are subjected to different regimes, despite the common legislation which regulates the social security system. Therefore, the legal qualification of voluntarily insured periods reveals importance while determining the pension regime. In principle, these periods are considered as periods passed under Article 4/I-b of Act No. 5510. Exemption to this principle is contributions paid by part-time workers. The voluntarily insured periods paid by part-time employees are deemed as periods passed under Article 4/I-a of Act No. 5510 (Article 50/2, 4 of Act No. 5510).

B. Dependants and Beneficiaries

94. The social insurance system is based on the contributions of wage earners and their employers. However, the group under an obligation to pay contributions does not coincide with the one receiving social insurance benefits. For example, the family members of the insured worker benefit from some social insurance benefits without paying any contributions. The dependants of contributors constitute an important percentage of beneficiaries.

95. The social security coverage of family members is divided into two categories: dependants and beneficiaries. As long as the insurance holder is alive, his/her family members benefit only from healthcare services, while their cost of living is provided by the insurance holder. Therefore, family members do not get any monetary benefit from the Institution. By the death of the insurance holder, family members become a 'beneficiary' in the system. According to Article 3/7 of Act No. 5510, the spouse, children and parents of an insurance holder become beneficiaries if the

104. A. Güzel/A.R. Okur, 10. ed., p. 124; C. Tuncay/Ö. Ekmekçi, 11. ed., pp. 144–145.

insurance holder or those who receive permanent incapacity allowances or those who receive pensions due to old-age, invalidity or job invalidity become deceased.

III. Spatial Scope of Application

96. While applying legal provisions about social security, workplace carries an important place, because the social security system is based on the monitoring of insurance holders via workplace numbers. The workplace is the principal administrative unit that the Social Security Institution uses as a controlling power. In addition, the place wherein the insurance holder works determines the risks of industrial accident and occupational disease.

97. A workplace is a unit wherein material and immaterial elements, as well as insurance holders, are organized by an employer to produce goods and services.[105] The employer may have many production units. The problem is whether these different units may be considered under the organizational frame of one workplace. Under Turkish Law, the workplace is recognized as organizational integrity. Article 11 of Act No. 5510, as well as Article 2 of the LA, provides that affiliated units, annexes and vehicles belong to the integrity of the workplace. Affiliated units are those units wherein the common organizational targets are pursued under the common management with the main unit. Although the close location of the affiliated unit to the workplace is not required, the distance between units may prevent common management.

Not only production units but also social facilities are considered under the frame of the workplace. Facilities such as restrooms, nurseries, dining rooms, dormitories, medical examination and maintenance, body or vocational training places, and courtyards also belong to the workplace. Any kind of vehicle, either motorized or not, such as cranes, buses, cars, trucks, fork-lifts etc. are also part of the workplace.

98. The employer is under a duty to notify the Social Security Institution of the workplace. According to Article 11/3 of Act No. 5510, the employer is responsible for delivering the workplace notification either directly or via the internet when he/she starts to employ an insurance holder. Therefore, whenever an insurance holder enters into a workplace to work, the place draws the attention of the Institution. Each workplace should have a registration number given by the Institution. Such a number constitutes the basis for social security procedures related to that workplace. If a workplace or undertaking employing insurance holders is transferred to another employer or moved up to another address in another city, a workplace notification should be submitted to the Institution. The notification has no legally founding effect. Therefore, no or late submission of the workplace notification shall not abolish the rights and duties arising from Act No. 5510.

---

105. For the concept *see*, K. Doğan Yenisey, *İş Hukukunda İşyeri ve İşletme, -Alman ve Fransız Hukuklarıyla Karşılaştırmalı Bir İnceleme*(Istanbul, 2007), pp. 17–51; T. Dereli, n. 91, paras 127–131.

99. In the case of non-submission of the workplace notification in the time and manner due, the Institution is authorized to issue the necessary certificates. The non-observance of a legal duty is the pre-condition for the use of ex-officio authority of the Institution (Article 32 of RSIP). By detection of non-submission of workplace documents, the Institution officially notifies the employer that the relevant document must be submitted within a month. If the employer does not deliver the required documents within the month, the Institution prepares them ex-officio. In addition, non-submission of documents is sanctioned by administrative fines.

100. Under the social security system, although the Act recognizes the organizational structure, the workplace has a physical subsistence, which is reflected as an address and registration number. However, technological developments have transformed this physical presence substantially. Through information technology, the insurance holder may perform his/her task from his/her own home without the need for being present in a workplace. Such practices create important problems from practical points as the administrative system needs to have a registration number given to a workplace to assess the submitted information.

§2. Calculation of Contributions

101. Based on the Bismarckian tradition, contributions of employees and employers are the main source of the financing of social insurance. Except in the case of unemployment insurance, the state did not share the financial burden of social insurance under the previous system. The state is under a duty to contribute to the Institution at a rate of one-fourth of the total amount of invalidity, old age and survivors insurance and universal health insurance contributions. The state contribution to the finance of social insurances is one of the positive aspects of the reform.

102. The Act recognizes the obligatory nature of paying contributions with regard to insurance holders. Spending ways of contribution incomes are determined by Act No. 5510 to prevent the state from using social security funds to make up budgetary deficits. Therefore, the Institution has the right to collect contributions only to afford every kind of payment foreseen by the Act related to short and long-term insurance branches, universal health insurance and managerial expenses (Article 79 of Act No. 5510).

103. The workers' contribution is deducted from wages by the employers, who must add their share and remit the entire contribution to the Social Security Institution.

I. Calculation Base

104. Article 80 of Act No. 5510 determines in a very detailed manner the nature of the income of the insured, which shall be the basis for contributions. Not only the gross wage but also some other payments on the part of the employer are taken into contributions calculation. Article 80/I classifies the income types into the three sub-categories discussed below.

A. *Wages That Insured Employee Is Entitled During the Month That Contribution Is Paid*

105. According to Article 80/I, a, 1 of Act No. 5510, wage that an insured employee is entitled to receive for the month in question constitutes the basis for the calculation of contribution amount. It is irrelevant whether the employee received the wage or not. It is sufficient that the wage is accrued. Article 32 of LA No. 4857 gives this definition of wage: 'wage is, in general terms, the amount of money to be paid in cash by an employer or by a third party to a person in return for work performed'.[106] Besides the basic wage, this definition includes overtime pay, pay for national and public holidays, as well as a weekly day of rest. While calculating the contribution amount, seniority payments, shift payments, hardship premiums, social assistance, etc. are also taken into consideration.[107]

106. Wages paid to the insured employee during sickness and confinement periods are also subjected to contribution deductions. In fact, an employer is not obliged to pay wages to an employee who cannot work due to sickness or pregnancy. An insured employee has the right to temporary disability allowances paid by the Social Security Institution. However, employees whose salaries are paid on a lump-sum monthly basis are entitled to remuneration during sickness or confinement. In this case, an employer ought to pay the difference between the wage and temporary disability allowance. Such payment is also subjected to contribution deductions.[108]

107. The wage increments paid retroactively due to collective agreements caused certain problems. The conclusion of a new collective agreement, following the termination of another one, takes, in most cases, a long time. It may take more than one year between the termination of a collective agreement and conclusion of a new one, which means employees are not entitled to any wage increments during this period. In order to compensate employees' losses, that would have been due during this period; a retroactive entry put into force of a collective agreement has

---

106. *See* T. Dereli, n. 91, paras 267–271.
107. Y. Alper, '5510 Sayılı Kanunda 4/1-a Kapsamındaki Sigortalılar Bakımından Prime Esas Kazançlar', *Sicil Der.*(Aralık, 2008), pp. 166–179; Ö. Ekmekçi, 'Primlere İlişkin Hükümler', in *Yeni Sosyal Güvenlik Sistemi* (Istanbul Barosu Yayınları, 2010), pp. 131–138; A. Güzel/ A.R. Okur/N. Caniklioğlu, n. 7, p. 230; C. Tuncay/Ö. Ekmekçi, n. 7, p. 164; F. Uşan, n. 28, p. 135; A.N. Sözer, n. 70, pp. 200–201; B. Öztürk, *Türk Sosyal Güvenlik Hukukunda Primler*(Ankara, 2016), pp. 165–169; Ö. Ekmekçi, '506 Sayılı Sosyal Sigortalar Kanununda Prim Oranları ve Prime Esas Olan–Olmayan Kazançlar', *İHD*, 1(1991), pp. 240–248.
108. Ö. Ekmekçi, 'Primlere İlişkin Hükümler', p. 232; A. Güzel/A.R. Okur/N. Caniklioğlu, n. 7, p. 231; C. Tuncay/Ö. Ekmekçi, n. 7, pp. 164; A.N. Sözer, n. 70, pp. 199–200.

been decided. Therefore, a sum of wage increments, which arise from the retroactive implementation of a collective agreement, is paid to the employee on a lump-sum basis, which is subject to contribution deduction. However, a contribution deduction on the month of effective payment caused contribution losses of the Institution because the payments beyond the upper limit are exempted from deductions.[109] Facing this problem, the Court of Cassation held that the wage increments which would have been due in previous months, arising from the retroactive application of the collective agreement, were to be taken into contributions calculations.[110]

B. Premiums, Bonuses, Gratuities and All Similar Payments Which Have Been Paid to Insured Employees in the Month in Question

108. Premiums are designed to reward the employee for hard work, increased effort or superior performance. Bonuses are also a special form of remuneration granted by an employer on certain occasions, such as the end of a working year, secular and religious holidays, birthdays, etc. From any other similar payments, the employer is to also remit the contributions (Article 80/I, a, 2 of Act No. 5510).

109. Certain earnings of employees are exempted from insurance deductions;[111] for example, allowances in kind, death, birth and marriage benefits, travel allowances, severance payments, notice period and cash indemnities, food, child and family assistance, at an amount to be fixed annually by the Institution. In addition, private health insurance contributions and personal retirement contribution fees, the total amount of which do not exceed 30% of the monthly minimum wage paid by employers on behalf of insurance holders, are exempted (Article 80/I, c of Act No. 5510). These exemptions are exhaustively listed by the Act.[112] Any other exemptions provided by special acts are abrogated by Act No. 5510, and such payments are also submitted to deductions.[113] If allowances in kind are paid in cash, they will also be taken into calculation when contributions are deducted (Article 80/I, c of Act No. 5510).

110. Unlike wages, only the monthly amount, which is actually paid to the insured employee, is taken into calculation. If the employee is entitled to a bonus but has not received it totally or in part, contributions are deducted only on the sum actually paid out. However, such a system caused premium losses for the months when the amount of bonuses was higher than the upper limit of contributions, as

109. A. Güzel/A.R. Okur/N. Caniklioğlu, n. 7, pp. 234–235.
110. Court of Cass., HGK, 17 May 1989, 10-250/361, *YKD*(Şubat, 1990), pp. 171–172.
111. *See* A. Güzel/A.R. Okur/N. Caniklioğlu, n. 7, pp. 240–245; Tuncay/Ö. Ekmekçi, n. 7, pp. 168–174; A.N. Sözer, n. 70, pp. 204–205; M. Şakar, n. 7, pp. 149–150; B. Öztürk, *Primler,* pp. 179–182.
112. A. Güzel/A.R. Okur/N. Caniklioğlu, n. 7, p. 241; F. Uşan, n. 28, pp. 138–139; Y. Alper, *Prime Esas Kazançlar,* pp. 168–170; A.N. Sözer, n. 70, p. 205; B. Öztürk, *Primler*, p. 179.
113. *See also* F. Uşan, '5510 Sayılı Kanun Karşısında İlave Tediyelerden Sosyal Sigorta Primi Kesilemeyeceğine İlişkin Kuralın Yürürlükte Olduğu Söylenebilir mi?', *Sicil Der.*(Mart, 2010), pp. 253–257.

payments beyond the upper limit are exempted from deductions. Act No. 5510 provides a new calculation method to prevent such loss. If the amount of payments is beyond the upper limit, that exempted amount shall be added to the amounts due of the following two months, unless the total amount of contributions for these months goes beyond the upper limit.

C. Payments Due to Administrative Decisions or Judicial Verdicts

111. If the wages, bonuses or any kind of payment concerned is paid due to an administrative decision or judicial verdict, contributions are deducted not from the earnings of the relevant month, but from the earnings of the month in which that effective payment is made (Article 80/I, a, 3 of Act No. 5510).

II. Daily Earnings of Employees' Basis for Contribution

112. The gross wage of the worker is the basis for the calculation of contributions. The gross wage is composed of the basic wage, deductions for tax reasons and workers' contributions to the Social Security Institution. Employers' contributions do not constitute part of the gross wage. According to Article 80/I, g of Act No. 5510, the daily earnings are to be taken as a basis for the calculation of contributions. This amount equals one-thirtieth of monthly earnings, subject to contributions. However, if the insurance holder has not been entitled to wages for certain days of the week because he/she has not worked, the total of earnings is divided by the number of days worked on calculating the daily earnings of the insurance holder. Therefore, the number of days taken into account while calculating daily earnings also indicates the number of contribution paid days for insurance holders.

113. The number of contribution paid days is revealed as important when determining whether the insurance holder is entitled to social insurance allowances. If the insurance holder works part-time, the number of contribution paid days is calculated by dividing the total amount of working hours by 7.5 as daily working hours (Article 80/I, h of Act No. 5510). Part-time employment contracts must be in writing.

114. If the insurance holder works for several employers in the same period, each employer shall pay his/her own contribution amount according to the above-explained rules. Nevertheless, if the total monthly amount of contributions paid by different employers is beyond the upper limit, the exceeding part shall be refunded to the insurance holder at a rate of his/her share at the latest within one month following his/her written request. The Institution refunds only the insurance holder's share of the contribution, but not the employers' share. Such a regulation is not compatible with the upper limit restrictions.[114]

114. M. Çenberci, n. 80, p. 450; A. Güzel/A.R. Okur/N. Caniklioğlu, n. 7, p. 246; Tuncay/Ö. Ekmekçi, n. 7, p. 179.

115. Furthermore, the Act sets limits to the amount of daily earnings, the basis for the calculation of contributions. The lower and upper limits are to be taken into consideration. Article 82 states that one-thirtieth of the monthly minimum wage is the lower limit for daily earnings. Various commentators have long put the importance of establishing a link between the minimum wage and the upper limit of the social insurance contributions forward.[115]

The upper limit of the daily earnings is 7.5 times the daily minimum wage. Thus, that part of wages beyond the upper limit is exempted from deductions for social security contributions.

III. Contribution Amount

116. On the basis of the daily earnings, employer and employee pay specific contribution rates for each branch of social insurance. Three different contribution types exist: contributions for long-term insurance branches, contributions for long-term insurance branches and universal health insurance contributions (Article 81 of Act No. 5510).

117. Long-term insurance branches cover the monetary risks of industrial accidents and occupational diseases, sickness and maternity insurances. The Act has a fixed contribution rate for long-term insurance branches to 2% regardless of the degree of risk of the work. Short-term contributions are only to be paid by the employer.

118. Contribution for long-term insurance branches covers the risks of disability, old age and death of the insurance holder. The contribution is paid at the rate of 20% of the earnings of the insurance holder. 9% of this amount is to be paid by the insurance holder. 11% of the amount falls on the employer's share. Act No. 5510 brings for the first time the state's financial support to the insurance system. According to Article 81/III of Act No. 5510, the state is under an obligation to contribute to the Institution at a rate of one-fourth of invalidity, old age and survivors insurance and universal health insurance premiums collected by the Institution.

119. If the insurance holder is covered by short and long-term insurance branches, the contribution amount of universal health insurance is 12.5%, of which 5% imputes on the insurance holder and 7.5% on the employer of the earnings based for contribution. Nevertheless, if the insurance holder is subjected only to universal health insurance, the contribution amount is 12% of the contribution basis.

120. The unemployment insurance is regulated by the special Act No. 4447, which entered into force on 1 June 2000. The rate of contribution for this insurance

115. A. Güzel/A.R. Okur, 10. ed., p. 167; C. Tuncay, *Sosyal Güvenlik Hukuku Dersleri* (Istanbul, Beta, 2002), p. 170; K. Arıcı, '4447 Sayılı Kanunla Sosyal Sigortalar Kanununda Yapılan Değişiklikler', *Kamu-İş Der.*(Ocak, 2000), p. 23; A. Güzel/E. Özkaraca, '506 Sayılı Sosyal Sigortalar Kanunu'nda 4958 ve 5073 Sayılı Kanunlar İle Yapılan Değişiklikler', 2, *Legal-İSGHD*(2004), p. 438.

is 4% of the basis for contribution, of which 1% is the insurance holder's share, 2% is the employer's share, and 1% is the share of the state.

Table 1 Contribution Amounts Applied under the Frame of Social Insurance and Universal Health Insurance Act

Insurance Branches	*Employee*	*Employer*	*State*	*Total*
Long-term insurance branches (Disability, old age and survivors)	9	11	-	**20**
Universal health insurance	5	7.5	–	**12.5**
Long-term insurance branches (Industrial accidents and occupational diseases, sickness and maternity)	–	2	–	**2**
Unemployment	1	2	1	**4**
TOTAL	**15**	**22.5**	**1**	**38.5**

121. Act No. 5510 abolishes the insurance holder's opportunity for going back to work while drawing old-age pensions. If those who gain the insurance holder status for the first time according to Act No. 5510 resume work while drawing an old-age pension, the pension shall be cut-off at the beginning of the payment period following the date of their resume to work (Article 30 /III of Act No. 5510).[116] However, those who have gained the insured status before the entry into force of Act No. 5510 may resume working under a contract of employment while drawing an old-age pension. If he/she submits a request in writing, pension payments continue. However, a special contribution called 'social security support contribution' is deducted from their earnings at a rate of 30%.[117] One-fourth of the contribution (7.5%) is to be paid by the insured employee and three-fourths (22.5%) by the employer (Prov. Article 14/I, a of Act No. 5510). In addition, Act No. 5510 provides that the employer is also to pay contributions for industrial accidents and

116. *See infra* paras 482–484.
117. The ratio of 25% is replaced by 30% by Act No. 4447 which is valid from 1 Oct. 1999.

occupational diseases while recruiting pension holders with a contract of employment. Therefore, the total amount of employer's share shall be 24.5% (22.5%+ 2%) of the basis for contribution.

Since the amount of pensions is low in general, there existed many complaints about the deductions for social security contribution. The legislator has made an exception by Act No. 6663[118] for those who resume working as subjected to Article 4/I, b, mainly Self-Employed persons. Therefore, those who gain an insurance holder status for the first time according to Act No. 5510 could resume working while drawing an old-age pension and without paying any social security contribution, if this new work is subjected to Article 4/I, b. Nevertheless, they have the right to request the cut-off from their old-age pensions and be insured with respect to all insurance branches[119] (Amended Article 30/III, b of Act No. 5510).

§3. Reduction and Exemptions

122. To counter the criticisms that the amount of social security contributions is too high to create new employment, certain reductions and subsidizations are envisaged both by special acts and Act No. 5510.[120] The number of special provisions has been increased since 2004. Each act provides special conditions and special rates of subsidization. The main principle that an employer could only benefit from one subsidization rate is revealed by Act No. 6111. Therefore, the employer may benefit from more than one subsidization available for his/her situation (Article 81/I, ı of Act No. 5510).

123. Act No. 5510 provides that 5% of the employer's contribution rate of disability, old-age and survivals insurance contribution is paid by the Treasury (Article 81/I, ı of Act No. 5510). Only private sector employers may benefit from this reduction. If there is more than one subsidization available, 5% reduction shall be applied.

The employer is to deliver monthly insurance certificates to the Institution within the deadline fixed by the Act and pay monthly contributions on time. Also, the employer is to be out of debt against the Institution. If the employer delays in delivering certificates or paying contributions, his/her right to the benefit from this reduction does not end but is interrupted. By the delivery or payment, 5% of the reduction is re-deducted.[121] The employer cannot benefit from such reduction for employees working abroad and employees drawing an old-age pension.

124. Due to Article 30 of Act No. 4857, employers who have fifty or more employees in their workplaces within the boundaries of the same municipality are obliged to employ people who are disabled, ex-convicts or victims of terror. The

118. OJ, 10 Feb. 2016, No. 29620.
119. For details, *see* A. Güzel/A.R. Okur/N. Caniklioğlu, n. 7, pp. 562–568.
120. For details, *see*, N. Caniklioğlu, *Sosyal Sigortalarda Prim Teşvikleri* (Istanbul, 2011); B. Öztürk, *Primler*, pp. 116–156.
121. N. Caniklioğlu, *Prim Teşvikleri*, pp. 21–29; H. Ergin, 'İşverenlere Getirilen Beş Puanlık Prim İndirimi', *Sicil Der.*(Aralık, 2008), pp. 176–186; A.Güzel/A.R. Okur/N. Caniklioğlu, n. 7, pp. 291–292; C. Tuncay/Ö. Ekmekçi, n. 7, pp. 183–186; F. Uşan, n. 28, pp. 153–154.

ratio of disabled employees shall not be less than 3% of the total number of employees in the private sector workplaces. In public sector workplaces, employers are obliged to employ disabled employees at a ratio of 4% and ex-convicts at a ratio of 2% of the total number of employees.[122] Article 30/VI of the LA provides that the employer's contributions for disabled employees recruited mandatorily shall be paid by the Treasury. Therefore, the legislation encourages the employment of disabled persons.

125. The contribution amount of the insurance holder is calculated on the amount of the lower limit of their daily earnings. If the wage of a disabled employee is more than the amount of the lower limit, the contribution to the difference is for the employer to pay. In order to benefit from this subsidization, the employer is to deliver monthly insurance certificates to the Institution on time and to pay all contribution obligations to the Institution within the legal due time.

126. To subsidize the employment of young and female employees, many special subsidizations have been adopted. If the insurance holder is male and is older than 18 years and younger than 29 years or if the insurance holder is female and older than 18 years, the employer shall get subsidization for contributions on a decreasing rate until 31 December 2020.[123] Some other conditions are also required to benefit from this opportunity; for example, the employee should have been unemployed during the last six months before the employment. In addition, the employer needs to increase the number of employees over the average number of workplace recruitment within the previous six months. Furthermore, this subsidization has a temporary nature. The subsidization period varies in accordance with the employee's age, sex, professional education, and being registered as a job seeker on the agency of the Turkish Employment Institution.[124]

The employer benefits from another subsidization for the recruitment of an insurance holder who is older than 18 years and younger than 29 years and who has completed the On-the-Job training programmes, which are organized by the Turkish Unemployment Institution by 31 December 2017. The employer needs to increase the number of employees over the average number of workplace recruitment within the previous year (Trans. Article 15 of Act No. 4447).

127. Since the unemployment rate is considerably high in some regions of the country, different acts were adopted with the aim of encouraging investments and employment in underdeveloped regions. For the private sector, 5% of the employer's contribution rate is paid by the Treasury (Article 81/I, ı). In addition, the Council of Ministers is authorized to determine the cities and the validity period of additional subsidization by taking into account the socio-economic development index. In those cities, 6% of the employer's contribution rate, which is calculated on the basis of the minimum daily earning of the employee, is paid by the Treasury

122. *See* T. Dereli, n. 91, para. 186.
123. The Council of Ministers is authorised to extend the subsidization period for five years by transitory Article 10/12 of Act No. 4447.
124. For details, B. Öztürk, *Primler*, pp. 134–140; C. Tuncay/Ö. Ekmekçi, n. 7, pp. 194–199.

(Article 81/II of Act No. 5510). Therefore, 5% of the employer's contribution rate is calculated on the basis of the daily earnings and 6% of the contribution rate is calculated on the basis of the minimum daily earnings of the employee.[125]

128. Under the framework of decisions on state aids for investment, the full amount of employers' contribution to insurance holders recruited for subsidized investments is paid by the Treasury. The contribution amount is calculated on the upper limits for contributions. The Council of Ministry has the authority to determine the duration, amount, rate and cover of the payment provided by the Treasury, as well as the sector and the size of the investment. The employer is to deliver insurance certificates monthly to the Institution within the deadline fixed by the Act. In addition, the employer has to pay monthly contributions on time to benefit from that subsidization (Article Supp. 2 of Act No. 5510).[126]

129. Act No. 5746 dated 28 October 2008[127] on the Supporting Research and Development Activities provides that 50% of the employers' contributions are paid by the Ministry of Finance for those who are not public officers and who work in research and development centres or programmes and undertakings as R&D or support personnel (Article 3/III of Act No. 5764). Only employees, whose salaries are exempted from income tax according to Act No. 4691 on Technology Development Regions, benefit from this contribution subsidization. According to Article 8/III of Act No. 4691, all payments made to R&D personnel, researchers and software engineers are exempted from all kinds of tax for ten years starting from the foundation date of the region.[128] Besides R&D, a special Act No. 5225 dated in 2004[129] supports the investments for culture.[130]

130. To increase employment, Act No. 5921 dated 11 August 2009[131] provides a special exemption for the recruitment of those benefiting from unemployment insurance. However, each employment of an insurance holder receiving benefits from unemployment insurance does not lead to contribution reduction. Only if the employer increases the number of employees employed during the last six months starting from the previous month of the employment of unemployed, the Unemployment Fund meets the employee's and employer's contributions and contribution for universal health insurance for the rest of the period that the insurance holder would receive unemployment benefit. The subsidized amount of the employer's contribution is limited to the upper limit of the contribution amount, regardless of the employee's wage. In addition, the contribution subsidization shall not be more than 1% of the long-term insurance contributions regardless of the exact amount of

125. A. Güzel/A.R. Okur/N. Caniklioğlu, n. 7, pp. 294–295.
126. *See* N. Caniklioğlu, *Prim Teşvikleri,* pp. 61–74; A. Güzel/A.R. Okur/N. Caniklioğlu, n. 7, pp. 296–297; C. Tuncay/Ö. Ekmekçi, n. 7, pp. 189–191.
127. OJ, 12 Mar. 2008, No. 26814.
128. *See* N. Caniklioğlu, *Prim Teşvikleri,* pp. 194–219.
129. OJ, 21 Jul. 2004, No. 25529.
130. *See* N. Caniklioğlu, *Prim Teşvikleri,* pp. 219–237.
131. OJ, 18 Aug. 2009, No. 27323.

contribution (Article 50/III of Act No. 4447). In order to benefit from this subsidization, the employer is to deliver monthly insurance certificates to the Institution on time and pay all contribution obligations to the Institution within legal due time.[132]

131. Turkish employees who are sent by private sector employers to work in workplaces established abroad are deemed to be an insurance holder with respect to long-term insurance branches and universal health insurance. Since they work abroad, their employers do not benefit from the 5% of the Treasury subsidization. Nevertheless, Article 81/I, i provides that 5% of the employer's contribution rate of general health insurance is paid by the Treasury. Therefore, 5% of the7.5% of the general health insurance contribution is subsidized.

132. Since the number of industrial accidents is quite high, another subsidization in order to prevent industrial accidents is implemented by Act No. 4447 (Supp. Article 4/I, c.1 of Act No. 4447). The subsidization is provided to workplaces which are classified as 'very hazardous' under the frame of Act No. 6331 on Occupational Health and Safety. The employer should employ more than ten employees in workplaces classified as very hazardous throughout Turkey. Moreover, if no industrial accident which causes the death or the permanent incapacity of a worker has occurred during the previous three years, the employer's contribution rate for unemployment insurance is paid at a rate of 1% in the upcoming three years. If an industrial accident which causes a worker's death or a permanent incapacity occurs, the subsidization is cancelled starting from the month following the accident.

§4. Administration

133. The Social Security Institution is charged with the administration and collection of wage earners social insurance premiums. Not only the collection of social insurance and health insurance contributions but also the collection of unemployment insurance contributions is among the duties of the Institution.

I. Collection of Contributions

134. Employers are to pay the total amount of contributions, including insured's share deducted from wages not later than the end of the following month (Article 88/I of Act No. 5510). If the employer fails to deduct the insured's share from wages, the employer is also charged with the payment of this part. The Institution has no right to acquire from the insured any insurance contribution, which has not been deducted by the employer.[133]

132. *See* N. Caniklioğlu, *Prim Teşvikleri,* pp. 152–173.
133. M. Çenberci, n. 80, p. 533; A. Güzel/A.R. Okur/N. Caniklioğlu, n. 7, p. 283.

II. Certificates of Contribution

135. As mentioned above, the employer must notify the Institution both the workplace and insured employees employed in that workplace. However, due to the widespread practice of employing non-registered employees, a strict notification process is established with the aim of strengthening the inspection and supervision of the Institution's records. According to Article 86/I of Act No. 5510, the employer is responsible for submitting to the Institution a 'certificate of insurance and service' wherein the names and national identification numbers of insurance holders, the total insurable earnings, the number of days of the contribution payment, and original and additional records, the nature of which is determined by Institution regulations, are included. The Institution is authorized to determine the date of submission. Employers are under obligation to submit this document within one month, following the month that those records belong to, by the end of the date fixed by the Institution. The details of the certificate are regulated by the Regulation on Social Insurance Process. The notification is to be submitted to the Institution via the internet.

136. An employer is under a duty to notify about not only recruited insurance holders and their contributions but also the fact that he employs no insurance holder anymore. If an employer interrupts in employing an insurance holder in the workplace, he/she should notify the Institution of this issue within fifteen days following the end of employment (Article 86/XII of Act No. 5510).

137. It happens quite often that despite the employee being registered, the number of working days, which are the basis for the contributions, has been declared to be a number lesser than it actually is. Therefore, Article 86/IV states that for an insured person for whom it has been stated that he has not been employed for certain days of a month and for which he has received no wages, the employer is to annex to the certificate of insurance and service notes and documents demonstrating that the insured had worked for less than thirty days. These documents should be enclosed in the monthly certificate of insurance and service.

Chapter 2. Contribution Regulation for Those Who Are Subjected to Article 4/I-b (Mainly Self-Employed Persons)

138. The last group covered by the statutory compulsory social security regime is self-employed persons. Act No. 1479, the Institution of Social Insurance for Craftsmen and Artisans and Other Self-Employed Workers (Bağ-Kur), was adopted in 1971. In 2000, by Decree-law No. 619, the organizational structure and financial status of the Institution, as well as the benefits were modified substantially. Pursuant to the annulment of Decree-law No. 619 by the Constitutional Court,[134] these amendments were made part of Act No. 4956.[135] Lastly, by Act No. 5502, as was the Social Insurance Institution, Bağ-Kur was also transferred to the Social Security Institution with all its assets and obligations (Trans. Article 1 of Act No. 5502).

§1. Field of Application

I. Territorial Field of Application

139. Act No. 5510 regulates the social security of self-employed persons in Turkey. Article 4/I-b, like abrogated Act No. 1479, covers those who engage in an occupational activity in an independent manner in Turkey. Article 4/I-b of Act No. 5510 states that to be covered by Act No. 5510, the candidate must be a taxpayer or member of professional associations because of activities carried out under his/her own name and account, or be a partner in certain types of companies, or carry out agricultural activities. The nationality of a self-employed person has no importance. Thus, foreigners are also covered by compulsory insurance for self-employed.[136]

140. A self-employed person may exercise certain activities abroad. However, as long as that person resides in Turkey, the social security system for self-employed persons finds the place of application. However, if those who carry out activities in Turkey reside abroad and are subjected to the social security legislation of that country, they are not considered as compulsory insurance holders (Article 6/I, e of Act No. 5510). If such persons have a social security relationship, for example, before commencing an independent activity in Turkey they prove that they are registered or have paid contributions to the social security system of their own country, or are receiving a pension, they shall be considered out of the scope of the self-employed foreigners; if they carry out an independent activity in Turkey, and they are not able to prove their subjection to a social security system in their foreign country, they are deemed to be insurance holders under Act No. 5510, even if he/she resides abroad.[137]

134. Cons. Court, 26 Oct. 2000, 61/34, OJ, 8 Nov. 2000, No. 24224.
135. OJ, 2 Aug. 2003, No. 25187.
136. A. Güzel/S. Ocak, '1479 Sayılı Bağ-Kur Kanununda 4956 ve 5073 Sayılı Kanunlar İle Yapılan Değişiklikler', 3, *Legal-İSGHD*(2004), pp. 883–886.
137. M. Bulut, 'Yabancıların Sosyal Güvenlikleri', p. 213; A.N. Sözer, n. 70, p. 108.

II. Personal Field of Application

141. According to Article 4/I-b of Act No. 5510, in order to be considered a compulsory insured self-employed, the insurance holder must carry an occupational activity under his/her own name and account without being engaged with a contract of employment. Before the reform, self-employed insurance holders were divided into two different groups: compulsory and voluntary insured self-employed persons. By Act No. 5510, the compulsory insured status is expanded. Nevertheless, self-employed persons may also benefit from voluntary insurance if they fulfil the required conditions, as explained above.

142. Article 4/I-b divides self-employed persons into five groups:

(1) The elected heads of villages or districts are covered by Article 4/I-b. Apart from Act No. 5510, the social security of elected heads of villages has also been regulated by Act No. 2108 on Allowances and Social Security of the Elected Heads of Village or District. According to Article 4/I-b of Act No. 5510, the social security of elected heads is regulated by Article 4/I-b, without any other requirement. However, Act No. 2108 states another condition: The social security of elected heads is regulated by Article 4/I-b, only if they do not carry out any other activity which is subjected to other paragraphs (a and c) of Act No. 5510. In other words, only if they are not covered by any other social security regime, the elected heads shall be subjected to the regime of self-employed persons. Since Act No. 2108 is *lex specialis,* its application has priority, that is, for example, the elected head is also working with an employment contract, his status of insurance will be determined according to Article 4/I-a, like employees.[138]

(2) Self-employed persons who are income taxpayers because of their commercial earnings or because of income received from independent occupational activities are subjected to Article 4/I-b of Act No. 5510. Independent activity constitutes the fundamental characteristic of being self-employed.

(3) Self-employed persons whose names have been entered in the Craftsmen and Artisans Register are covered by Article 4/I-b. In cases where the self-employed persons are exempted from income tax, Act No. 5510 covers those whose names have been entered in the Craftsmen and Artisans Register.

(4) Shareholders of commercial companies are covered by Article 4/I-b. Except for joint-stock and commandite companies, all shareholders of a company, such as limited company, maritime joint-ventures, are deemed to be insurance holders under Article 4/I-b of Act No. 5510. Shareholders of a joint-stock company are covered by Article 4/I-b, only if they are a member of the board of directors. With respect to commandite company with shareholders, only commandite shareholders are covered by Article 4/I-b.

(5) Those working in the agricultural sector are also covered by Article 4/I-b. Before Act No. 5510 came into force, the social security of self-employed persons in the agricultural sector was regulated by a specific Act No. 2926 in a

138. A. Güzel/A.R. Okur/N. Caniklioğlu, n. 7, p. 101.

voluntary manner. By Act No. 5510, they are covered by the compulsory insurance system. However, if they document the amount of the remaining monthly activity income, after deducting costs, is less than thirty times the lower amount of daily earnings based to contributions, they fall out of the scope of Article 4/I-b (Article 6/I, ı of Act No. 5510).

143. In addition, the social security of jockeys and trainers subject to Law No. 6132 in a Horse Race is also provided under Article 4/I-b of Act No. 5510.

144. In spite of their independent activities, Article 6 of Act No. 5510 exempts those who are mentioned below from the cover of insured persons:

- Those who have not reached 18 years of age fall out of the cover of insured persons, even if they carry out an independent activity in their own name and account (Article 6/I, h of Act No. 5510).
- Those whose monthly income is low are not covered by Article 4/I-b. Although the insured status is based on the nature of the activity, Act No. 5510 provides an important exemption to that rule: Self-employed persons, who are exempted from income tax and who are registered on the Craftsmen and Artisans Register, fall out of the cover of Article 4/I-b of Act No. 5510 if they document the amount of their remaining monthly activity income, after deducting costs, is less than thirty times the lower amount of daily earnings based to contributions. Therefore, the amount of income becomes determinant in subjection to the compulsory insurance system. Considering the importance of the informal economy in Turkey, such an exemption constitutes a significant deficiency to the compulsory nature of the social security system.
- Those who carry an independent activity in the agricultural sector also fall outside the scope of Article 4/I-b if they document that their remaining monthly activity income, after deducting costs, is less than thirty times the lower amount of daily earnings based to contributions (Article 6/I, ı of Act No. 5510). Therefore, the amount of income becomes determinant in determining who is compulsorily insured.[139]
- Those who have reached 65 years of age and who carry an independent activity in the agricultural sector may require to be left out of the scope of Article 4/I-b. The written requirement is necessary (Article 6/I, ı of Act No. 5510).
- Those who resume carrying an independent activity while drawing an old-age pension under the frame of Article 4/I, b may continue to work without a cut-off from their old-age pension. Therefore, they fall out of the compulsory scope of insurance holders, unless they request otherwise (Article 6/1, n of Act No. 5510).

145. The beginning of the status of insurance holdership varies in accordance with the nature of the activity (Article 7/I, b of Act No. 5510). With respect to those who have a tax liability, the compulsory insurance commences with the acquirement of taxpayer status. This group consists of the shareholders of an unlimited

139. A. Güzel/A.R. Okur/N. Caniklioğlu, n. 7, p. 104; K. Arıcı, n. 7, p. 258.

liability company, commandite and commanditer shareholders of regular commandite companies, and shareholders of maritime joint-ventures. Shareholders of limited companies, as well as commandite shareholders of commandite companies shareholders become insured from the date of the company registration by the Trade Registry Office. The board members of a joint-stock company become insured from the date they are elected to the board. The registry date to the Craftsmen and Artisans Register is also considered as the starting date of the insured status. The concerned tax offices, artisan registry offices, administrative bodies are under a duty to notify the Institution of the insurance holder's employment status. In certain cases of the self-employed, he/she may notify the Institution of his/her own employment status. The Social Security Institution announces the enrolled insurance holder within one month that his/her rights and duties have started.

§2. Calculation of Contributions

146. Although the insured status is compulsory in nature, the insured Self-Employed had the right to choose an available income level, which would be the basis for insurance contributions, as they do not have a regular income coming in every month. Before the reform, in order to calculate the insurance contributions required and the pension that the insured would be entitled to, an income table consisting of twenty-four stages was determined. These stages were to be fixed each year. The amount of the insurance premium was 20% of the chosen income level (Articles 49, 50 of Act No. 1479).

Act No. 5510 provides a much simpler system: The Self-Employed person declares to the Institution the amount of their daily earnings based for contributions between lower and upper limits. The amount of the contribution basis is thirty times their daily earnings. If the insurance holder omits to declare the level of his/her income, the lower limit of the daily earnings is taken as the basis for contributions (Article 80/II, a of Act No. 5510). The minimum wage is the lower limit for daily earnings.

§3. Administration

147. After the transfer, the Social Security Institution is the institution authorized to govern the social insurance of craftsmen and artisans. The Institution collects the contributions of and administers the benefits for, the insured self-employed. Insured Self-Employed or others mentioned under Article 4/I-b, or voluntarily insurance holders are to pay their contributions to the Institution by the date fixed by the Institution within the following month. The insurance holders under item 4/I-b are to pay thirty days of contribution for each month. The Act enables Self-Employed insurance holders to advance payment of contributions for a maximum of 360 days. In the case of advance payments, for each day in advance, discount provisions of Act No. 6183 on Procedure for Collection of Public Claims shall apply. Nevertheless, discounts for pre-payment are not deducted from the earnings based for contribution (Article 88/VI of Act No. 5510).

Chapter 3. Contribution Regulation for Those Who Are Subjected to Article 4/I-c (Mainly Civil Servants)

148. Civil servants were the first group to acquire social security under abrogated Act No. 5434, the Pension Fund, in 1949.[140] The Pension Fund was the only social security institution which the state took part in the financing. By Act No. 5502, the Pension Fund had also been transferred to the Social Security Institution. With regard to other provisions of Act No. 5434, certain provisions are abrogated (Article 106/I, 8 of Act No. 5510), a quite considerable number of its provisions retains its validity with respect to those who are covered by Act No. 5434 before the entry into force of Act No. 5510 (Prov. Article 4 of Act No. 5510). Therefore, despite the common legislation, civil servants are divided into two categories with regard to the system of social security: Civil servants, who were entered into the system before the entry into force of Act No. 5510, are mostly subjected to the provisions of Act No. 5434. However, those who are first covered by Act No. 5510 are subjected to the provisions of Act No. 5510, which we will examine below.

§1. Field of Application

I. Territorial Field of Application

149. Since the Article 4/I-c of Act No. 5510 covers civil servants only, in principle its territorial field of application is restricted to Turkey. However, as long as civil servants are on a mission, the place where these duties are performed has no bearing on their insurance coverage.

II. Personal Field of Application

150. In order to be covered by Article 4/I-c of Act No. 5510, two conditions are required: employment in public entities and not be covered by Article 4/I a and b, in other words, by the other social security regimes. Public entities in the sense of this provision are mainly public administration such as the ministries and their subdivisions, municipalities, public economic enterprises, their affiliated entities and corporations with more than 50% of their capital belonging to public entities.

151. Those who work in permanent cadres of public entities fall into the scope of application of Article 4/I-c if they are not subjected to Article 4/I-a of Act No. 5510. Similarly, those who are not covered by Article 4/I a and b of Act No. 5510 and who work with an administrative contract and those who are assigned proxy according to Article 86 of Act No. 657 on Civil Servants are considered insurance holder under Article 4/I-c of Act No. 5510.

140. OJ, 17 Jun. 1949, No. 7235.

152. Article 4/IV of Act No. 5510 sets out the positions entitling the insurance holder status as those of civil servants:

- Those who are elected or assigned to duty on public administrations are covered by Article 4/I-c if they are not working with a contract of employment and if they are granted pension rights with those of civil servants.
- Prime minister, ministers, mayors, members of the Turkish Parliament, members of the city council.
- Presidents and board members of unions and confederations founded by public officers.
- Cadets attending military academies, faculties and upper high schools.
- Cadets attending police academies, faculties and upper high schools.
- Cadets attending the Academy of Gendarmerie and Coast Guard, faculties and upper high schools are covered by Article 4/I-c of Act No. 5510.

153. Those who are elected to the presidency or management boards of public servants' trade unions, union branches are also covered by Act No. 5510 (Article 4/IV, c of Act No. 5510).[141] Public officers who are elected to the presidency or board of public servants' trade unions maintain their status of a public officer. However, if they wish, during their office, they may take a non-paid leave with a written request (Article 18/III of Act No. 4688 on Public Servants' Trade Unions). During their non-paid leave, they are also covered by Act No. 5510.

154. Although in order to be a public officer the age of 18 must have been attained, the complex nature of the employment relations in the public sector makes it possible to recruit a person who is younger than 18 in certain cases. In that case, in spite of their activities in public entities, Article 6 of Act No. 5510 exempts those who have not reached 18 years of age from the cover of insured persons (Article 6/I, h of Act No. 5510). In a similar way, those who are recruited with an administrative contract in representative offices abroad fall out of the scope of Article 4/I-c if they have the nationality of that country or a permanent residency permit and if they document that they are subjected to the social security system of that country because of the compulsory nature of this country or because of a bilateral social security agreement (Article 6/I-l of Act No. 5510).

155. The insured status under Article 4/I-c commences with the date the insurance holder take office or starts education (Article 7/I c of Act No. 5510).

§2. Calculation of Contributions

156. As we mentioned above, with respect to civil servants, two different systems are in force: For those who are entered into the system before the Act No.

141. A.N. Sözer, n. 70, p. 90; K. Arıcı, n. 7, p. 245.

5510, the provisions of Act No. 5434 keeps its validity. However, for those who first gained insured status under Act No. 5510, the provisions of Act No. 5510 shall apply.

157. According to Act No. 5434, deductions from insurance holders (called 'participants' by Act No. 5434) and their establishments, as well as contributions of the Treasury are the main financial sources. Deductions from participants are of three sorts: entry deduction, monthly deduction, and increment deduction, actual or assumed service increment:

- The entry deduction is equal to 25% of the first salary forming the basis for contributions.
- The monthly deduction is 16% of the salary on which contributions are based.
- The increment deduction is paid whenever the monthly salary of the participant is increased; the first difference is paid into the Fund.
- The actual or assumed service increment deduction equals half of 10% of the contributions relating to the additional length of time because of either actual or assumed services.

Public entities or institutions to which the participant is appointed are obliged to pay 20% of the monthly salary, which is the basis for contributions. Furthermore, for other benefits provided by the Fund, the public entities or organizations concerned are to pay contributions, such as invalidity pensions, administration expenses of the Institution, retirement gratuity, and death assistance paid to survivors.

In addition, the Institution is refunded certain pensions from the Treasury after having paid them to participants. Presidential pensions and those widow's and orphan's pensions paid to the president's survivors are subjected to such a refund. The most important state contribution is made if the budget of the Fund shows a deficit at the end of the year. In this case, a contribution is made from the general budget (Supp. Article 146 of Act No. 5434).

158. For those who are first covered by Act No. 5510, different methods of calculation are set up, since Article 4/I-c covers different groups. For those who receive their monthly salaries according to personnel statutory regulations, the monthly earnings based for contribution consist of monthly salaries calculated on the basis of monthly indicators and additional indicators, public service basis and seniority basis increments, different sorts of allowances, such as position, representation, duty and other envisaged by the special acts. Act No. 657 on Civil Servants, the main statutory regulation regarding the personnel matters of civil servants, determines the calculation of salaries according to a system of indicators and coefficients.

159. The amount of contributions is determined pursuant to income items of insurance holders pursuant to their relevant status. In certain cases, the Act refers to the contribution basis set up under Article 4/I-a. For example, for those who are employed with an administrative contract corresponding staff position, the earnings based for contribution is calculated on the amounts taken into account under Article 4/I-a of Act No. 5510.

§3. ADMINISTRATION

160. Public entities in which a civil servant is working are responsible for deductions and the collection of contributions. Public entities and institutions are to deduct the public officers' share from the salary and are to pay it to the Institution not later than the day that will be fixed by the Institution (Article 88/IX of Act No. 5510). The public entity carries the responsibility against the Institution for the share of the non-paid insurance holder.

161. Public entities are responsible for submitting to the Institution a 'certificate of insurance and service' wherein the names and national identification numbers of insurance holders, the total insurable earnings, the number of days of the contribution payment, and original and additional records – the nature of which is determined by Institution regulations – are determined, at the latest, on the date fixed by the Institution.

Chapter 4. Consequences of Failure to Perform Social Insurance Duties

162. Despite all legal regulations, the employment of non-notified employees is quite extensive in Turkey. In addition, the Institution envisages considerable difficulties in collecting contributions. The inadequacy of administrative supervision is the ground on which this illegal practice is based. Act No. 5510 provides a series of notification duties enforced by administrative fines, as explained above. In order to eliminate illegal employment, Act No. 5510 equips the Institution with a considerable number of ex-officio powers. Moreover, all claims of the Institution are regulated under Act No. 6183 on Procedure for Collection of Public Claims to facilitate the collection of contributions. Public authorities are donated with considerable powers to enforce individuals to pay their public debts, such as the sequestration of overdue payments. The Social Security Institution is also donated with these powers.

§1. Personal Scope of Those Charged with Social Security Duties

I. Employer, Employer's Representative and Managers

163. Act No. 5510 designates not only the employer but also many other persons as responsible for social security duties. The employer is the real or legal person or institution, without having a legal personality, who employs an insurance holder (Article 12/I of Act No. 5510). In employment law, the employer is a party to the contract of employment.[142] However, in social security law, the term has a more general meaning. In order to be an employer, the determinant factor is to employ an insurance holder either to Article 4/I-a or to 4/I-c. Even the work relation is not based on the employment contract, for example, the state as employing public officers or the business owner in the apprentice relationship, and Penitentiaries and Prisons Employment Institutions for which convicts and detainees work are considered employers under Act No. 5510. An employer bears all responsibilities arising from Act No. 5510.

164. The employer's representative is the person who acts on behalf of the employer and who carries out the entire management of the job. In order to be considered an employer's representative, the person should act in the name and on behalf of the employer, and he should manage the entire business. The employer's representative is also an insurance holder in the sense that he/she works under both a contract of employment and a statute relationship. However, the managerial position that he/she is charged with lies on the basis of his/her responsibility. According to Article 12/II of Act No. 5510, the term 'employer' also covers 'employer's representative'. Therefore, an employer's representative shares the joint responsibility with the employer for all duties, even monetary ones, arising from Act No. 5510.

142. *See* T. Dereli, n. 91, paras 109–110.

For example, in the case of non-payment of contribution debts by the employer, the employer's representative shall also be liable for contributions.[143]

165. In order to foster the sensitivity of managers with regard to the payment of social insurance contributions and any other claims of the Institution, the Act enjoins a joint and successive responsibility towards the Institution. In addition to the employer's representative, Act No. 5510, like abrogated Act No. 506, also renders some other managers liable.[144] Those who are public officers, accountants in charge and treasurers of the public institutions, agencies and those who are high level managers, including members of the board of directors,[145] authorized persons and legal representatives in private legal companies, are responsible for unpaid debts against the Institution on the due date unless a just reason can be shown (Article 88/XX of Act No. 5510). The scope of high-level managers is more extensive than the one of employer's representatives as to be an employer's representative the management of an entire business is required. Although the Act fixes responsibility in a very broad manner, only those who carry out a task and are financially authorized to deal with the affairs of the company can be held responsible towards the Institution.[146] The liability of managers covers not only the payment of contributions but also any kind of claims, such as non-paid fines.[147] If the non-payment of contributions is based on a just reason, for example, the authorized manager attempted to conduct the payment. However, the employer did not pay the necessary amount, and the liability of the manager is disclaimed.[148]

166. The responsibility of managers in public institutions is another debatable issue. All board members, general directors, mayors and account officers charged with the duty of accrual and payment in public institutions are responsible for social security contributions.[149] Either because of the financial difficulties faced by municipalities or because of the deliberate behaviour, municipalities have considerable debts to the Social Security Institution. Due to the above-mentioned Article, the Court of Cassation held mayors responsible for insurance contributions due to

143. A. Güzel/A.R. Okur/N. Caniklioğlu, n. 7, p. 189.
144. *See* K. Arıcı, 'Tüzel Kişi İşverenlerin Üst Düzey Yönetici veya Yetkililerinin Prim Ödemeden Doğan İşverenleri ile Birlikte Müştereken ve Müteselsilen Sorumluluğu', *Sicil Der.*(Mart, 2006), pp. 116–117; A. Güneren, 'Üst Düzey Yönetici veya Yetkililerin İşverenin Prim Borcundan Müteselsil Sorumluluğu ve Primlerin Ödenmemesinin Yaptırımı', *Sicil Der.*(Haziran, 2007), pp. 151–160.
145. *See* Z. Ayan, 'Anonim Şirket Yönetim Kurulu Üyelerinin Şirketin Sosyal Sigorta Borçlarından Sorumluluğu', in *Osman Güven Çankaya Armağanı* (Ankara, 2010), pp. 407–428.
146. *See, as example,* Court of Cass., 10th Ch., 26.9.2000, 5121/6113, Kazancı Bilişim Sistemleri; Court of Cass. 21th Ch., 1 Apr. 2002, 517/2702, www.hukukturk.com; 21th Ch., 27.4.2004, 457/4186, 5, *Çalışma ve Toplum Der.*(2005/2), pp. 316–318; 10th Ch., 9.11.2005, 9155/11377, *Çalışma ve Toplum Der.*(2006/4), pp. 284–285.
147. A. Güzel/A.R. Okur/N. Caniklioğlu, n. 7, p. 304; C. Tuncay/Ö. Ekmekçi, n. 7, p. 224.
148. K. Arıcı, 'Üst Düzey Yöneticilerin Sorumluluğu', p. 118; A. Güneren, 'Üst Düzey Yönetici ve Yetkililerin Sorumluluğu', pp. 153–154; 156–157.
149. Memorandum No. 16-145 Annex of 11 Aug. 1997.

the municipality's employees.[150] However, such a personal financial responsibility of elected mayors has been criticized by some commentators.[151]

II. Sub-contracting, Temporary Work Relationship and Transfer of Workplace

167. Employee outsourcing is one of the characteristics of new management practices. Sub-contracting and temporary work relations are the most common ones. Under Turkish law, the problem of decentralization of production processes is dealt with the liability approach. Turkish law provides joint liability of different employers against employees and the Social Security Institution to guarantee employees' rights.

168. The responsibility of the principal employer against employees of the sub-contractor employers has been regulated by specific provisions since 1936. In order to be protected by the joint liability of different employers, the relationship between the main employer and the sub-contractor should carry certain conditions set up by Act No. 5510. Quite similar but not the same conditions are also set up by LA.[152]

169. Article 12/6 of Act No. 5510 names the sub-contractor as a 'sub-employer' and defines them as the third person who undertakes to perform work from a principal employer and charges his insurance holders with a duty to perform that work in the workplace of the principal employer. The work that is undertaken by the sub-employer must be related to the main business or part thereof, the production of goods and services in the workplace, or should be executed in the facilities.

170. To hold both employers principal and sub-employer responsible for social security duties against the Social Security Institution, the contractual relationship between the two employers must fulfil the below-mentioned conditions:[153]

- The main employer, who awards the contract, must be an employer, which means he/she is to employ insurance holders in the workplace where the sub-contractor performs his activities. Therefore, the Act renders liable employers who recruit insurance holders, whether employees or public officers, in his/her own workplace.[154]
- The sub-employer must also be an employer. In other words, he/she is to perform his/her activities via his/her own employees.

150. Court of Cass., 10th Ch., 25.6.1992, 866/7260, *Çimento İşv. Der.*(Kasım, 1992), p. 44; 21th Ch., 9 Oct. 2000, *YKD.*(Mayıs, 2001), p. 720.
151. C. Tuncay/Ö. Ekmekçi, n. 7, pp. 226–227.
152. *See* T. Dereli, n. 91, paras 119–126.
153. A. Güzel/A.R. Okur/N. Caniklioğlu, n. 7, pp. 193–195; C. Tuncay/Ö. Ekmekçi, n. 7, pp. 337–338.
154. Court of Cass., 10th Ch., 19.10.2010, 9170/13928, 29, *Çalışma ve Toplum Der.*(2011/2), pp. 559–562; 10th Ch., 19.4. 2010, 20353/5609, Hukuk Türk Veri Tabanı.

– The work undertaken is to be carried out in the workplace of the principal employer. This plant becomes the sub-contractor's own workplace as well. Therefore, one production plant constitutes two different workplaces from the legal point of view. Sub-contracting activities performed at the workplace out of the principal employer's workplace do not fall under the cover of Article 12 of Act No. 5510. The principal employer is held responsible for insurance holders who work in the same workplace.
– The work contracted-out must be related to the main business or part thereof, the production of goods and services in the workplace, or should be executed in the facilities. For example, repairing jobs, which fall out of the scope of the main activity, do not cause the responsibility of the main employer.[155]

171. If all of these conditions are fulfilled, although employees have an employment relationship with the sub-employer, the principal employer is jointly liable with the sub-employer for any duties arising from Act No. 5510. The content of the response is determined widely. The principal employer is responsible for all kinds of sub-contractor duties in his capacity as an employer, such as notification of insurance holders, duties of depositing certain documents, contribution payments, etc. The Court of Cassation held the principal employer responsible for recourse indemnities due from industrial accidents.[156] In case of an industrial accident, if the insurance holder suffers an industrial accident because his employer failed to take the necessary health and safety measures, the Social Security Institution grants all necessary services and benefits to the insurance holder. However, the Institution has the right to demand from the employer the reimbursement of its expenses. The Social Security Institution may bring an action against both the sub-employer as well as the principal employer, in a case where the conditions for joint responsibility are fulfilled.

172. Temporary work relations are one of the most debated provisions of LA. The legislator, with the aim to prevent abusive practices, brought restrictions to these practices:[157] According to Article 7 of LA, temporary employment relationships shall only be concluded between companies which lay down under the same holding structure. If the employee will be leased to another company, which falls out of the group of companies, temporary work contracts may be concluded. The employee, who will be sent to work under the surveillance of another employer, must give his/her written approval at the moment of the transfer. Lastly, the temporary work contract may be concluded for a period not exceeding six months, and if required, it may be renewed twice. The consent of the employee is required for each renewal.

173. By a new amendment with regard to temporary work,[158] agency work has been introduced to labour law. Heretofore, according to the jurisprudence of the

155. Court of Cass., 10th Ch., 3.3.2004, 750/2567, 5, *Çalışma ve Toplum Der.*(2005/2), pp. 299–302.
156. Court of Cass., 10th Ch., 18 May 1999, 3208/3311, *YKD*(December 1999), pp. 1667–1668.
157. *See* T. Dereli, n. 91, paras 170–176.
158. Act No. 6715, OJ, 20 May 2016, No. 29717.

Court of Cassation, if the employee was recruited through a temporary work agency, the contract between the agency and the employee shall have been deemed as a contract for job intermediary, and a direct employment relationship had been accepted between the user company and the employee.[159] Amended Article 7 of LA enables employers to employ employees via employment agencies under certain conditions. The main idea is to restrict the use of agency employees in place of permanent employees of the establishment. Agency employees can be employed for seasonal agricultural works, domestic works, incidental jobs that fall out of daily routine tasks, urgent jobs related to health and safety, unpredictable work that increases above the average production capacity of the enterprise, periodical work increases except for seasonal works, or for works during the suspension period of the permanent employees due to maternity leave, sickness periods, military service, etc. (Article 7/II of Act No. 4857). No employment relationship exists between the temporary agency worker and the user company.

174. Although the main employer carries all obligations arising from the contract of employment, LA No. 4857 and Act No. 5510 on Social Insurance and Universal Health Insurance provides a joint liability of the temporary employer if the temporary employee has a regular employment relationship with the hiring employer. In that case, the user-employer shall also be responsible for wages and social security contributions during the length of time that the temporary work relation is continued. Furthermore, the temporary employer has a duty of care for temporary employees, which means that an employee who suffers an industrial accident may sue against the temporary employer, as well as his own employer for material and immaterial damages. With respect to employment agencies, Article 19/II of Act No. 4904 provides the responsibility of the employment agency for duties arising from Act No. 5510. Nevertheless, there exists no provision which provides the responsibility of the user company for agency employees' social security contributions. Nevertheless, despite the absence of a clear provision, Article 12/II of Act No. 5510 provides that the temporary employer is liable for all duties of the main employer under the frame of Act No. 5510. These provisions should cover the use of agency employees.

175. In case of a transfer of workplace, both employers, transferor and transferee, are held liable against the Institution for social security duties of the transferor employer. If the workplace, wherein the insurance holder works, is transferred with all active and passive assets, or if the workplace joins in or merges with another workplace, the new employer is jointly responsible for the debts of the former employer (Article 89/I of Act No. 5510). This joint responsibility covers not only the debts of contributions but also all kind of administrative fines, penalties for delay and overdue increments etc. Any agreement against such joint responsibility is invalid.

---

159. Court of Cass., 9th Ch., 4 Apr. 2005, 774/11838, *Legal-İSGHD* (2005) 8, pp. 1754–1757; also *see* Court of Cass., 9th Ch., 8.7.2004, 17098/17432, Judgment and notes by D. Ulucan, 3, *Çalışma ve Toplum Der.* (2004/3), pp. 145–152.

§2. Overdue Payments and Administrative Fines

I. Penalty for Delay and Overdue Increase

176. The difficulty in collecting contributions has caused a series of legal regulations about unpaid contributions. If contributions or any other credits of the Institution are not paid completely in due time, the unpaid amount is increased by 2%[160] on the due date for the following three months;[161] this amount is called a penalty for delay. In addition, an overdue increase, which is not considered as interest from the legal point of view,[162] is calculated over this total amount when the due date has passed. The increase rate is calculated on a compound basis for each month separately at the monthly average interest rate of Government bonds to be declared by the Treasury (Article 88/II of Act No. 5510). The Council of Ministers has the authority to increase the amount of the penalty for delay up to doubling it and can reduce it by up to 1%. For the month that the payment is made, overdue interest is calculated on a daily basis. Even if a lawsuit and execution prosecution is in progress, the penalty for the delay and overdue increase on the non-paid amount shall be collected.

177. The above-mentioned overdue increments are also valid for the non-payment of administrative fines in due time (Article 89/II of Act No. 5510).[163] Therefore, administrative fines which have not been paid within fifteen days following the date of notification by the Institution are increased by 2% on the due date for the following three months. An overdue increase shall also be applied to administrative fines.

II. Administrative Fines

178. If the employer fails to perform his duties arising from Act No. 5510, for example, if he does not submit the necessary certificates to the Institution or if he does not notify the Institution of the insurance holder or of the workplace, Article 102 of the Act provides administrative fines that vary the amount levied in accordance with the nature of the document not submitted, original or additional, the issue of certificates ex-officio by the Institution and the non-submission of documents despite the written notice by the Institution. For example, if the employer does not notify the Institution of an insurance holder, the amount of the fine equals the minimum wage for each insurance holder. However, if the non-notification is revealed by the examination of the Institution's officers, the amount of the fine is

160. The amount of penalty for delay was reduced from 3% to 2% by a Council of Ministers Decision starting from the first day of the following month to 28 Apr. 2010.
161. Amended by Art. 6 of Act No. 5458 of 22 Feb. 2006, OJ, 4 Mar. 2006, No. 26098.
162. Court of Cass., Unif. Judg., 22.11.1991, 1990/5, 1991/4, Kazancı Bilişim Sistemleri, İçtihat Bilgi Bankası; C. Tuncay/Ö. Ekmekçi, n. 7, pp. 216–217.
163. A. Güzel/A.R. Okur/N. Caniklioğlu, n. 7, p. 302.

doubled. In order to keep the whole employment life under control, the Act provides quite detailed provisions, which we have given certain examples of as mentioned below.

179. With respect to original documents, such as a certificate of insurance and service, the amount of the fine equals one-fifth of the minimum wage for each registered, insured worker who must be mentioned in the document. Nevertheless, the total amount of the fine shall not be more than two times the monthly minimum wage (Article 102/I, c, 1 of Act No. 5510). If the document in question is an additional one, a fine of one-eighth of the minimum wage for each insured worker in consideration, under the condition that the total amount of the fine is less than two times the monthly minimum wage, is levied against the employer.

180. If the additional document is issued ex-officio by the Institution, the employer shall be charged with a fine equalling one-half of the minimum wage for each registered insurance holder who must be mentioned in the document, unless the total amount of the fine is more than two times the minimum wage. If the employer has not supplied any of the certificates or documents mentioned, and this omission is found out, based on information and documents received from banks, organizations having revolving funds, public administrations and institutions and administrations established by law, or on court judgments, or on examinations carried out by Institution's officers charged with the duty of inspection and control, or on investigations, inspections and examinations carried out by the control officers of other public administrations pursuant to their legislation, two times the minimum wage fine is levied against the employer (Article 102/I, c, 4 of Act No. 5510). Moreover, the employer, who does not fulfil his duty to display certificates, is sentenced to a fine equalling two months minimum wage.[164]

181. An administrative fine is incurred upon written notification to the concerned party. He/she may either deposit the required amount to the Institution within fifteen days starting from the date of notification or make an objection to the Institution and request a review within the same period. An objection shall suspend the collection. If the Institution refuses the objection grounds, the concerned party may bring an action in the competent administrative court within thirty days following the notice of refusal. The penalties or charges shall not be cancelled during the appeal. If the concerned party does not recourse an objection within fifteen days, the administrative fine shall be finalized (Article 102/IV of Act No. 5510). If the fine is paid within fifteen days without any objection, three-fourths of this amount shall be recovered. Even after payment in advance, the concerned party has the right to appeal.

164. For more details, *see* A. Güzel/A.R. Okur/N. Caniklioğlu, n. 7, pp. 261–266.

182. The time limitation is ten years with regard to administrative fines. The time limit starts on the date of the action; in other words, the failure to perform duties arising from the Act.[165]

III. Statute of Limitation and Refund of Contributions

183. Contributions and other claims of the Institution shall be subject to a ten years statute of limitation, starting from the beginning of the calendar year following the date on which the term is matured (Article 93/II of Act No. 5510). The starting date of the statute of limitation varies in accordance with the facts that the Institution is acquainted: If the claim for contribution arises from a court decision, the statute of limitation starts from the date on which the judgment of the court is finalized; if it arises from the audits and supervisions of the Institutions' officers, it starts from the date on which the Institution received the results of the investigation; if it arises from the investigations, inspections and examinations conducted by public authorities, it begins from the date on which the results of the investigation are received by the Institution.

184. The Institution admits the payment after the expiry of the time limit. However, for those who are insured under Article 4/I-b, mainly Self-Employed persons, non-contribution paid periods expired by the statute of limitation are not considered among insured periods. Therefore, all rights and duties related to these periods are barred by the statute of limitation (Article 93/IV of Act No. 5510).

185. Contributions which are collected wrongly or inappropriately by the Institution shall be refunded to employers, insurance holders and right holders unless a period of ten years has expired (Article 89/III of Act No. 5510). Legal interest shall be applied starting from the month following the date on which contributions are deposited. The refund of the wrongly collected contributions may affect conditions to get benefits from the social security system. Therefore, such a refund may lead to the cutting-off of granted benefits to the insurance holder.

186. It is also possible that the Institution makes expenses wrongly or they are inappropriately claimed by the insurance holder. Such expenses shall be taken back from the concerned parties (Article 89/IV of Act No. 5510). The cover of the refund varies in accordance with the reasons for the expenses. If the insurance holder or benefiter causes these expenses with deliberate or negligent conduct, these expenses may be refunded within ten years starting from the date of finding the erroneous transaction. If the Institution made an erroneous transaction, the Institution is entitled to ask for a refund within five years starting from the date of finding the erroneous transaction (Article 96/I of Act No. 5510). Even in cases of an erroneous transaction by the Institution, the Institution is entitled to ask for legal interest if the

165. For more details, *see* N. Caniklioğlu, '5510 Sayılı Kanuna Göre Sosyal Güvenlik Kurumunun Alacaklarında Zamanaşımı', *Prof. Dr. Ali Rıza Okur'a Armağan, Marmara Üniversitesi Hukuk Fakültesi Hukuk Araştırmaları Dergisi,* Y. 2014, C. 20, S. 1, pp. 825–849.

total amounts of erroneous payments are not paid within twenty-four months pursuant to the written notice. Although it is hard to find just that the Institution is able to refund expenses made owing to its own mistakes, the Act provides legal interest in case of non-payment of these expenses.

§3. Ex-officio Powers of Social Security Institution

I. The Issue of Certificates Ex-officio

187. In case of the non-submission of required certificates in due time or in a due manner, the Institution is authorized to issue the necessary certificates and fix the amount of contributions (Article 86/VII of Act No. 5510). Further, if on the basis of information derived from the de facto situation or workplace documents or documents issued by public authorities, it is established that there exist insured employees whose certificates have not been submitted or which have been incompletely submitted, the Institution officially notifies the employer that the relevant documents must be submitted within one month. In case of non-submission or incomplete submission of these documents, the Institution prepares them ex-officio and fixes the amount of contributions to be paid by the employee.

188. The non-observance of the legal duty to supply the necessary certificates to the Institution is the pre-condition for the use of ex-officio authority of the Institution. Pursuant to that provision, the Institution has the authority to issue notification of insured status, a certificate for insurance and service, as well as assess the amount of contributions that should be paid by an employer ex-officio. The employer may contest the notice with respect to the amount of the contributions debt to the competent office of the Institution within one month following the notification. An objection shall suspend the collection of contributions. In case of their appeal being rejected, the employer may bring a case before the competent labour court. Application to the court neither halts the pursuit of the debt nor its collection.[166]

189. As mentioned above, for an insured person, for whom it has been stated that he has not been employed for certain days of a month and for which he has received no wages, the employer is to annex to the certificate of insurance and service notes and documents demonstrating that the insured had worked for less than thirty days. These documents should be enclosed to the monthly certificate of insurance and service. If these documents are not submitted, or if the Institution invalidates these documents, such documents shall be issued by the Institution ex-officio. The Institution also assesses the correspondent contributions. The objection may be made to the Institution within one month. The employer also has the right to appeal against the final decision of the Institution in labour courts.

166. For further information, *see* A. Güzel/A.R. Okur/N. Caniklioğlu, n. 7, pp. 256–257; C. Tuncay/Ö. Ekmekçi, n. 7, pp. 232–234; F. Uşan, n. 28, pp. 157–158; A.N. Sözer, n. 70, pp. 162–164.

II. The Ex-officio Calculation of Contribution Amounts

190. The Institution is authorized not only to demand and vet documents and assess contributions pursuant to these documents ex-officio but also to fix the amount of contributions ex-officio.[167] The contribution amounts may be calculated ex-officio either with regard to individual insurance holders or with regard to the total workforce in the workplace.

191. Such a minimum workforce assessment requires an authority to assess the minimum workforce necessary to effect the activity taking place in the workplace and determining the contributions accordingly. Pursuant to Article 85/I of Act No. 5510, if the Institution detects an understatement of the number of required insured workers, their working times, or amounts of insurable earnings, the officers of the Institution charged with the inspection and control are authorized to determine the minimum amount of labour required to operate the work in question. Criteria such as the characteristics of the work done, the technology utilized within the workplace, the size of the enterprise, the number of workers employed in similar enterprises and the opinions of relevant occupational or public organizations are applied. Written records prepared by inspectors are in effect unless proved otherwise.

192. Since the non-registered employee recruitment rate is quite high in the construction sector, the Act also provides an investigative procedure regarding construction contracts adjudicated to real or legal persons by institutions and establishments specified in Article 85/II of the Act. These are mainly public institutions such as establishments dependant on the general or supplemental budget, provincial and municipal administrations, construction contracts awarded by banks, constructions carrying special characteristics. If the investigation results in a declaration that the number of workers notified for the construction is insufficient, the amount of the contribution cost over undeclared labour costs is calculated on the basis of an assumption. The employer is to pay these additional costs with a penalty for the delay and an overdue increment within one month following the notification. If the employer gives a written commitment that he/she would pay the officially communicated contributions, the contribution debt will be finalized. In case of non-payment of the communicated contributions, overdue increment, as well as the penalty for delay or for non-submission of a written commitment, the Institution conducts further investigation. The Institution may also consider an investigation necessary.

193. A Commission for Determining Minimum Workmanship composed of seven members is established under the organizational structure of the Institution in order to define the method to be used in assessing the required minimum labour, to investigate if sufficient numbers of workers have been declared to the Institution and

167. *See* A. Güzel/A.R. Okur/N. Caniklioğlu, n. 7, pp. 257–260; C. Tuncay/Ö. Ekmekçi, n. 7, pp. 234–239; F. Uşan, n. 28, pp. 158–161; A.N. Sözer, n. 70, pp. 164–167.

to decide employers' appeals regarding the minimum labour rates (Article 85/VI of Act No. 5510). The minimum workmanship rates are published in the Official Journal.

194. The employer is notified of the amount of accrued contributions calculated ex-officio by the Institution on the basis of the insurance inspections, and they may object to the amount of the contribution debt to the competent office of the Institution within one month following the date of notification. In case of their appeal being rejected, the employer may bring a case before the competent labour court. Application to the court neither halts the pursuit of the debt nor its collection.

195. A reconciliation process is provided with regard to minimum wage assessments. If officers of the Institution detect a failure while investigating minimum labour in workplaces founded permanently, before the submission of the investigation report, the Institution and employer may conduct a settlement on the amounts of contributions, overdue increments and fines. The reconciliation amount is written in minutes and is finalized. The employer has no right of appeal or objection. The settled amount should be paid within one month following the reconciliation minutes. In case of non-payment of settled amounts, fully or partly, within one month, the reconciliation is annulled (Article 85/IX of Act No. 5510).

§4. The Establishment of Insured Period

I. The Establishment of Insured Period by the Social Security Institution

196. As mentioned above, the Institution is authorized to issue non-submitted certificates for an insurance holder. Issuing such certificates means the establishment of the insured periods by the Institution. Both Institution's officers and officers charged with other public authorities may detect the uninsured periods while auditing or inspecting the workplace. According to Article 86/VIII of the Act, if, on the basis of information derived from the de facto situation in the workplace, it is established that there exist, insurance holders, whose certificates have not been submitted or which have been incompletely submitted, the Institution, while calculating the insured periods and earnings based for contribution, takes into account a maximum of one year retrospectively beginning from the date of control.

If the aim of such regulation is to prevent the employment of uninsured employees, it is incomprehensible to restrict the Institution's authority within one year, in cases where the Institution detects that an employee has worked for many years without being notified. Such a restriction may have the ability to weaken the Institution's authorities while fighting against non-registered employment.[168] Nevertheless, if the information on the non-registered employment relationship is derived from workplace documents, all period retrospectively is taken into account (Article 26 of RSIP).

168. A. Güzel/A.R. Okur/N. Caniklioğlu, n. 7, p.267; A.N. Sözer, n. 70, p. 164.

II. The Establishment of Insured Period by Court Decision

197. If the certificates of the insured employee have not been submitted to the Institution by the employer or the employment relationship has not been detected by the Institution's officers, even if such an employee has become automatically insured, as from the date on which he/she entered into the employment relationship (Article 7 of Act No. 5510), the legally insured employee has no right to benefit from the unregistered years of employment, with respect to social insurance allowances. Therefore, Article 86/IX of the Act enables the insured employee to sue the employer with the aim of establishing the actual employment period, with respect to social insurance. The insurance holder may benefit from this right if the employer has not submitted required certificates to the Institution or if the Institution has not detected the insurance holder ex-officio. The employee may apply to the court, within a period of five years immediately preceding the end of the year, that she/he had terminated the employment concerned. This judgment is a declaratory judgment by its nature.[169]

198. The legal nature of the five-year period is a debatable issue. Although certain commentators advocate the application of the statute of limitation,[170] the Court of Cassation has accepted the five-year period as a strict time limit.[171] This period is calculated from the end of the year in which the insured employee left the job. In case of the death of the employee, his/her successors may also bring the action. In that case, the five-year period is calculated from the day of the inheritor's demise.[172] If the employer has submitted the required certificates to the Institution but not paid contributions or paid contributions less than the due amount, the insurance holder may sue the employer anytime regardless of the five-year limitation.

199. The basic condition for the establishment of the insured period is that the employment relationship and workplace in question must be covered by Act No. 5510.[173] Aside from the employer, those who are held jointly responsible and the Institution must be taken as a counterparty in action.[174] Although it is up to the insured employee to prove the amount of wages accrued, as well as the length of

169. K. Tunçomağ, n. 7; p. 193; A. Güzel/A.R. Okur/N. Caniklioğlu, n. 7, p. 269; C. Tuncay/Ö. Ekmekçi, n. 7, p. 271; C. Saraç, 'Sigortalı Hizmetlerin Hükmen Tespiti', in *Osman Güven Çankaya'ya Armağan* (Ankara, 2010), p. 465.
170. K. Tunçomağ, n. 7; pp. 193–194; A. Güzel/A.R. Okur/ N. Caniklioğlu, n. 7, p. 269; A.N. Sözer, n. 70, p. 455.
171. *See, as example,* Court of Cass., General Council, 28.2.1986, 10-37/184, Kazancı Bilişim Sistemleri, İçtihat Bilgi Bankası; C. Tuncay/Ö. Ekmekçi, n. 7, pp. 262–263; F. Uşan, n. 28, p. 162; M. Şakar, n. 7, p. 138; Saraç, 'Sigortalı Hizmetlerin Hükmen Tespiti', p. 466.
172. Court of Cass., 11 Jul. 2005, 3052/7320, İBD, 2006/1, pp. 347–348; A. Güzel/A.R. Okur/N. Caniklioğlu, n. 7, p. 271; C. Tuncay/Ö. Ekmekçi, n. 7, p. 263; C. Saraç, 'Sigortalı Hizmetlerin Hükmen Tespiti', p. 468.
173. *See, as example,* Court of Cass., General Council, 16.6.1999, 21-508/525, Kazancı Bilişim Sistemleri, İçtihat Bilgi Bankası.
174. *See, as example,* Court of Cass., 10th Ch., 26.9.1991, 4998/7272, *YKD*(Aralık, 1991), pp. 1826–1827; A. Güzel/A.R. Okur/N. Caniklioğlu, n. 7, pp. 274–275; C. Tuncay/Ö. Ekmekçi, n. 7, pp. 260–261; A.N. Sözer, n. 70, p. 457; C. Saraç, 'Sigortalı Hizmetlerin Hükmen Tespiti', pp. 460–465.

period that has been worked, the judge is to investigate the case ex-officio, while the social insurance issue is part of the public order.[175] Therefore, the judge shall consider all kind of evidence to determine the employment relationship. Nevertheless, the Court of Cassation requires meticulous investigation by the first instance courts in order to prevent sham claims.[176]

200. If the court brings down a decision in favour of the insured employee, the total amount of the monthly earnings and the number of contribution days will be taken into account, with respect to social insurance benefits. Thus, it is held that if the number of working days has been declared a number lesser than it actually is, the insurance holder will receive benefits from sickness and maternity insurance branches (Article 86/X of Act No. 5510).

201. The Institution collects the contributions belonging to the past periods including the insured's share, along with overdue increments. However, the employer cannot recourse to recovering the employee's share from the employee himself/herself. The employer shall also be imposed with a fine because of the failure to submit the required certifications to the Institution.

202. In addition, if the workplace notification has not been made to the Institution, by the declaratory judgment, workplace wherein the insurance holder has worked shall be registered ex-officio.

§5. The Postponement and Re-structuring of Contribution Debts

I. The Postponement of Contribution Debts

203. If the workplace or house of employer or self-employed is destroyed or heavily damaged because of a natural disaster such as fire, flood or earthquake, and if the self-employed or the employer proves this damage with the required documents and submits these relevant documents to the Institution by the end of the following three months, the overdue contribution payment, as well as those contributions due for the period of the following three months, may be deferred for a period up to one year following the disaster (Article 91 of Act No. 5510). This opportunity is extended for employers who suffered from commercial or financial loss due to force majeure such as serious illness, serious accident, imprisonment or sabotage by a legislative amendment.[177] In addition to employers and self-employed persons, insurance holders who pay their own contributions are also entitled to benefit from this postponement. In order to benefit from this opportunity, the insolvency of the employer or the self-employed for paying contributions must

175. A. Güzel/A.R. Okur/N. Caniklioğlu, n. 7, pp. 276–278; C. Tuncay/Ö. Ekmekçi, n. 7, p. 264; C. Saraç, 'Sigortalı Hizmetlerin Hükmen Tespiti', p. 474.
176. *See, as example,* Court of Cass., General Council, 6.7.2005, 21-437/448, *Çalışma ve Toplum Der.*(2005/4), S. 7, pp. 109–112; C. Tuncay/Ö. Ekmekçi, n. 7, pp. 267–268.
177. Article 49 of Act No. 6728, OJ, 9 Aug. 2016, No. 29796.

be revealed by the investigation of the Institution. Such an insolvency condition is brought by Act No. 5510.[178] An overdue increase is not paid at that time.

204. The Act empowers the Institution with a general postponement authority, in case of natural disaster, regardless of any time restriction. According to Article 91/III of Act No. 5510, the Institution is authorized to determine or postpone due dates for submitting certificates, payment of contributions and other debts. The Institution has this power only in cases where the natural disaster affects the common life pursuant to Act No. 7269 on the Aids to be Made and Measures to be Taken for Disasters Affecting General Life. Any employer inside the disaster area, who has suffered damage either directly or indirectly, or insurance holders or dependants may benefit from this postponement.

II. Deduction of Contributions from Progress Payments

205. Difficulties in collecting contributions and other Institution's claims lead it to take different kinds of measures in collecting contributions, such as deducting at the source. Public entities, institutions with revolving funds, institutions subject to the Banking Act or any kind of institution founded by statue are obliged to notify the Institution within fifteen days of the contractors and their addresses who undertook a work by tender (Article 90 of Act No. 5510). These institutions are to pay progress payments to the contractor, unless the contractor has any obligation, either contribution or contribution-related debts or administrative fines, against the Institution. The public entity, which will make progress payments to the contractor, is obliged to ask the Institution whether the contractor has any debts against the Institution. The Institution notifies the public entity within one month about the debts of the contractor and its subcontractors. The public entity shall not make any payment to contractors until receiving the Institution's response. If the contractor or his subcontractors have debts, the public entity deducts this amount from the progress payment. In addition, performance bonds of the contractor shall be returned after it is determined that the contractor and its subcontractors have no debt against the Institution.

206. Correspondingly, the public authorities are obliged to ask for documents which certify that the contractor has no debt against the Social Security Institution while granting certain permissions and licenses. Particularly, in the construction sector, such permissions have an important scope of application. Such provisions aim to prevent the use of non-registered employees at works which are carried out pursuant to public licences or financed by public authorities.[179]

178. A. Güzel/A.R. Okur/N. Caniklioğlu, n. 7, p. 308.
179. For further information, *see* A. Güzel/A.R. Okur/N. Caniklioğlu, n. 7, pp. 310–311.

III. Re-structuring of Contribution Debts

207. Faced with difficulties in collecting contributions, the legislator has adopted high overdue increases and penalty payments. However, imposing high penalties is far from solving the problem. On the contrary, considering the fact that the amount of overdue increases is higher than the amount of the main debt, employers or self-employed persons abstain from paying their debts for as long as possible. This practice renders a big gap between the number of insurance holders who are legally considered as insured and the number of those for whom contributions are paid. In order to prevent social problems, the government has adopted many regulations which bring amnesties to penalties and overdue increments for the delay and re-structure the main contribution debts. However, the frequency of such amnesty acts almost provokes the non-payment of contributions in practice.[180]

180. For further information, *see* A. Güzel/A.R. Okur/N. Caniklioğlu, n. 7, pp. 309–310.

Part III. Short-term Insurance Branches

Introduction

208. Act No. 5510 describes short-term insurance branches like those of industrial accidents and occupational diseases, sickness and maternity insurances (Article 3/I, 4 of Act No. 5510). Contributions and benefits granted under the frame of these insurance branches are also very common.[181]

209. One of the fundamental changes implemented by the reform is the exclusion of healthcare services from the cover of social insurance branches. Only monetary benefits are allocated under cover of the short-term social insurance branches. Healthcare services are provided according to universal health insurance principles. Therefore, social insurance schemes compensate for the material needs of the insurance holders and benefiters.

181. For evaluation of the reform, *see* N. Caniklioğlu, 'Kısa Vadeli Sigorta Kolları Açısından Yeni Mevzuatın Getirdiği Değişiklikler', in *Yeni Düzenlemeler Çerçevesinde Sosyal Güvenlik Mevzuatı Semineri* (Ankara, 2007), pp. 59–105;The same author, 'Sosyal Sigortalar ve Genel Sağlık Sigortası Kanun Tasarısına Göre Kısa Vadeli Sigorta Hükümleri', 8, *Çalışma ve Toplum Der.*(2006/1), pp. 50–92; R. Korkusuz, 'Anayasa Mahkemesinin İptal Kararı'ndan Sonra Sosyal Güvenlik Hukukumuzda Kısa Vadeli Sigorta Türlerinin Hukuki Durumunun İncelenmesi', *Sicil Der.*(Aralık, 2007), pp. 140–165; T. Canbolat, 'Kısa Vadeli Sigora Hükümleri', in *Yeni Sosyal Güvenlik Sistemi* (Istanbul, 2010), pp. 15–39.

Chapter 1. Industrial Accidents and Occupational Diseases

210. The high number of industrial accidents is one of the big problems of industrial relations. The insurance for industrial accidents and occupational diseases is regulated as a separate insurance branch. Both risks, industrial accidents and occupational diseases, are regulated under the same insurance branch in Turkish law. Thus, the scope of application and the extent and types of benefits are the same for both risks.

§1. Field of Application

I. Territorial Field of Application

211. The Social Insurance and Universal Health Insurance Act does not determine either territorial or personal fields of application for each insurance branch separately. The territorial scope is determined by referring to the personal field of application. Those who are considered 'insurance holders' according to Article 4/I a and b, on suffering an industrial accident or occupational disease at a workplace in Turkey are entitled to benefits according to the insurance provided for industrial accidents and occupational diseases.

212. Even if the accident has occurred abroad, if both parties to the contract of employment have Turkish nationality, the Act declares itself applicable. Thus, with respect to Turkish employees sent to work abroad, pursuant to 5/1, g of Act No. 5510, if an employee is working in the workplace of a Turkish employer in a foreign country with whom the Turkish Republic has no bilateral agreement, that employee shall be deemed to be an insurance holder according to Article 4/I-a of Act No. 5510. However, the cover of their compulsory insurance status is restricted to short-term insurance branches and universal health insurance. Therefore, if those employees suffer an industrial accident whilst abroad, the Institution shall provide all necessary benefits arising from short-term insurance branches. In that case, the accident occurred abroad may be qualified as an industrial accident according to the provisions of Act No. 5510.[182,183]

II. Personal Field of Application

213. Under the previous system, in a real sense, only wage earners benefited from insurance for industrial accidents and occupational diseases. According to the

182. A.N. Sözer, n. 70, pp. 313–314.
183. Court of Cass., 21th Ch., 25.10.2010, 2009/13391, 2010/10434 noted by H. Ergin, 'Türk Vatandaşı İşçinin Yabancı Bir Ülkede Geçirdiği İş Kazasına Uygulanacak Hukuk', *Sicil Der.*(Eylül, 2011), pp. 234–242; 21th Ch., 19.12.2016, 881/15225, *Çalışma ve Toplum Der.*(2017/2), pp. 1083–1085.

abrogated Act No. 1479, Self-Employed persons rarely benefited from the insurance protection against industrial accident because the abrogated Act stated an analogical application of the provisions of Act No. 506, applicable to wage earners. However, the nature of these provisions was not appropriate to an analogical application in the case of industrial accidents of Self-Employed persons. Therefore, it was rare to meet with industrial accidents application under the previous system.[184]

214. Act No. 5510 extends the personal field of application, since, in addition to wage earners, self-employed persons are covered by short-term insurance branches of the Act.[185] Therefore, as mentioned in the heading of the short-term insurance branches in the Act, those who work under a contract of employment and who are self-employed persons shall benefit from the insurance for industrial accidents and occupational diseases.

A. *Wage Earners and the Self-Employed Persons*

215. The victim of an accident or disease must be covered by the scope of Article 4/I-a and b of Act No. 5510 to qualify the accident as an industrial accident. As mentioned above,[186] certain groups are partly covered by short-term insurance branches. Convicts and detainees, apprentices, trainees who do an internship during their education at a vocational high school or higher education, students who work part-time in universities, participants to vocational training organized by the Turkish Employment Institution are also covered by the provisions regarding industrial accidents and occupational diseases.

B. *Civil Servants*

216. Act No. 5510 deals with industrial accidents for civil servants under only the case of job invalidity. Civil servants who gain insurance holder status for the first time, according to Article 4/I c of Act No. 5510, are subjected to Article 47 of Act No. 5510, which regulates job invalidity. For those who gained civil servant status before the entry into force of Act No. 5510, Act No. 5434, Pension Fund will be applicable (Trans. Article 4/4 of Act No. 5510).

---

184. L. Akın, 'Sosyal Sigortalar ve Genel Sağlık Sigortası Kanunu Tasarısı'nın İş Kazası Tanımı', *İşveren*(Kasım, 2005), p. 61.
185. For details, *see* F.B. Mutlay, 'Bağımsız Çalışanlar Bakımından İş Kazası Halleri Yenilik midir?', *Prof. Dr. Sarper Süzek'e Armağan,* C. III (İstanbu, 2011), pp. 2434–2467.
186. *See supra* para. 85.

§2. The Concept of 'Industrial Accident'

217. Instead of defining the concept of 'industrial accident', Act No. 5510 lists circumstances, whereby if an accident occurs, it is considered an industrial accident. Industrial accidents in the sense of Act No. 5510 differ from industrial accidents resulting in employer liability. In order to hold the employer liable for the accident, the circumstances of the accident must be related to the performance of the work under a contract of employment. However, Act No. 5510 describes a larger framework for the industrial accident to provide social security benefits for a greater number of insured employees.[187]

I. Industrial Accident

218. An industrial accident is defined by authors as a sudden, unexpected and external event, and which produces physical or mental injuries to the insurance holder.[188]

219. In order for an accident to qualify as an industrial accident, first of all, the victim of the accident must be covered by the scope of Article 4/I a or 4/b of Act No. 5510. Those who are left out of the scope of short-term insurance branches of the Act may be injured by accident; however, such an accident is not considered an industrial accident. The commencement of the insured employee's employment under a contract of employment is sufficient for him/her to fall under cover of Article 13. Therefore, registration of the insured worker with the Social Security Institution is not required to benefit from insurance for industrial accidents and occupational diseases.

220. Second, the insured employee must suffer from an industrial accident producing physical or mental injuries. It does not matter if the effect of the injury is immediate or delayed. If an accident causes only material damages to the goods of an employee, it is not deemed to be an industrial accident.[189] Third, there must be causality between the accident and the injury of the insurance holder. The authority of the employer is considered as evidence to prove the causality lien in many cases.

221. Lastly, the accident must be due to a sudden and external effect. 'Sudden' means a quick happening or lasting for a certain duration of time. An external effect must cause the accident. Therefore, suffering a heart attack or any other sickness in

187. S. Süzek, İş Hukuku, 12. ed. (Istanbul, 2016), pp. 63–464; L. Akın, İş Kazasından Doğan Maddi Tazminat (Ankara, 2001), pp. 39 et seq.; 46 et seq.; A.N. Sözer, n. 7, pp. 314–317; The same author, 'Türk Sosyal Sigortalar Hukukunda İş Kazası Kavramı ve Unsurları', in *Prof. Dr. Nuri Çelik'e Armağan*, C. II (Istanbul, 2001), pp. 1897–1898, 1916; C. Tuncay/Ö. Ekmekçi, n. 7, p. 312.
188. R. Atabek, *İş Kazası ve Sigortası* (Istanbul, 1978), pp. 40–49; M. Çenberci, n. 80, pp. 115–116; A. Güzel/A.R. Okur/N. Caniklioğlu, n. 7, p. 331; F. Uşan, n. 28, p. 172; S. Taşkent, 'İş Kazası Kavramı', in *Prof. Dr. Nuri Çelik'e Armağan*, C. II (Istanbul, 2001), pp. 1951–1966.
189. M. Çenberci, n. 80, p. 116; K. Tunçomağ, n. 7; p. 264; A. Güzel/A.R. Okur/N. Caniklioğlu, n. 7, p. 346; C. Tuncay/Ö. Ekmekçi, n. 7, p. 384; Y. Alper, n. 7, p. 240.

the workplace shall not be considered as an industrial accident, unless an external effect triggers the attack.[190] Nevertheless, the Court of Cassation held to consider such sicknesses occurring at the workplace as an industrial accident.[191]

222. If authors are agreed upon the necessity of an external effect in the occurrence of an accident, there is no unanimity, with regard to, the intention of the insured employee. The question remains whether it would be considered an industrial accident, whenever the intention of the insured employee plays a role in its happening. According to some authors, we cannot talk about an industrial accident when the principal act causing the accident is intentional on the part of the insurance holder.[192] However, the majority argues that an intentional act of the insurance holder does not prevent the accident from being qualified as an industrial accident.[193] The wording of Article 22 of Act No. 5510, which deals with the insurance holder who has suffered from an industrial accident because of his/her fault, supports this view. The negligence of the insurance holder affects only the scope of monetary benefits. Thus, the Court of Cassation considered suicide in the workplace as an industrial accident.[194]

II. The Circumstances Enumerated in Article 13 of Act No. 5510

223. Act No. 5510 envisages amending not only the personnel field of application but also the concept of an industrial accident. Abrogated Act No. 506 listed the situations under which an accident will be considered an industrial accident. The Act takes this regulation as a basis but with certain amendments.

224. Article 13 of Act No. 5510 lists the circumstances where an accident is considered an 'industrial' accident:

(a) the accident occurs in the workplace;
(b) in connection with the work carried on by the employer, if the insurance holder works in his own name and account, the accident occurs in connection with that activity;
(c) if the insured employee is sent by the employer to another place to perform a task and the accident occurs during related free time;

190. C. Tuncay/Ö. Ekmekçi, n. 7, pp. 377–378; F. Uşan, n. 28, p. 174.
191. Court of Cass., 21th Ch., 21.11.2002, 9004/10005, cited and noted by N. Caniklioğlu, 'Sosyal Sigorta Türleri', in *Yargıtayın İş Hukukuna İlişkin Kararlarının Değerllendirilmesi 2002* (Ankara, 2004), p. 342; Court of Cass., 21th Ch., 3.11.2004, 8871/9254, 5, *Çalışma ve Toplum Der.*(2005/2), pp. 310–311; 21th Ch., 8.2.2011, 2010/9728, 2011/801 noted by C. Saraç, 'İşyerinde Kalp Krizinden Ölüm ve İşverenin İş Kazasından Dolayı Sorumluluğu', *Sicil*(Haziran, 2012), pp. 125–130.
192. C. Tuncay/Ö. Ekmekçi, n. 7, pp. 371–372; F. Uşan, n. 28, p. 173.
193. M. Çenberci, n. 80, p. 117; K. Tunçomağ, n. 7; p. 278; A. Güzel/A.R. Okur/N. Caniklioğlu, n. 7, p. 338; A.N. Sözer, n. 70, pp. 315–316; M. Şakar, n. 7, p. 197; R. Korkusuz/S. Uğur, n. 83, p. 289.
194. Court of Cass., 9th Ch., 29.3.1979, 8413/2759, *YKD*(Ağustos, 1979), p. 1167; 10th Ch., 5.7.2004, 4465/6425, *Legal-İSGHD*(Ağustos, 2004), pp. 2267–2269.

(d) the accident occurs during the periods set aside for the employee to nurse a child;
(e) the accident occurs during the collective transfer of employees in a vehicle provided by the employer.

225. First of all, all accidents occurring in the workplace are 'industrial' accidents. Only insured employees may benefit from this provision. There is no need for a direct link between the accident and the performance of the work. This implies that an accident may happen while the actual work has stopped. From the moment of entry into, until the leaving of the workplace, the employee is under the protection of Act No. 5510, without any further need to examine whether he/she is under the authority of the employer at the time the accident occurred. Thus, even accidents which occur outside working hours but in the workplace are 'industrial' accidents. For example, during the lunch break, if an employee breaks his leg while running in the garden, it is also considered an 'industrial' accident.[195]

226. If the insured employee has suffered an accident in connection with work carried out by the employer (Article 13/I, b of Act No. 5510), this accident is also deemed to be an industrial accident. Accidents occurring in the workplace is regulated by Article 13/I, a, but accidents occurring outside of the workplace is regulated by 13/I, b. If the insured employee is sent by the employer to another place to perform a task, the employee is under cover of insurance for industrial accidents against any accidents which may occur during this period. The basis of the accident affects the benefit of entitlement. A work-related activity or any other external or internal reason may be the cause of the accident.

The second part of the provision regulates industrial accidents for Self-Employed persons. Only accidents in connection with the activity carried out by the Self-Employed person are deemed to be an industrial accident. Thus, an accident occurring in the workplace has to be related to the activity carried out to be considered as an industrial accident, with regard to, self-employed persons.

227. The employer may charge the employee with a task which must be performed in another city or abroad. Accidents which occur while travelling to or while spending time in such places are also covered by insurance for industrial accidents (Article 13/I, c of Act No. 5510). Thus, an insured person, who lost his life in a plane accident, was also considered to be a victim of an 'industrial' accident.[196] Furthermore, any accident that happens during the period, when the insured employee spent his time not doing his main tasks, falls under cover of insurance for industrial accidents. To qualify as an industrial accident, the Court of Cassation requires that

195. M. Çenberci, n. 80, pp. 118–119; K. Tunçomağ, n. 7; pp. 259–260; A. Güzel/A.R. Okur/N. Caniklioğlu, n. 7, pp. 339–340; A.N. Sözer, n. 70, pp. 322–324; Y. Alper, n. 7, p. 244; M. Şakar, n. 7, p. 197; comp. C. Tuncay/Ö. Ekmekçi, n. 7, pp. 375–376; F. Uşan, n. 28, pp. 175–176.
196. Court of Cass., 9th Ch., 29.12.1981, 11284/15904, Judgment and notes by C. Tuncay, *İHU* 1982/I, SSK. 11(No. 2).

the activity must be among customary activities performed over the course of normal life. Due to the principles of social security law, the insured employee must be protected against all risks which may appear in the course of normal daily life.[197]

228. Accidents occurring during the periods allocated to insured employees to nurse children are also 'industrial' accidents (Article 13/I, d of Act No. 5510). Nursing female employees have the right to leave their workplace for periods of forty-five minutes, twice a day, once before and once after their lunch. If the nursing employee has an accident in the course of this time, the accident constitutes as an 'industrial' accident. For example, an insured woman hit by a car, while crossing the road after returning from nursing, is deemed to have lost her life in an 'industrial' accident.[198]

229. If the insured employee suffers an accident, while on the way to and from work, in a vehicle supplied, this constitutes an 'industrial' accident (Article 13/I, e of Act No. 5510). The accident may be a traffic accident or any other accident occurring underway or while the employee is entering or leaving the vehicle. Two requirements exist in order for an accident to be classified as an industrial accident. First, the vehicle must be provided by the employer. The nature of the legal relationship between the employer and the provider has no relevance. If the vehicle belongs to the employer, it makes it part of the 'workplace', and every accident which occurs at the workplace is an industrial accident. Second, the accident must have occurred on the way to and from work. Act No. 5510 removes the requirement that insured employees must be transported collectively.

230. The legal nature of these circumstances is a debatable issue. Certain authors and the Court of Cassation argue that if an accident occurs under the circumstances mentioned in Article 13/I of Act No. 5510, no other condition is required to consider an accident as an industrial accident.[199] Some other authors argue that the accident must occur under the authority of the employer to be considered as an industrial accident.[200] In our view, the authority of the employer is revealed as important with respect to indemnities. This insurance branch aims to provide for the losses of the employee due to an industrial accident. A restricted interpretation of the Act may leave the insurance holder alone to face the losses.

III. Notification of the Accident

231. The employer of the insurance holder, who is subjected to Article 4/I-a or to Article 5, must notify the authorized police forces immediately and the Institution, within three working days following the accident. The time period starts with

197. A. Güzel/A.R. Okur/N. Caniklioğlu, n. 7, p. 343; A.N. Sözer, n. 70, pp. 326–327.
198. Court of Cass., General Council, 10.6.1983, 328/652 cited in M. Çenberci, n. 80, pp. 120–121.
199. Court of Cass., General Council, 13 Oct. 2004, 21-529/527, www.hukukturk.com; A. Güzel/A.R. Okur/N. Caniklioğlu, n. 7, p. 345; A.N. Sözer, n. 70, p. 318; The same author, 'İş Kazası Kavramı', p. 1898.
200. C. Tuncay/Ö. Ekmekçi, n. 7, p. 370; F. Uşan, n. 28, pp. 175–176.

the date of being informed of the accident if the industrial accident occurs at a place out of the control of the employer (Article 13/II, a of Act No. 5510). The notification may be made directly or via registered mail.

232. Self-employed persons are under a duty to notify the Institution of the accident within three working days starting with the date of his/her accident and, at the latest, within one month following the accident (Article 13/II, b of Act No. 5510).

233. The Institution has the authority to investigate whether the accident is an industrial accident or not. The investigation may be carried out by the Institution's officers or labour inspectors. If at the end of the investigation, it is found that the notified issues are not true or the accident is not an industrial accident, inappropriate payments made by the Institution shall be refunded from the parties who gave false notification (Article 13/III of Act No. 5510).

IV. Job Invalidity for Civil Servants

234. Article 47 defines job invalidity similar to abrogated Act No. 5434. If the invalidity occurs while the civil servant is performing his/her job, while performing duties belonging to another public entity, or while performing duties with the aim of protecting the interest of his/her public entity and the loss of capacity to works reaches 60%, such an invalidity is considered as job invalidity. Furthermore, invalidities arising from accidents occurring in the workplace or in vehicles provided by the employer, while on the way to and from work, are also considered as job invalidity. Act No. 5510 extended the cover of job invalidity. Before the Act, accidents which occurred in the workplace had to have arisen from the nature of the workplace or the subject of the work. However, Act No. 5510 requires no other condition than occurring in the workplace, with regard to, the conditions of job invalidity. In addition, accidents occurring on the way to and from home are also covered by job invalidity. In the Draft Bill, such criteria had been provided for, with respect to employees and self-employed persons. However, in Parliament, this provision was amended, in such a way, to restrict its application.[201]

235. Therefore, the protection against industrial accidents for civil servants is provided for, only if, the degree of invalidity attains a certain degree. Act No. 5510 requires that either the insurance holder must lose his/her capacity to work to a minimum of 60% or lose earning capacity to the degree that the victim is unable to perform his/her duties (Article 25 of Act No. 5510).

201. *See* A.N. Sözer, n. 70, pp. 284–292.

§3. THE CONCEPT OF 'OCCUPATIONAL DISEASES'

I. Occupational Diseases

236. According to Article 14/I, an occupational disease is defined as a temporary or permanent disease, invalidity or mental problem that the insurance holder suffers because of a continuing causal factor, characteristic of the nature of work that the insured performs, or arising out of conditions required for the execution of such work.

237. In order to be covered by insurance, first of all, the insurance holder suffering from an occupational disease must be deemed to be insured in the sense of Article 4/I a and b of Act No. 5510.

Second, the insurance holder must have suffered a physical or mental injury. This sickness may cause a temporary or permanent incapacity to work. The insurance for industrial accidents and occupational diseases also covers the survivors of the insurance holder who has lost his/her life due to an accident or occupational disease.

In this case, sickness or death should arise from the nature of the work which the insured had performed. The causality relationship between the disease and the specific task is very important. Unlike an industrial accident, the occupational disease must arise from the task that the insured employee performs under a contract of employment or the Self-Employed carries out.[202]

Finally, the diagnosis of the occupational disease must be confirmed by an Institution's Health Board report. Act No. 5510 brought in a procedure of two steps: First, the occupational disease must be diagnosed by the authorized service providers; therefore, all service providers of the Institution are not authorized anymore to diagnose an occupational disease. Second, the medical report and other documents shall be examined by the Institution's Health Board. The Board may request to examine the inspection reports about the workplace working conditions and related medical consequences (Article 14/II of Act No. 5510). Lastly, the final decision is given by the Institution's Health Board.

238. The list of occupational diseases is regulated by a Bylaw, the Evaluation the Loss of Capacity for Working and Capacity for Earning Rate, issued on 11 October 2008.[203] According to this Bylaw, for a disease to qualify as an 'occupational' disease, the sickness must correspond to one of those on the official list, and it must have occurred during the determined time period, thus, indicating causality between the performance of the work and the disease. The time period between the termination of the causal work and the appearance of the illness, called 'the engagement period', varies between three days to fifteen years. However, the engagement period is not restrictive. Thus, if a disease is diagnosed and the causes of such disease are found out to be from the workplace following an official examination, the disease is to be deemed as an 'occupational disease', even if the engagement period has

202. M. Çenberci, n. 80, p. 124; A. Güzel/A.R. Okur/N. Caniklioğlu, n. 7, p. 354; C. Tuncay/Ö. Ekmekçi, n. 7, pp. 387–388; F. Uşan, n. 28, p. 178; A.N. Sözer, n. 70, p. 336.
203. OJ, 11 Oct. 2008, No. 27021.

expired. The Supreme Health Institution decides upon the request of either the insurance holder or the Institution itself (Article 14/III of Act No. 5510).

239. Under the Turkish social insurance law, a mixed system to define occupational diseases is accepted. Therefore, even if a sickness is not registered in the official list, the victim is allowed to prove the occupational origins of the disease. In that case, the victim is charged with the burden of proof. The conflict appears between the victim and the Social Security Institution. If the Institution refuses the insured's request to benefit from the insurance for occupational diseases, the appeal is brought before the Supreme Health Institution. Against the decisions of this Institution, the parties may appeal to the labour courts.[204] In case of an action brought directly to the court without applying to the Supreme Health Institution, the labour court should postpone the hearing of the case until the plaintiff has had time to consider the opinion of the Health Institution.[205] However, the Court of Cassation, in its more recent judgments, has held that even though the plaintiff sues the Institution without having reviewed the opinion of the Health Institution, the court should examine the case. However, the judge may also ask the Council of Forensic Medicine for its opinion.[206]

240. Silicosis due to sandblasted jeans constitutes an occupational disease. However, the fact that many employees working on blasting jeans with sand are non-registered in Turkey prevents to provide necessary health protection to those persons. Certainly, these workers may claim the establishment of their insured periods by a court decision. However, such a trial takes time. In addition, silicosis develops in certain cases five to ten years after the first exposure to higher concentrations of silica dust. Thus, the sickness appears after many years that the exposed worker has left the job, which reveals the case much more complicated. Faced with problems to include silicosis among occupational diseases, the legislator preferred, by an amendment made to Act No. 2022,[207] a cross-cut solution to provide protection to those persons.

241. According to transitory Article 2 of Act No. 2022, those who do not work as being subject to social security legislation and who do not receive any income or pension from social security institutions or an institution abroad may request a pension, if they suffer a loss of 15% earning power due to silicosis. A monthly pension shall be allocated.

The amount of monthly pension is calculated by the multiplication of indicator by monthly coefficient fixed by the budgetary act. The indicator shall be determined according to the loss of earning capacity. If the loss of earning capacity is between 15% and 34%, the indicator is set to 7,000; between 35% and 54%, it is set to 8,000; between 55% and above, it is set to 9,000.

204. Court of Cass., Unif Judg. 28.6.1976, 6/4, Judgment and notes by M. Cuhruk, *İHU* 1977, SSK 109 (No. 2).
205. M. Çenberci, n. 80, p. 127; A. Güzel/A.R. Okur/N. Caniklioğlu, n. 7, p. 358, fn. 132.
206. Court of Cass., 2 Oct. 1990, 6864/10113, *YKD*(Nisan 1991), pp. 564–565; 21th Ch., 16.11.2009, 5752, K. 14932, *Legal-İSGHD*(26/2010), pp. 840–841.
207. Act No. 6111 dated of 13 Feb. 2011, OJ, 26 Jun. 2012, No. 28335.

If the silicosis pension receiver dies, the pension shall be distributed among his/her spouse, sons and daughters.

The biggest deficit of the regulation is that only those who made a request within three months starting from the date of publication of this article (26 June 2012) may benefit from such pension. It seems that the legislator found a temporary solution to defeat public pressure.

II. Notification of Occupational Disease

242. The employer of the insurance holder, who is subject to Article 4/I-a or to Article 5, must notify the Institution of the occupational disease within three working days following the date of being informed about the disease. A self-employed person must notify the Institution within three working days starting with the date the insurance holder learns of the diseases.

243. The Institution has the authority to investigate whether the accident is an industrial accident or not. The investigation may be carried by the Institution's officers or labour inspectors. If at the end of the investigation, it is found out that the notified issues are not true or the accident is not an industrial accident, inappropriate payments made by the Institution shall be refunded from the parties who gave false notification (Article 13/III of Act No. 5510).

§4. Benefits Provided

I. Type of Benefits

244. With respect to employees and self-employed persons, benefits provided to the victims of an industrial accident or to those who suffer an occupational disease are the same. Under the abrogated Act No. 506, healthcare was provided under cover of industrial accidents and occupational disease insurance. However, Act No. 5510 provides healthcare within the framework of universal health insurance.

245. With respect to civil servants, a job invalidity pension is awarded to those who suffered from job invalidity. Survivors pensions, funeral allowance, as well as, marriage assistance, are also provided in case of the death of the civil servant due to a reason related to his/her invalidity.

A. Temporary Incapacity Allowance

246. After having suffered an industrial accident or occupational disease, the recovery of the victim takes a certain time. During this period, victims lose the capacity to work and even, in some cases, their jobs. The employer is not obliged to pay the wages of the period that the insured employee is absent. In order to compensate for the absence of regular income, the Institution pays a temporary incapacity allowance to those who are subjected to Article 4/I-a, mainly employees. Neither the length of the insurance period nor the amount of paid contributions are determinant in benefiting from the allowance. Unlike the insurance coverage for health and maternity, the insured employee, who meets with an accident on the very first working day, without having paid any contribution for insurance for industrial accidents and occupational diseases may benefit from temporary incapacity allowance. The only requirement for entitlement allowance is the medical report proving temporary incapacity to work.

247. If the aim of the allowance is to make up for the loss of income, it does not compensate for the entire amount of the loss. The amount of the allowance varies in accordance with the method of treatment. In case of inpatient victims, that is, the treatment provided while the victim stays in a hospital or other nursing facility, the amount of the allocation is half of the daily wage up to the limits fixed by Act No. 5510. For outpatients, those receiving medical services or treatment on an outpatient basis in a hospital or health institution, the amount of the temporary allowance equals two-thirds of the daily wage (Article 18/III of Act No. 5510).

248. Although self-employed persons are protected against the risk of industrial accident and occupational disease under the same provisions which regulate the insurance for employees, the required conditions to get these benefits are different, with respect to self-employed insurance holders. Unlike wage earners, a self-employed insurance holder must settle all kinds of debts related to contribution payments, including contributions for universal health insurance, to benefit from temporary incapacity allowance. Despite criticisms against such a distinction,[208] the Constitutional Court declined the unconstitutionality claim about this provision.[209] In addition, such an allowance shall be paid only to inpatient self-employed victims (Article 18/II of Act No. 5510). Therefore, outpatient self-employed persons do not get temporary incapacity allowance.

B. *Permanent Incapacity Allowance*

1. Permanent Incapacity to Work

249. The treatment may lead to full recovery of the victim. However, in some cases, the victim cannot be entirely cured. At the end of the treatment, if the victim has lost at least 10% of his/her earning capacity as a result of the industrial accident or occupational disease, that person is considered to be suffering a permanent incapacity (Article 19 of Act No. 5510). If the degree of incapacity is less than 10%, permanent incapacity does not exist. The Court of Cassation held that if the victim

208. N. Caniklioğlu, 'Sosyal Hukukta Ayrımcılık', pp. 659–660; A. Güzel/A.R. Okur/N. Caniklioğlu, n. 7, p. 363.
209. Cons. Court., 15.12.2006, 111/112, OJ, 30.12.2006, No. 26392 (Mük.).

has suffered from accident or disease at different times and the cumulative incapacity caused by these accidents exceeds 10%, and the insured may also benefit from a permanent incapacity allowance.[210]

250. The notion of permanent incapacity includes the loss of earning capacity in the victim's current profession, even though the victim retains the ability to work in another profession.[211] A profession is defined as the job that the insured employee performed, in accordance with a contract of employment, at the time of the occurrence of the accident or occupational disease. The ability of the victim to do another job does not prevent permanent incapacity.

251. The degree of incapacity to work is determined according to schedules fixed by Regulations of Social Security Procedures on the basis of medical reports issued by the medical board of the service providers authorized by the Institution. If the insured person has suffered a 100% loss of the capacity to work, a permanent total incapacity exists. However, partial incapacity to work exists if more than 10% but less than 100% of the person's labour capacity has been lost.

2. Permanent Total Incapacity Income

252. A victim suffering total incapacity to work is entitled to a life-long permanent total incapacity pension. The amount of the pension is equal to 70% of the total monthly income of the insured (Article 19/III of Act No. 5510). If the victim is in need of permanent attendance, the pension's amount is to be increased by 100% (Article 19/III of Act No. 5510).

3. Permanent Partial Incapacity Income

253. If the degree of incapacity to work varies between 10% and 100%, the victim is entitled to a partial incapacity income. The amount of income awarded to the insured is to be calculated in proportion to the degree of incapacity to work. As is the case for those suffering total incapacity, the amount of pension is increased to 100% in the cases of those needing an attendant (Article 19/3 of Act No. 5510).

254. The rule is that a permanent partial incapacity income is paid over the life of the insured. Since the amount of the income is determined in proportion to the degree of incapacity to work, a change in that degree affects the amount of the income paid. Either the insured victim or the Institution may ask for the effect of the change on the income to be determined. Thus, the insured may demand an increase in the degree of incapacity to work to be determined. The need for a nurse may also be proven. Similarly, the Institution may request the insured to be

210. Court of Cass., 10th Ch., 3 Oct. 2000, 5889/5884, *YKD*(Şubat, 2001), pp. 206–208.
211. A. Güzel/A.R. Okur/N. Caniklioğlu, n. 7, p. 370; F. Uşan, n. 28, p. 182.

re-examined. The change in the state of the degree of incapacity to work must be proven by a report issued by the service provider authorized by the Institution.

255. If the insurance holder re-suffers another industrial accident or occupational disease, the total disability degree and the amount of the last wage are taken as a basis for calculating the incapacity income. However, if the amount of later incapacity income is less than the former one, the incapacity income shall be calculated on the basis of the daily income of the former work (Article 19/VIII of Act No. 5510).

256. To award total or partial incapacity income to those who are subject to Article 4/I-b of Act No. 5510, the self-employed insurance holder must be out of all kinds of debts related to contribution payment including contributions for universal health insurance.

C. Death Allowances

257. If the insured victim has died due to an industrial accident or occupational disease, the survivors are entitled to certain benefits provided by the insurance for industrial accidents and occupational diseases. These benefits are summarized as follows: payment of funeral expenses, awarding of incomes to survivors and marriage assistance.

1. Death Income Awarded to Survivors in Case of Death of the Insurance Holder

258. If the insurance holder lost his/her life due to an industrial accident or occupational disease, a death income would be awarded to their survivors (Article 20/I of Act No. 5510). Unlike survivors' insurance, the only requirement to award survivors' income is that the insurance holder dies due to an industrial accident or occupational disease. In addition, if the insurance holder receiving permanent incapacity income loses his/her life afterwards, his/her survivors are entitled to receive death income, even if the death has no relevance to an industrial accident or occupational disease.

2. Funeral Expenses

259. An allowance for funeral expenses is paid to the family of the insured who died due to an industrial accident or occupational disease or who died while receiving permanent incapacity income. The amount of the allowance is fixed by the board of directors of the Social Security Institution and approved by the Minister of Labour and Social Security (Article 37 of Act No. 5510). If the funeral is arranged by a private or public person in lieu of the family, whoever has arranged the funeral is entitled to these benefits. Funeral expenses shall be granted to the insurance holder's spouse, if not to the children, if not to the parents and if not to the siblings.

3. Marriage Assistance

260. In order to protect the daughters of the deceased insurance holder, the Act provides marriage assistance, while the death income payment shall be ceased at the marriage of the daughter. Act No. 5510 extends the personal field of application of this assistance in such a way as to include self-employed persons, who have no such right under the current system. If within two years following the discontinuance of the income, the daughter gets divorced, no income shall be awarded until the end of the two years period (Article 37/I of Act No. 5510). Nevertheless, they will receive benefits from universal health insurance (Article 60/I, f of Act No. 5510).

II. Amount of Benefits

A. Temporary Incapacity Allowance

261. While calculating the temporary or permanent incapacity allowance to be paid under the framework of insurance for industrial accidents and occupational diseases, the daily income of the insured is calculated as set out above.[212] Nevertheless, Act No. 5510 brought in certain restrictions: If there exist premiums, bonuses and any other similar payments, the monthly amount which is actually paid is taken into consideration while calculating daily earnings based for contribution. Nevertheless, while calculating temporary incapacity allowance, these amounts taken into calculation, shall not be more than the amount found by adding 50% of these payments. If there exist wages, bonuses or any kind of payment concerned is due to an administrative decision or judicial verdict; contributions are deducted not from the earnings of the relevant month but from the earnings of the month that effective payment is made. While calculating the daily amount of the allowance, only payments related to the three months shall be taken into calculation. Other payments related to the months prior to the last three months are not considered.

262. With regard to the income periods taken as a basis for the calculation of income periods, Act No. 5510 provides detailed regulations: The daily earnings to be taken as a basis for calculation of the allowance are to be calculated by dividing the total earnings obtained, as described above, in the course of the last three months in twelve months preceding the date on which the accident occurred by the number of days for which the contribution was paid (Article 17 of Act No. 5510).

If the insured employee has not worked and gained a wage regularly during these twelve months, all wages earned between the day he started to work and the day of temporary incapacity will be divided by the number of the working days to fix the

212. *See supra* paras 112–115.

amount of the temporary allowance. If the insured person suffered the accident on the day of commencing the employment, the amount of wage paid to an insurance holder, on the same or equivalent job, shall be taken into consideration (Article 17/II of Act No. 5510).

If the occupational disease occurred within one year, following the day the insurance holder quit work, the daily amount is calculated on the basis of the wage earned at that last work.

263. A self-employed person declares himself/herself to the Institution the amount of daily earnings based for contributions between lower and upper limits. The amount of the contribution basis is thirty times the daily earnings (Article 80/II of Act No. 5510). The minimum wage is the lower limit for daily earnings.

264. Temporary incapacity allowance is paid in the course of treatment without any time restriction. Unlike insurance for sickness, the payment starts from the first day of incapacity. The payment of temporary incapacity allowance for previous periods is made within seven days following the submission of the required documents to the Institution. In case of treatments which continue more than ten days, minimum ten days of allowance is paid.

265. If the insurance holder suffers from an industrial accident, while being assigned abroad, permanently or temporarily, or whilst being sent abroad, the employer is responsible for paying temporary incapacity allowance.

B. Permanent Incapacity Allowance

266. The amount of monthly income is thirty times the amount of daily income based for the temporary incapacity allowance. The amount of permanent total incapacity allowance is equal to 70% of the total monthly income of the insured (Article 19/III of Act No. 5510). The amount of partial incapacity allowance is to be calculated in proportion to the degree of incapacity to work. Due to the nature of the permanent incapacity allowance, they will be paid, as long as, the insured is in a condition of permanent incapacity, which means that the total loss of earning is more than 10%.

267. Nevertheless, the amount of either temporary or permanent payments may be reduced in case of negligent acts of the victim in the course of the treatment. If, because of the victim's negligence in disobeying doctors' recommendations, the treatment has to be extended or the insured becomes disabled or the degree of disability increases, the Institution may reduce the incapacity payments in proportion to the negligence of the victim. Nevertheless, such reductions may not exceed one-fourth of the temporary incapacity allowance or permanent incapacity income (Article 22/I, a of Act No. 5510). The degree of negligence is to be fixed by a medical report.

268. Likewise, if the victim suffers the industrial accident or occupational disease due to his/her intentional action or refuses the treatment offered by the health institutions in spite of the written notification of the Institution, temporary and permanent incapacity allowance is paid in half (Article 22/I, c of Act No. 5510). If the victim is in gross negligence, then the amount of temporary and permanent allowance is reduced up to one-third of its amount.

269. The insurance holder is not to resume working without having a medical certificate which proves that the treatment is over, and the insurance holder may start work. If the insurance holder starts working without receiving such certificate, no temporary incapacity allowance shall be paid. Those who have already been paid shall be refunded pursuant to Article 96 of Act No. 5510.

270. The Social Security Institution has the right to request a control examination at any time. If the victim refuses the control examination without any reasonable excuse, the payment of permanent incapacity income is suspended starting from the payment, which follows the control examination. However, for insurance holder who undergoes medical treatment within three months following the written notified day and whose permanent incapacity status is confirmed, the suspended income shall be granted again starting from the day of suspension (Article 94/VI of Act No. 5510). There is no retroactive payment for controls made after three months.

C. *Death Allowances*

1. Death Income Awarded to Survivors in Case of Death of the Insurance Holder

271. If the insured has died due to an industrial accident or occupational disease, an income will be awarded to his survivors. In order to award such an income to survivors, Act No. 5510 requires no condition as regards to the amount of the contribution made or the length of the insured period. If this is the case for insurance holders working with a contract of employment, for Self-Employed insurance holders, the Act requires that to award an income to the survivors of a Self-Employed insurance holder, the insurance holder has to have cleared all his debts related to contribution payments, including contributions for universal health insurance.

272. The benefit to be divided among the survivors is 70% of the monthly income of the deceased's insurance (Article 20/I of Act No. 5510). This amount equals that of the permanent total incapacity income awarded to insured persons suffering complete incapacity to work. Nevertheless, if someone receiving a permanent incapacity income, having lost 50% or more of earning capacity, dies, the amount of the survivors' income equals the amount of the total incapacity income. Even if the incapacity of the insurance holder is partial, his/her survivors receive the income as if it was total. Whether the death is due to an industrial accident or occupational disease, has no importance. However, if the loss of earning capacity is less than 50%, the insurance holder's partial income shall be divided among the survivors, if the death has no causal connection with the industrial accident or occupational disease (Article 20/ III of Act No. 5510). In cases of an industrial accident, survivors shall share the amount equal to the total incapacity income.

273. The widow or the widower is entitled to receive monthly income without any other pre-condition. If both widow and children have a right to the pension, the widow or the widower has the right to 50% of the total amount. In that case, it is of no importance whether he/she works or receives an income under the framework of the Social Security Institution. If there is no child benefiting from income, the widow is entitled to 75% of 70% of the yearly income of the insured, only if he/she does not work under the frame of Act No. 5510 or in a foreign country, and he/she does not receive any pension or income due to his/her own work. Therefore, to get an income equal to 50% of the total amount, the Act requires no other condition. However, to get an income equal to 75% of the total income is subject to some other conditions. Such a difference is criticized.[213] In the case of remarriage, the widow/widower ceases to receive income. However, if this second marriage ends due to the death and the widow/widower is entitled to receive income due to the second spouse, he/she has right to choose the income to be allocated (Article 54/II b, 5 of Act No. 5510).

274. If a person is entitled to death allowance due to his/her spouse and due to his/her parents, he/she has right to choose the allowance to be allocated (Article 54/I, b, 4 of Act No. 5510).

275. Each child of an insured person, who has died in an industrial accident or from an occupational disease, is entitled to an income equalling 25% of the total amount of the income. However, if both parents are dead or have, subsequently, died or if there was no matrimonial tie between the parents or if the father/mother remarries, subsequently, or if the child is the sole right holder receiving income, this amount is increased by 50% (Article 34/I, c of Act No. 5510). As regards infants, the Act requires certain conditions to award death income: First, infants must not work under the frame of Act No. 5510, thus, neither as an employee and self-employed nor as a public officer. Also, infants must not work as subject to foreign legislation. In addition, infants must have no other benefits from the Social Security Institution due to their own employment. Therefore, pensions awarded in his/her survivor's capacity does not prevent receiving death income. Lastly, the Act provides age requirements depending on the sex of the infant. If the orphan is a son, the payment of income continues as long as he has no income, of any kind, up to the age of 18. However, the age limit is increased, in accordance with the educational stage. If he attends secondary school, the benefits continue to be paid up to the age of 20 – the orphan who continues in higher education benefits from the allocations up to the age of 25. Nevertheless, if the orphan has lost a minimum 60%

213. A. Güzel/A.R. Okur/N. Caniklioğlu, n. 7, pp. 379–380.

of his work power and his invalidity is proven by a medical report issued by the Institution Health Committee, he shall receive income regardless of his age.

276. For sociological reasons, the law sets no upper age limit regarding daughters. Whatever her age is, as long as, the daughter of the victim has not got married, nor performed an activity covered by Act No. 5510, nor drawing pensions from the Social Security Institution because of her own employment,[214] she has the right to a monthly income due to the death of her father/mother in an industrial accident or occupational disease. If it is certain that the opportunity to work and establish a social security relation is not equal for men and women, whether such a difference should be made up by the act or a non-contributory regime is a debatable issue.[215] If she draws a pension, if she is married or resumes work under a contract of employment or as self-employed or as a public officer, the death income ceases following the due date she is entitled to a wage or other pensions (Article 23/I C of Act No. 506). If the married daughter, who had previously drawn an income, loses her husband or is divorced, the payment of the income resumes as from the beginning of the month following the date of application to the Institution (Article 35/III of Act No. 5510).

277. As has been mentioned, the total of the monthly payments may not exceed 70% of the monthly income of the insured. In order not to exceed this limit, proportional reductions are made in the incomes payable to survivors. If, for example, in addition to the widow, more than two children exist, income assistance due to the survivors is reduced in proportion to their shares. Thus, for example, survivors with 25% have one share; the survivor with 50% has two shares. All of the shares are cumulated, and the total income is divided by the number of the shares and then distributed to the owners as one or two shares.[216]

278. The dependent parents of the victim are entitled to benefits only if the total of the income provided to the widow and the children of the insured does not reach 70% of the monthly earnings calculated as thirty times the daily earnings. Thus, if the deceased insured left one widow and two children and parents, the parents have no right to draw an income. In any case, each of the parents cannot receive more than 25% of the 70% of monthly earnings. The second requirement for parents to be able to benefit from a monthly income is that their income obtained from any kind of earning and rent must be less than the net amount of the minimum wage, and they must not receive a monthly pension or/and income except for pensions or/and incomes allocated due to other children (Article 34/I, d of Act No. 5510). The total amount of income shall not be more than 25% of the total income. Thus, if the deceased insured left one widower and one child and parents, widower shall have the 50%, the infant shall have the 25%, and parents shall have 25% (12.5% for each)

214. A. Güzel/A.R. Okur/N. Caniklioğlu, n. 7, p. 381; C. Tuncay/Ö. Ekmekçi, n. 7, p. 402.
215. N. Caniklioğlu, 'Tasarıya Göre Kısa Vadeli Sigorta Hükümleri', p. 75.
216. A. Güzel/A.R. Okur/N. Caniklioğlu, n. 7, p. 382fn. 177.

of the total income. If the mother and father are above the 65 years of age, the parent shall receive 25% of the total income regardless of the left over share (Article 34/I, d of Act No. 5510).[217]

279. If the parents are entitled to receive allowances due to many children, among allowances, he/she is awarded the full amount of the highest and the one-half of the second-highest allowance (Article 54/II, b, 3 of Act No. 5510).

2. Funeral Expenses

280. The amount of funeral expenses is determined by the Board of directors of the Social Security Institution. Therefore, not the total amount of funeral expenses, but a fixed amount over a tariff is paid as a funeral benefit (Article 37/III of Act No. 5510).

3. Marriage Assistance

281. Upon the marriage of the daughter receiving death income, a total amount of two years income is paid in a lump-sum (Article 37/I of Act No. 5510). This aid is called marriage assistance and is paid only once and on a written request by the daughter.

§5. Civil Liability

282. Due to Article 417 of the TCO, the employer is obliged to protect the health and security of employees against industrial accidents and occupational diseases. To ensure the health and security of employees, the employer is under the obligation to take all due measures and to provide all necessary equipment. In addition, the employer is to supervise the employees and inform them of the occupational risks they face. Act No. 6331 on Occupational Health and Safety dated 20 June 2012, entered into force from 1 January 2013, abrogated related provisions of LA. In order to ensure and improve occupational health and safety in workplaces, the new Act regulates all duties, powers, responsibilities, rights and obligations of employers and employees (Article 1 of Act No. 6331). Having also the character of public law, if the employer fails to conform to these duties, he/she will be subjected to administrative and penal sanctions.

283. Whenever an accident occurs, or disease appears, the insurance first provides all necessary allowance for industrial accidents and occupational diseases to the victim. Universal health insurance also provides healthcare. However, social insurance does not eliminate the civil liability of the employer. The liability of the

217. A. Güzel/A.R. Okur/N. Caniklioğlu, n. 7, pp. 383–384; C. Tuncay/Ö. Ekmekçi, n. 7, pp. 402–403.

employer is determined according to the rules governing breach of contract (Articles 112 and 417 of TCO).[218] Damages, which may be claimed, consist of material and moral damages. If the damage to the insured or his/her survivors has only been partially compensated by benefits of the Social Security Institution, the insured victim may bring a civil liability action against the employer. Since the Social Security Act does not meet moral damages, moral indemnity may only be claimed from the employer. It should be underlined that indemnity rights and social insurance benefits do not accumulate.

I. The Liability of Employer to the Social Security Institution

284. Due to the social nature of social insurance, the mere fact that contributions to the Institution have been paid does not preclude further liability of the employer to the Institution. The very fundament of this regulation is also to encourage preventive measures with the aim of protecting the life and property of the employee. Additionally, it is aimed to compensate financial losses to the Institution due to accidents caused by employers.[219]

285. Once the Institution has granted benefits, it may bring an action against the employer for reimbursement of its expenses. The responsibility of the employer is determined in accordance with whether the employer has performed his duties arising from the Social Insurance and Universal Health Insurance Act or not. According to Article 8, the employer has to give a written notice for the employee to be registered with the Social Security Institution before the date on which the person starts work. Thus, if the employer has notified the Institution regarding the insured employee, any liability to the Institution must be based on negligence. However, if the employer fails to register the insured with the Social Security Institution, while the non-registered employee is, nevertheless, considered insured under Act No. 5510, there is no need to determine employer's negligence for holding the employer liable to the Institution.

286. The new Act No. 5510, keeps the main principles of the previous system; despite all the criticisms, the employer is liable to the Institution. However, while referring to the employer, although the personal field of application has been extended, only employers in the strict meaning of the term, who are a party to a contract of employment, are meant. Therefore, the Act exempts public entities of responsibility towards the Institution for accidents suffered by civil servants, soldiers and other persons performing their duties (Article 21/V of Act No. 5510).

---

218. About civil liability of employer, *see* S. Süzek, *İş Hukuku* (Istanbul, 2012), pp. 426–469; L. Akın, *İş Kazasından Doğan Maddi Tazminat* (Ankara, 2001); G.B. Seratlı, *İş Kazasından Doğan Destekten Yoksun Kalma Tazminatı* (Ankara, 2003).
219. M. Çenberci, n. 80, p. 187; A. Güzel/A.R. Okur/N. Caniklioğlu, n. 7, pp. 386–387; C. Tuncay/Ö. Ekmekçi, n. 7, p. 407.

Moreover, since the Act calls for reimbursement of the employer, the Institution has no right to bring an action against Self-Employed persons for reimbursement of expenses made on their behalf.[220]

A. Liability Based on the Negligence of the Employer

287. If the employer acts in conformity with his duties arising from Act No. 5510, Article 21 states a special liability on the grounds of the negligence of the employer. Thus, negligence is the constitutional element of liability. Nevertheless, Article 21 enumerates two circumstances whereby the employer is held liable against the Institution in an exhaustive manner.[221]

288. The responsibility of the employer is restricted to these two situations:

- If the work accident or occupational disease is the result of an intentional act of the employer.
- Employer conducts contrary to legislation concerning the protection of employees' health and safety. Health and safety legislation includes all acts, by-laws, regulations and decrees.[222] Health and safety measures under the framework of Act No. 6331 on Occupational Health and Safety and 417 of the TCO are of particular importance. According to these provisions, the employer is to take all necessary measures and ensure all equipment is without defect for the protection of employee's health and safety in his/her workplace – even if such measures are not specifically mentioned in the legislation. The Court of Cassation holds the employer responsible by referring to the sacred nature of human life. The employer is required to take all necessary measures and must also follow the latest developments in science and technology to ensure the health and security of the working conditions and provide all necessary equipment to protect the health and safety of his/her employees. The Court ruled by its jurisprudence that except for unavoidable circumstances, the employer should be held responsible for accident or disease. Even slight negligence by the employer is sufficient for holding him/her responsible to the Social Security Institution.[223]

Article 21/I of Act No. 5510 clearly sets forth that the principle of unavoidability is taken into account when determining the responsibility of the employer, as well

220. N. Caniklioğlu, 'Tasarıya Göre Kısa Vadeli Sigorta Hükümleri', p. 78.
221. K. Tunçomağ, n. 7, pp. 293–294; A. Güzel/A.R. Okur/N. Caniklioğlu, n. 7, pp. 389–397; C. Tuncay/Ö. Ekmekçi, n. 7, p. 407.
222. M. Çenberci, n. 80, p. 195; A. Güzel/A.R. Okur/N. Caniklioğlu, n. 7, p. 392; C. Tuncay/Ö. Ekmekçi, n. 7, p. 412.
223. *See, as example,* Court of Cass., 10th Ch., 21.10.1985, 4787/5604, *YKD*(Mayıs, 1986), pp. 685–686; 10th Ch., 27.5.2008, 2626/7283, www.hukukturk.com noted by A. Güzel, 'Sosyal Sigortaların Genel Hükümleri ve Türleri', in *Yargıtay'ın İş Hukuku ve Sosyal Güvenlik Hukuku Kararlarının Değerlendirilmesi 2008*(Ankara, 2010), pp. 321–323; for ciriticism of this issue *see* M. Şakar, 'İş Kazası veya Meslek Hastalığı Sebebiyle Sosyal Sigortaların İşverene Rücuunda Kusur Şartının Sınırlanması Sorunu', *Sicil Der.*(Haziran, 2006), pp. 129–135.

as the employee. If the employer does not take the necessary measures indicated in the legislation, the possibility of 'unavoidability' is excluded (Article 45/3 of RSIP).[224]

289. The legal nature of the Institution's right to demand reimbursement from the employer is a much-debated issue. One group of authors argue for an ordinary right of recovery.[225] However, the majority of authors are in favour of legal subrogation to explain the legal nature of this recovery.[226] The Court of Cassation has shared this latter view in many decisions which unify different judgments. The Supreme Court qualified the recovery right as a sui generis legal subrogation.[227] The provisions which restrict the amount of indemnity that the Institution may ask from the employer with the amount of indemnity amount that the insured employee or his survivors may demand from the employer constituted the ground for legal subrogation. However, the Constitutional Court had annulled these provisions.[228] Such an annulment, which is related to the legal nature of the right of recovery, resumed new debates.[229] Nevertheless, by the adoption of Act No. 5510, which again restricts the amount of indemnity, the debates have calmed.

Therefore, the legal ground for the recovery of expenses is that the Institution subrogates into the injured employee's rights. Thus, the amount of indemnity that the Institution may ask from the employer extends up to the indemnity amount that

224. A. Güzel/A.R. Okur/N. Caniklioğlu, n. 7, pp. 395–396; C. Tuncay/Ö. Ekmekçi, n. 7, pp. 413–415; A.N. Sözer, n. 70, pp. 151–152; *see also* C. Tuncay, 'Kurumun İşverene Rücuu-Olayda Kaçınılmazlık Durumu', *Sicil Der.*(Aralık, 2006), pp. 184–188; H. Keser, 'İşverenin İş Kazası ve Meslek Hastalığı Dolayısı ile Kurumun Yaptığı Harcamalardan Sorumlu Olmasının Koşulları ve Kaçınılmazlık', *Sicil Der.*(Haziran, 2006), pp. 137–146.

225. R. Aslanköylü, 'Kurumun 506 Sayılı Sosyal Sigortalar Kanununun 10. ve 26. Maddesinden Doğan Rücu Hakkının Hukuksal Temeli', in *Yargıç Dr. Aydın Özkul'a Armağan, Kamu-İş*, C. 6(2002), pp. 230–235.

226. M. Çenberci, n. 80, p. 188; K. Tunçomağ, n. 7; p. 293; A. Güzel/A.R. Okur/N. Caniklioğlu, n. 7, pp. 387–388; C. Tuncay/Ö. Ekmekçi, n. 7, p. 409; O.E. Civan, 'İş Kazası veya Meslek Hastalığından Doğan Rücu Hakkının Hukuki Niteliği ve Sosyal Güvenlik Kurumu Karşısında Sorumluluğun Koşulları', AÜHFD, 64(3)(2015), pp. 543–544.

227. Court of Cass., Unif. Judg. 31 Mar. 1954, 17/10, OJ, 15 Jul. 1954, No. 8755; Unif Judg. 17 Jan. 1972, 2/1, OJ. 20 Mar. 1972, No. 14134; Unif. Judg., 1 Jul. 1994, 3/3, OJ, 20 Oct. 1995, No. 22439; Court of Cass, General Council, 20 Feb. 1991, 10-488/87, www.kazanci.com; General Council, 8 Nov. 2006, E. 2006/10-696, K. 2006/704, www.hukukturk.com.

228. Cons. Court, 23 Nov. 2006, 2003/10, 2006/106, OJ, 23 Nov. 2007, No. 26469.

229. E. Turan, 'Anayasa Mahkemesi'nin 2003/10 E., 2006/106 K., 23.11.2006 Tarihli Kararı Karşısında 506 Sayılı Yasanın 26. Maddesine Dayalı Rücuan Tazminat Davaları', *Sicil Der.*(Haziran, 2007), pp. 161–184; U. Araslı, 'Rücu Davalarında Tavan Sınırlamasının İptali ve Ortaya Çıkardığı Sorunlar ve 1.7.1994 Günlü YİBBGKK', *Sicil Der.*(Haziran, 2007), pp. 185–205; C. Erbaş, 'Sosyal Sigortalar Kurumu'nun Rücu Davaları, Anayasa Mahkemesinin İptal Kararı Karşısında Öngörülen Hukuki Sonuçlar ve Uygulamadan Örnekler', *Sicil Der.*(Eylül, 2007), pp. 94–113; A. Güzel, 'Sosyal Sigortaların Genel Hükümleri ve Türleri', in *Yargıtay'ın İş Hukuku ve Sosyal Güvenlik Hukuku Kararlarının Değerlendirilmesi 2008*(Ankara, 2010), pp. 323–335; C. Tuncay/Ö. Ekmekçi, n. 7, pp. 409–410.

the insured employee or his survivors may demand from the employer.[230] Moreover, subrogation permits the Institution to use preferential rights and securities held by the injured employee or his survivors.[231]

290. In addition to the legal subrogation, the statute of limitations within which the Institution may bring an action against the employer is the one applicable to breach of contracts, ten years. However, as regards the commencement of the statute of limitations, the Court of Cassation held that the limitation is reckoned from the day on which the Institution approves the increase or the date on which the expenses were incurred.[232] Act No. 5510 adopted these judgments as a legal provision. According to Article 93/III, the statute of limitations is ten years. As regards to the expenses and pensions reckoned, the statute of limitations starts with the approval date of the Institution, as with regards to expenses and payments, it starts from the day of incurring the expense or payment.

291. In making such a claim, the Institution may demand the total amount of expenses incurred or to be incurred in the future for the insured person or his survivors from the employer. If any income has been awarded, the capital value of the income is to be retrieved from the employer (Article 21/I of Act No. 5510). The Institution recovers not only the expenses already made but also the expenses which will be incurred in the future. Furthermore, such payments must have been related to the industrial accident or occupational disease. Since the upper limit of the recovery has been harshly criticized by employers, Act No. 5510 restricts the liability of the employer by the capital value of income (Article 21 of Act No. 5510). Therefore, the Institution is not entitled to claim from the employer the increments of the income due to the state's regulation, with respect to the amount of such payments. Nonetheless, the recovered amount is restricted to the amount of indemnity that the insured may demand from the employer. If the insurance holder contributed to the harm by his own negligence, contributory negligence is taken into consideration while fixing the indemnity by the court. Therefore, the employer shall be liable against the Institution for this amount.

B. Liability of an Employer Failing to Perform His or Her Legal Duties

292. If the employer failed to notify the Institution regarding the employee before the employee commenced employment, Article 23 assigns strict liability of the employer to the Institution. Thus, even if he has no negligence, the employer may be held responsible for an industrial accident.[233] The employer is responsible for the recovery of the full amount of benefits paid in accordance with the Act. All

230. M. Çenberci, n. 80, pp. 203–204; A. Güzel/A.R. Okur/N. Caniklioğlu, n. 7, pp. 398–399; C. Tuncay/Ö. Ekmekçi, n. 7, p. 416.
231. *See* Civan, 'Rücu Hakkının Hukuki Niteliği', pp. 540–541.
232. Court of Cass., Unif. Judm., 1 Jul. 1994, 3/3, OJ, 20 Oct. 1995, No. 22439.
233. Court of Cass., 10th Ch., 13 Jul. 2010, 9495/11209, Hukuk Türk Veri Tabanı; 10th Ch., 5 Mar. 2013, 2012/21515, 2013/13762, Çalışma ve Toplum Der.(2013/4), pp. 535–538.

expenses of any kind incurred or, subsequently, to be incurred by the Institution are to be reimbursed by the employer. If a pension is awarded, its capital value is reclaimed from the employer without consideration to any actual negligence.

293. The legal nature of the Institution's right to recourse does not arise from legal subrogation. Therefore, the amount of indemnity that the Institution may ask from the employer is not restricted to the indemnity amount that the insured employee may ask for. However, the Court of Cassation held that it is due to bona fides to restrict the employer's liability to such an amount.[234] Therefore, in cases where the recovery of expenses is demanded, first of all, the actual amount of the indemnity the employer owes to the insured employee or survivors is calculated. Thus, there is no relevance whether the employer is at fault or not in the industrial accident or occupational disease. However, the causality link between the act and the damage must be established. If the damage is unavoidable, the employer cannot be held responsible for it.

294. If the accident is the result of negligent conduct on the part of the employer, other than in case of failure of notification, both Articles 21 and 23 will be applicable. However, Article 23 takes precedence over Article 21.

295. Besides the case of non-registered employees, Act No. 5510 envisages the legal responsibility of the employer, in case of, failure of certain other duties. Thus, according to Article 76, the employer is under obligation to ensure all necessary medical care required by the victim's state of health until the Institution can take the appropriate action. If, because of negligence or delay in providing this care, the treatment of the insured person must be extended or if the victim remains disabled, or the degree of the disability is increased, the employer is to refund to the Institution all expenses incurred as a result of these failures (Article 76/II of Act No. 5510).

296. When an industrial accident occurs, or an occupational disease appears, the employer shall notify the Institution in writing, at the latest, within three days. (Articles 13/II, a, 14/II, a of Act No. 5510). If the employer delays in notifying the Institution, temporary incapacity allowance due during this non-notified period shall be reimbursed from the employer.

297. The employer is also responsible for any damage caused or will be caused in the future through the Institution not having been informed in due time, either intentionally or by gross negligence or by supplying incomplete or erroneous information concerning the industrial accident (Article 13/III of Act No. 5510).

298. If the Self-Employed person has not notified the Institution of his/her own employment status within the periods fixed by the Act and an industrial accident or

234. *See, as example,* Court of Cass., General Council, 25 Mar. 1994, 13378/5740, *YKD*(Haziran, 1994), pp. 916–917; 10th Ch., 26 Apr. 2011, 5625/6114, Hukuk Türk Veri Tabanı.

occupational disease occurs during this non-registered period, the Self-Employed victim does not benefit from any income and allowance.

II. The Liability of Third Persons Against the Institution

299. If the insured suffers an accident or a sickness through a negligent act of a third person and if benefits are paid under Act No. 5510, the Institution is entitled to recover from the faulty third person all payments which have been done and will be done in the future to insurance holders and right owners, as well as half of the capital value of the granted income. Third persons are those other than the insured and employer.[235] Nevertheless, in case of death of the insurance holder, the Institution is not entitled to recourse the right holders who acted negligently to cause such accident or occupational disease or the survivors of the negligent insurance holder who lost his/her life in the accident (Article 21/end of Act No. 5510).

300. Not only third parties but also the employer who employed the third party is responsible against the Institution if he/she is at fault for the occurrence of the industrial accident (Article 21/IV of Act No. 5510). Although the employer is responsible for the acts of his/her personnel regardless of his/her fault, Act No. 5510 renders employers responsible against the Institution only if he/she acted negligently in causing the industrial accident. It is up to the Institution to prove the negligence of the third party's employer.[236]

301. The statute of limitation is ten years. However, if the accident is also a traffic accident, the statute of limitations is two and ten years.

235. M. Çenberci, n. 80, p. 258; A. Güzel/A.R. Okur/N. Caniklioğlu, n. 7, p. 408; C. Tuncay/Ö. Ekmekçi, n. 7, p. 417; A.N. Sözer, n. 70, p. 189.
236. A. Güzel/A.R. Okur/N. Caniklioğlu, n. 7, pp. 408–409.

Chapter 2. Sickness Insurance

302. The fundamental change implemented by the reform is on the health insurance system. Before the reform, healthcare services were regulated under each social security system as an insurance branch called 'sickness insurance'. By the reform, monetary aids and healthcare benefits are separated from each other. Monetary aids are regulated under the social insurance system; however, healthcare services are provided with other healthcare insurance that will be examined below.[237]

303. Before the reform, sickness insurance covered, for wage earners and civil servants, all kinds of sicknesses which did not fall under industrial accidents and occupational diseases coverage. Even in cases of miscarriage, necessary help was provided by sickness insurance but not by maternity insurance. However, for self-employed persons, the 'sickness branch' covered all kinds of ill-health, including industrial accidents and occupational diseases. Under Act No. 5510, sickness is defined as all kinds of illnesses which do not fall under industrial accidents and occupational diseases coverage (Article 15/1 of Act No. 5510). The sickness must cause sickness absence to be covered by the insurance.[238] It should be underlined that the cover of the sickness reveals importance only with respect to receiving monetary benefits.

§1. Field of Application

I. Territorial Field of Application

304. With respect to the territorial field of application, sickness insurance does not carry any particularity, since only cash benefits are provided. As long as the insurance holder is under cover of social insurances, he/she receives benefits from sickness insurance.

305. If the insured employee residing in Turkey is sent abroad on duty, medical reports given by the competent authorities of this foreign country are considered sufficient to pay temporary incapacity allowance (Article 39/3 of RSIP). The foreign agencies of Turkey must approve the competency of the health institutions that render the medical report. In a similar way, Self-Employed persons may benefit from temporary incapacity allowance, if he/she is abroad due to his/her carried activity.

II. Personal Field of Application

306. Sickness insurance covers only those who are subjected to subparagraph 4/I a. Candidate apprentices, apprentices and those who do an internship during their

237. *See infra* Part V.
238. A.N. Sözer, n. 70, pp. 225–226.

vocational education also benefit from sickness insurance (Article 5/I, b of Act No. 5510). In addition, Turkish employees sent abroad are also under the personal scope of sickness insurance.

307. Under Act No. 1479, self-employed persons were not entitled to temporary incapacity payment during their sicknesses. Although Act No. 5510 mentions those who are subjected to Article 4/I, while defining sickness, Article 18/II does not enumerate self-employed persons among those who receive temporary incapacity allowance during hospitalization and the period of recuperation. Therefore, self-employed persons fall out of the scope of sickness insurance.[239]

308. Likewise, civil servants fall out of the scope of short-term insurances. Their benefits during their sickness are regulated by Act No. 657, Civil Servants. In principle, they receive their wages without any reduction during their sickness.

309. Dependant family members of the insured person are under cover of universal health insurance which provides healthcare services. However, it is obvious that they do not receive cash benefits.

§2. Benefits

I. Type of Benefits: Temporary Incapacity Allowance

310. By the separation of healthcare services from the cover of sickness insurance, the sickness insurance provides only temporary incapacity allowance as a benefit. Due to the principle of 'no work no wage', the employer is not under an obligation to pay wages when an employee is absent from work due to illness. To make up for the loss of income during a period of illness, Act No. 5510 provides a temporary incapacity allowance for sick insured employees (Article 16/2 of Act No. 5510).

311. Although the employer is not obliged to pay wages to a sick employee, he/she may pay the wage without any reduction. Even if the employer pays the total amount of the wage while the insured employee is sick, the insurance holder is entitled to receive temporary incapacity allowance. The Court of Cassation ruled that such employer payments are a concession on the employers' part, which does not provide the Institution with grounds for the withdrawal of the allowance.[240] However, if such payments are made during the long period of time absences, the Court of Cassation requires examining the circumstances more carefully, although it is not common that the employer pays the full amount of the wage for a long period without receiving any work in return for doing so.[241]

239. C. Tuncay/Ö. Ekmekçi, n. 7, p. 423; A.N. Sözer, n. 70, pp. 230–231.
240. Court of Cass., 4th Ch., 8 Apr. 1963, 3898/3475; 9th Ch., 24 Dec. 1973, 15914/35008 cited by A. Güzel/A.R. Okur/N. Caniklioğlu, n. 7, p. 417.
241. Court of Cass., 10th Ch., 2 Jul. 1974, 3400/4789 cited by M. Çenberci, n. 80, p. 295.

II. Amount of Benefits

A. Those Who Are Subjected to Article 4/I, a

312. The amount of temporary incapacity allowance in case of sickness equals the amount paid in the case of industrial accidents and occupational diseases. This amount depends on the form of treatment: If the insured patient is hospitalized or enjoys another care facility, the amount of the allowance is half the daily wage up to the limit fixed by Act No. 5510. For outpatients, the amount of temporary allowance is two-thirds the daily wage up to the limit stated by Act No. 5510 (Article 18/III of Act No. 5510).

313. The amount of temporary incapacity allowance is based on the daily income of the insurance holder (Article 17/I of Act No. 5510). The calculation method for the allowance is the same for allowances paid in case of industrial accidents and occupational diseases. The insurance holder is entitled to a temporary incapacity allowance from the third day of sickness until he is cured. Previously, there was a regulation which restricted the payment of this allowance to eighteen months. However, the Constitutional Court annulled this provision, referring to the firm relations between the right to social security and the right to life.[242]

314. In order to prevent the deterioration of his/her own condition or an extension of the recovery period, the insured employee is also charged with certain duties, non-compliance with which results in a reduction or the cessation of the temporary incapacity allowance. If because of the sick insurance holder's negligence in disobeying the doctors' recommendations, the treatment has to be extended, the Institution may reduce the temporary incapacity allowance in proportion to the negligence of the insurance holder and the length of the extended treatment. Nevertheless, such reductions may not exceed one-fourth of the temporary incapacity allowance (Article 22/I, a of Act No. 5510).[243] Those who have criminal immunity or who have a reasonable excuse for not obeying doctors' recommendations are exempted from such reduction.

315. If the insurance holder becomes sick because of his/her own gross negligence, the amount of temporary incapacity allowance shall be reduced to one-third by the Institution in proportion to the negligence of the insurance holder (Article 22/I, b of Act No. 5510). However, if an intentional act of the insurance holder is the reason for his/her sickness, the temporary allowance shall be reduced.

316. In order to resume work, the insured employee is again obliged to obtain a report issued by doctors of the Institution stating that treatment has been completed, and the insured employee has regained the capacity to work. Without receipt of this document, the insured, on resuming work, will be deprived of the temporary incapacity allowance and if it has already been paid, the insured is obliged to reimburse

242. Cons. Court., 17 Nov. 1998, 35/70, OJ, 15 Jan. 2003, No. 24994.
243. Court of Cass., 10th Ch., 7.7.2004, 4856/6645, 4, *Çalışma ve Toplum Der.,* 2005/1, pp. 309–310.

the Institution (Article 22/I, d of Act. No. 5510). In addition, the expenses incurred for the treatment of the same sickness are recovered from the employer of the insured. The insured is responsible for these expenses if he/she has worked for another person (Article 22/I, d of Act No. 5510).

B. Those Who Are Subjected to Article 4/I, c

317. Unlike wage earners, civil servants keep their monetary and personnel rights, during the rest period stated by a medical report pursuant to Article 105 of Act No. 657 on Civil Servants. Thus, civil servants do not need any insurance coverage to compensate for their income loss as they receive the full amount of their salary. Their sick leave may be extended by up to twelve months; if there exists a sickness which requires a long-lasting treatment such as some cancers, tuberculosis or mental sickness, then up to eighteen months (Article 105/I of Act No. 657). Medical reports are issued pursuant to principles fixed by Act No. 5510 (Article 5 of Regulation on Medical Reports issued in case of Sickness of Civil Servants[244]). Medical reports for civil servants, who are permanently or temporarily on duty abroad, or who get sick during their holiday abroad, may be issued in accordance with the due procedures of that foreign country (Article 5/III of Regulation on Medical Reports issued in case of Sickness of Civil Servants). If the civil servant has not been able to recover at the end of the twelve or eighteen-month period, the civil servant may get retirement because of invalidity.

§3. Conditions

318. In order to receive a temporary incapacity allowance, the insurance holder must be covered by Article 4/I, a or Article 5 and must not have lost his/her insured status. If the insured status starts with the active work relation, with respect to sickness and maternity insurances, the legislator provides that the insured status shall be deemed to be lost starting from the tenth day of the termination of the employment status or independent activities. Through this provision, the insurance holder receives monetary benefits for periods not passed under a work relation. Before the reform, such an extension was meaningful, while sickness insurance also covered healthcare services. However, after the reform, it is difficult to explain its appropriateness, while the main benefit is temporary incapacity allowances.

319. Not only in cases wherein the work relation is terminated, but also during certain periods that work relation continues, the social insurance relation may terminate.[245] In cases where the insurance holder is on unpaid leave, participated in a strike or the employer announces a lock-out, the insured status for the sickness and maternity insurances ends starting from the tenth day following the end of such statuses (Article 9/II of Act No. 5510). During the suspension of the contract of

244. OJ, 20 Oct. 2011, No. 28099.
245. A.N. Sözer, n. 70, p. 61.

employment, although the employee is not entitled to wages, he/she profits from sickness and maternity insurance benefits. If the insured employee continues to work at the end of these periods, he/she benefits from sickness and maternity insurances without any break. However, if the insured employee does not resume work starting from the tenth day following the end of such suspension, the insured employee will fall out of the cover of sickness and maternity insurances.

320. Unlike the insurance for industrial accidents and occupational diseases, in order to prevent abusive demands, the Act grants this right in case of sicknesses which continue for more than two days. The insured person is entitled to cash benefits from the third day of the sickness. In addition, the incapacity must be confirmed by a medical report from a doctor or medical board designated by the Institution (Article 18/I, b of Act No. 5510).

321. Lastly, at least ninety days of sickness contribution must have been notified within the one year preceding the date on which the temporary incapacity commenced (Article 18/I, a of Act No. 5510). Since the Act refers to the notification, the actual payment of contributions plays no importance in receiving temporary incapacity benefits.[246] While calculating one year, time passed under strike or lock-out, the period that insurance holder receives temporary incapacity allowance because of not being able to work due to a sickness or industrial accidents, period on the military service or the period of arrest not concluded in conviction shall not be taken into consideration (Article 24 of Act No. 5510). It is not necessary that the insured employee had spent this period in the service of the same employer.[247] It should be noted that there is no obligatory contribution payment for civil servants to benefit from full paid sick leave.

§4. The Recovery Rights of the Social Security Institution

I. The Liability of Employers Against the Social Security Institution

322. An employer may be held liable against the Social Security Institution not only in cases of industrial accidents or occupational diseases but also in cases of the sickness of an insurance holder. The responsibility of the employer may arise from appointing an employee to jobs not suitable to his/her health conditions or from the failure of notification duties.

323. Regarding certain works, not necessarily hazardous works, and the employer needs to have a health certificate before recruiting an employee. If the insurance holder is employed without receiving a health certificate or is appointed to a post not suitable to his/her health conditions and such an employment causes sickness, other than an occupational disease, the Institution may bring an action

246. A.N. Sözer, n. 70, p. 227.
247. M. Çenberci, n. 80, p. 284; A. Güzel/A.R. Okur/N. Caniklioğlu, n. 7, p. 413; C. Tuncay/Ö. Ekmekçi, n. 7, p. 25.

against the employer for the reimbursement of temporary incapacity allowance paid to the sick employee (Article 21/III of Act No. 5510). Although the Act makes no difference between hazardous jobs and others, the Court of Cassation held that the medical report is required only for hazardous employment.[248] However, there is no legal basis for such a distinction. Either hazardous or not, the employer is under an obligation to require medical reports for all kinds of works.[249] In addition, by the adoption of a new Act No. 6331 on Occupational Health and Safety, the Court of Cassation may revise its jurisprudence, while pursuant to Article 15 of Act No. 6331, all employers are under the duty to provide a medical examination to their employees before the recruitment.

324. To hold the employer liable against the Institution, the negligence of the employer is not required. Whether there is a need for causality between the non-requirement of a medical report and the sickness of the employee is a matter of discussion. In its early jurisprudence, the Court of Cassation held the employer responsible just because of the failure of legal duty, regardless of causality.[250] However, in its recent jurisprudence, the Court looks for causality between the employer's failure and the sickness.[251] Certain authors argue that in case of such a failure, there is no need to investigate causality;[252] however, others welcome this new jurisprudence.[253] The fact of not having asked for a medical report is enough to be held liable for reimbursement.

325. As we mentioned above, the failure of the employer to notify the employee to the Institution does not prevent the acquisition of insurance holder status. If the sickness has occurred after the recruitment or before the notification to the Institution of the insurance holder, or before the detection of the employment relationship by the Institution, the insurance holder is entitled to receive temporary incapacity allowance. However, the total amount of this allowance shall be reimbursed from the employer who fails in his duties of notification (Article 23/I of Act No. 5510).

II. The Liability of Third Persons Against the Social Security Institution

326. A negligent third person may cause the sickness of an insurance holder. According to Article 21/IV of Act No. 5510, if the insurance holder gets sick because of an intentional or negligent act of a third person, for example, a traffic

248. Court of Cass., HGK, 31.1.1990, 10-597/37, Hukuk Türk Veri Tabanı noted by A. Güzel, 'Sosyal Sigorta Türleri Açısından Yargıtay'ın 1990 Yılı Kararlarının Değerlendirilmesi', in *Yargıtayın İş Hukukuna İlişkin Kararlarının Değerlendirilmesi 1990* (Istanbul, 1992), pp. 192–193; 10th Ch., 28.2.2000, 1065/1187, Hukuk Türk Veri Tabanı.
249. M. Çenberci, n. 80, p. 309; A. Güzel, 'Yargıtay'ın 1990 Yılı Kararlarının Değerlendirilmesi', p. 193; A. Güzel/A.R. Okur/N. Caniklioğlu, n. 7, pp. 419–420; C. Tuncay/Ö. Ekmekçi, n. 7, p. 352; A.N. Sözer, n. 70, p. 121, n. 2.
250. Court of Cass., 10th Ch., 6 Apr. 1984, 1447/1940, M. Çenberci, n. 80, p. 314.
251. *See, as example,* Court of Cass., HGK, 31 Jan. 1990, 10-597/37, Hukuk Türk Veri Tabanı; 10th Ch., 28 Feb. 2000, 1065/1187, Hukuk Türk Veri Tabanı.
252. M. Çenberci, n. 80, p. 312; A. Güzel/A.R. Okur/N. Caniklioğlu, n. 7, pp. 420–421.
253. C. Tuncay/Ö. Ekmekçi, n. 7, pp. 429–431.

accident, the Social Security Institution may ask for its expenses from this third person. The legal nature of the Institution's right to demand reimbursement is legal subrogation. In order to ask for reimbursement, the third person must be negligent. The Institution may demand half of its expenses, which means half of the total amount of the temporary incapacity allowance. Nevertheless, it is hard to explain why the negligent employer reimburses all expenses; however, negligent third persons reimburse only half of the Institution's expenses.[254]

327. The Act also holds the employer of third persons, if his/her employer is negligent in the occurrence of sickness, liable, for example, a traffic accident. Act No. 5510 requires the negligence of the employer, unlike the Code of Obligation, which holds employers responsible for the acts of his/her employees regardless of his/her fault.

254. A. Güzel/A.R. Okur/N. Caniklioğlu, n. 7, p. 422.

Chapter 3. Maternity Insurance

328. Maternity covers all sickness and invalidity related to pregnancy or maternity status starting from pregnancy up to the first eight weeks, and in the case of multiple pregnancies up to the first ten weeks following the confinement (Article 15/II of Act No. 5510). Unlike the previous system, maternity insurance covers miscarriage.

329. Maternity, as a risk, is covered both by the universal health insurance for the purposes of healthcare services and by a specific insurance branch, the maternity insurance. Unlike the previous system, maternity insurance covers only monetary benefits. Under Act No. 5510, the risk of maternity is regulated in a manner very similar to insurance for sickness.

§1. Field of Application

I. Territorial Field of Application

330. Territoriality is also the main principle, with respect to maternity insurance. If the female insurance holder is incapable of working due to her pregnancy while she is on a mission abroad, she will be entitled to receive temporary incapacity allowance for periods passed without working abroad. In that case, the Institution is not required to approve of any medical reports (Article 88/II of RSIP).

II. Personal Field of Application

331. The right to benefit from maternity insurance is granted to insured female insurance holders subjected to items 4/I, a and b, mainly employees and self-employed persons and uninsured wives of insured male employees and self-employed persons (Article 15/II of Act No. 5510). Although apprentices benefit from sickness insurance, they are excluded from maternity insurance coverage (Article 5/I, b of Act No. 5510). However, convicts and detainees who are employed in establishments, workshops and similar units structured under penal institutions, such as penitentiaries and jails, receive benefits from maternity insurance. In addition, Turkish employees abroad are also under cover of maternity insurance (Article 5/I, g of Act No. 5510).

332. Under Act No. 5510, self-employed insured women are also entitled to temporary incapacity allowance. Previously, these women had no right to receive such a payment. Such a difference was considered unfair and abrogated by Act No.

5510.[255] Article 4/I b covers five different groups such as the elected heads of village or district, income taxpayers, craftsmen and artisans, shareholders of commercial companies and those working in the agricultural sector.[256] Nevertheless, shareholders of commercial companies are left out of the scope of the temporary incapacity allowance, the main benefit of maternity insurance (Article 18/I c). The reason for such exclusion may be that the maternity of the female shareholders of the company does not cause a significant income loss.[257] They are only entitled to receive a nursery allowance.

333. Civil servants are excluded from the cover of maternity insurance as other short-term insurance branches. The reason of such exclusion is a female civil servant is entitled to receive her full salary during the rest period, before and after the confinement without any supplementary requirement, pursuant to Article 104 of Act No. 657 on Civil Servants.

§2. Benefits

334. Benefits arising from maternity insurance are divided in two: temporary incapacity allowance and nursery allowance.

I. Type of Benefits

A. Temporary Incapacity Allowance

335. Due to Article 74 of LA, it is prohibited to employ a female for eight weeks both prior to and following the confinement. Two weeks are added to this period prior to delivery in the case of multiple pregnancies. Nevertheless, if her state of health allows and the doctor approves, the female employee may work until three weeks prior to the delivery. The five weeks during which the employee has worked are added to the period after the confinement. The right to maternity leave is extended to those who fall under the scope of the Maritime Labour Act and the Code of Obligations by an amendment entered into force in 2016.[258] During these periods, the employer is not under obligation to pay wages, except journalists. Pursuant to Article 16/end of Act No. 5953, in case of the pregnancy of journalists, the pregnant journalist shall have a leave of absence from the seventh month of her pregnancy until the end of two months following the confinement. During this period, the employer is obliged to pay half of her wage.

336. In order to provide income guarantees to the women, maternity insurance grants a temporary incapacity allowance. Although the uninsured wife of the insured

255. N. Caniklioğlu, 'Tasarıda Kısa Vadeli Sigorta Hükümleri', p. 83.
256. *See supra* para. 142.
257. A.N. Sözer, n. 70, p. 241.
258. Act No. 6663, OJ, 10 Feb. 2016, No. 29620.

male employee, or the female insured person who receives income or pensions from the Institution, as well as uninsured wives of insured persons, who receive income or pensions from the Institution, benefit from healthcare services, temporary incapacity allowance is granted only to the insured female employee and self-employed.[259]

337. Act No. 6663 extended the scope of maternity leave to adoptive parents under the condition that the adopted child is younger than the age of three. An adoptive parent is also entitled to benefit this right. The eight weeks of maternity leave starts from the delivery of the child (Article 74/I of LA). However, adoptive parents are not entitled to receive temporary incapacity allowance because of the legislative absence.[260]

338. A female civil servant is also entitled to a paid leave for eight weeks both prior to and following the confinement. In the case of multiple pregnancies, two weeks are added to this period. The female civil servant receives her salary without any reduction during these periods, except those related to active work (Article 104/I, A and E of Act No. 657).

B. Nursery Allowance

339. Maternity insurance protects not only the health of the mother but also the health of the new-born child. Therefore, the insured woman or insured man because of his confined wife, or female insurance holder who obtains an income or pension because of her own employment relationship, or the uninsured wife of an insurance holder who receives an income or pension shall receive a nursery allowance for each child, under the condition that the new-born lives.

C. Confinement Grant

340. In addition to the nursery allowance, Act No. 6637 which entered into force on 7 April 2015[261] brought a new grant to the system. Parents are entitled to receive TRY300 for the first child, TRY 400 for the second child and TRY 600 for the third and following child(ren). This benefit is granted to the mother or father having Turkish nationality. If both parents have Turkish nationality, the mother receives the confinement grant. The Act provides no other condition than having Turkish nationality.

341. The individual employment contracts or collective agreements may also contain clauses providing payment in case of the confinement of the female worker or the worker's wife. The Act provides a deduction for the workers who are recruited by public institutions. If the amount of the confinement grant is more than

259. A. Güzel/A.R. Okur/N. Caniklioğlu, n. 7, p. 428; A.N. Sözer, n. 70, pp. 239–240.
260. A.N. Sözer, n. 70, p. 233.
261. OJ, 7 Apr. 2015, No. 29319.

the amount of the contractual benefit, the worker receives only the difference. If the amount of the contractual benefit is more than the amount of the legal grant, the worker is not entitled to receive the legal grant. However, workers in the private sector receive both of the benefits. It is hard to explain such a difference.[262]

D. Unpaid Leave Allowance

342. Act No. 6663 which entered into force on 10 February 2016 brings considerable improvement with respect to maternity protection and parental rights. Either a female or a male worker may benefit from an additional half week unpaid leave starting from the end of the maternity leave period in order to bring up their child. The length of the unpaid leave varies in accordance with the number of confinement, thus 60 days for the first child, 120 days for the second child and 180 days for the third child. Ten days are added to these periods in case of multiple pregnancies. If the child is disabled, the unpaid leave period is 360 days. During this period, the worker will continue to work for half of the working week. Therefore, the employer will pay only half of his/her wages. The Wage Guarantee Fund is the institution responsible for these allowances.

II. Amount of Benefits

343. The amount of the temporary incapacity allowance is two-thirds that of the daily income of the insurance holder. The amount of daily income is determined in the same way as for sickness insurance and industrial accidents and occupational diseases. However, unlike sickness insurance, the allowance is paid starting from the first day of the absence.

344. Temporary incapacity allowance is paid from the first day of the eight weeks period before the confinement until the end of the eighth week. However, if the female insurance holder is absent due to her pregnancy before this eight weeks period, temporary incapacity allowance shall be paid by the sickness insurance.[263] Even the pregnant insurance holder can take a rest without a medical report as she is entitled to receive temporary incapacity allowance.[264] However, if the incapacity of the woman continues for a longer period, whether these payments arising from maternity insurance will also continue is a matter of discussion. Certain authors argue that the wording of Article 15 prevents such a construction because the maternity status is defined as the length of time, which continues until the end of eight weeks after confinement. Therefore, absenteeism resulting from a sickness shall be considered under the framework of sickness insurance.[265] However, if Article 74 of

262. A.N. Sözer, n. 70, p. 240.
263. A. Güzel/A.R. Okur/N. Caniklioğlu, n. 7, p. 429; A.N. Sözer, n. 70, p. 236.
264. M. Çenberci, n. 80, p. 334; K. Tunçomağ, n. 7, pp. 328–329; A. Güzel/A.R. Okur/N. Caniklioğlu, n. 7, p. 429.
265. M. Çenberci, n. 80, p. 334; K. Tunçomağ, n. 7, pp. 328–329.

LA, where it is stated that with a doctor's report these periods may be prolonged, is taken as a basis, the rationale of maternity insurance would require the granting of temporary allowance payments also during these additional periods.[266]

345. If the insured woman has fallen ill or her sickness has been aggravated or her treatment has been extended by failure to take necessary precautions recommended by a doctor, up to one-fourth of the temporary incapacity allowance may be taken off in proportion to the length of time and the rate of aggravated incapacity (Article 22/I, a of Act No. 5510). As with sickness insurance, if the insurance holder resumes work without having had a medical report which states the end of the treatment, no temporary incapacity allowance shall be paid, and if paid the allowance shall be refunded.

346. The amount of the nursery allowance is determined by the board of managers of the Institution and approved by the Council of Ministers (Article 16/III of Act No. 5510).

347. The unpaid leave allowance aims to compensate for the income lost during the periods when the employee works only half of the weekly hours in the company. The amount of daily unpaid leave allowance is equal to the gross amount of the daily minimum wage regardless of the daily amount of his/her wage.

§3. Conditions

348. As regards temporary incapacity allowance, short-term insurance contributions must have been paid for the insured female employee for at least ninety days over the course of the year preceding the confinement (Article 18/I, c of Act No. 5510). However, if the insurance holder is self-employed, she must have settled all contributions and contribution-related obligations, including universal health insurance contribution (Article 18/II of Act No. 5510).

349. The Act envisages 120 days of contribution payment requirement to receive nursery allowances. Those who are subjected to Article 4/I-a must pay at least 120 days of contribution over the course of the year preceding the confinement (Article 16/IV, a of Act No. 5510). For those who are subjected to Article 4/I-b, they must have no contribution or contribution-related obligation against the Institution.

350. Since the nursery allowance is paid with an aim to keep the new-born baby, the legislator provides the payment even if the mother insurance holder has lost her insured status. Pursuant to Article 16/V, if the female insurance holder is entitled to the nursery allowance and the child was born within 300 days following the termination of her insured status, Act No. 5510 provides another possibility for nursery allowances. If the insurance holder who was entitled to the nursery allowance lost

266. A. Güzel/A.R. Okur/N. Caniklioğlu, n. 7, pp. 430–431; E. Pakin Akın, *Türk Hukukunda Kadın İşçilerin Sosyal Güvenliği*(Istanbul, 2005), p. 84.

her insured status, she has the right to require a nursery allowance under the condition that she has paid 120 days of contribution over the fifteen months preceding the confinement (Article 16/V of Act No. 5510).

351. Female civil servants receive their full wage during the confinement period. Act No. 657 provides no requirement to receive that salary.

352. The conditions to receive unpaid leave allowance are as follows: first, a minimum of 600 days of contribution should have been notified within the three years, which precede the confinement or the adoption. Second, the employee should work actively for half of the weekly working hours in accordance with Article 63 of LA. Lastly, the concerned employee should submit his/her request to the Turkish Employment Institution within thirty days following the end of the maternity leave. If the employee delays submitting the request to the Institution, except in cases of force majeure, the delayed period is deducted from the total period for which benefits are entitled (Supp. Article 5 of Act No. 4447).

Chapter 4. Family Allowances

353. The social security system provides protection against the risks of an industrial accident, occupational diseases, sickness, maternity, invalidity, old age, death and lastly, in 1999, unemployment. Although Turkey has ratified ILO Convention No. 102, family allowances are guaranteed neither under the previous system nor under Act No. 5510. In fact, family allowances have never attracted attention until recently. This reluctance comes from the insufficiency of social security funds.

354. Family allowances are regulated by a statutory regulation only in the case of civil servants. Act No. 657, Civil Servants, provides the family allowance and birth grants to married civil servants. Family allowances are granted to the children and to the spouse who does not work and draw a pension from the Social Security Institution. If the spouse resumes work in return for wages, family allowance is cut-off (Article 202 of Act No. 657). As regards children, allowances are paid until the children have not completed the age of 25. The family allowance is cut-off if the children start work in return for wages, are married or have a scholarship from the state (Article 206 of Act No. 657).

Family allowances are paid to civil servants each month with their salaries. If both spouses are civil servants, family allowances are paid to the husband only (Article 203 of Act No. 657).

355. Nevertheless, for wage earners, many collective agreements give place to family allowance. If one of the spouses receives a family allowance arising from the contract of employment or collective agreement, and the amount of the allowance is less than that given to civil servants, the spouse who is a civil servant will receive only the difference (Article 202 of Act No. 657).

356. In addition to monetary benefits, civil servants receive a modest parental leave for the birth of their child. By an amendment made in 2011, male civil servants receive ten days of parental leave in the confinement of their spouse. They also receive the full amount of their salary during this period (Article 104/I, B of Act No. 657).

Part IV. Long-Term Insurance Branches

Introduction

357. Act No. 5510 describes long-term insurance branches like those of invalidity, old age and survivors insurances (Article 3/I, 5 of Act No. 5510). Territorial and personal field of application of these insurances is common. There is only one contribution duty for three of these risks. However, conditions to receive benefits differ from each other.

358. Although different social security systems are unified under Act No. 5510, there still exist differences among insurance holders, particularly civil servants who are subjected to different propositions in terms of conditions leading to the entitlement to pension. As will be examined below, it is hard to talk about 'single roof', considering differences in entitlement conditions to insurance benefits.[267] In addition, the temporal application of Act No. 5510 reveals complicated problems. Under the current system, there exist effectively three sub-groups because of the temporal scope of Act No. 5510: those who acquired long-term insurance benefits before the entry into force of Act No. 5510, those who started work before the entry into force of Act No. 5510 and continue to work and those who started work under Act No. 5510.

267. For general evaluation of the system, *see* A.R. Okur, 'Sosyal Güvenlik Reformu: Uzun Dönemli Sigorta Dalları', 8, *Çalışma ve Toplum Der.*(2006/1), pp. 106–141; A.C. Tuncay, '5510 Sayılı Kanun Açısından Uzun Vadeli Sigorta Kolları', in *Yeni Sosyal Güvenlik Sistemi* (Istanbul, 2010), pp. 43–75; L. Akın, 'Uzun Vadeli Sigorta Kolları Açısından Yeni Mevzuatın Getirdiği Değişiklikler', in *Yeni Düzenlemeler Çerçevesinde Sosyal Güvenlik Mevzuatı Semineri* (Ankara, 2007), pp. 157–189; the principle of equality and different entitlement conditions *see* F.B. Mutlay, *Sosyal Sigorta Yardımlarına Hak Kazanma Koşulları ve Eşitlik İlkesi*(Istanbul, 2014), pp. 333–500.

Chapter 1. Field of Application

§1. Territorial Field of Application

359. The territorial field of application of long-term insurances coincides in principle with that of social insurance holdership.[268] The condition of having a work relationship in Turkey also applies to the payment of contributions for long-term insurance branches. Whoever has worked or paid contributions for long-term insurance branches in Turkey can, in principle, benefit from long-term insurance branches.

360. As with regards to wage earners, the insured person must perform, in principle, his/her services in Turkey. However, service periods of Turkish citizens working abroad cause problems with respect to the social security rights of these persons. If there is an international agreement between the Turkish Republic and the country where the employee works, the service periods performed there will be counted. However, in the absence of such an agreement, their service periods could not be aggregated to their service periods in Turkey. Therefore, there exist special acts which will be examined below.[269]

§2. Personal Field of Application

361. The personal field of application for long-term insurance is, in principle, the same with the personal scope of contributions. Nevertheless, it should be underlined that certain groups, such as apprentices, convicts and detainees, trainees who do an internship during their education at a vocational school, those who do internship during their vocational or technical secondary education or higher education, and technical or secondary school students who have vocational training or field education, scholarship holders who take part in projects supported by public institutions, students who work part-time in universities, participants to vocational trainings organized by the Turkish Employment Institution, and Turkish employees who are sent by employers who undertake work in countries with whom the Turkish Republic has no bilateral agreement are exempted from the cover of long-term insurance branches.[270] As regards to Self-Employed persons and civil servants, they fall under the personal field of application of Act No. 5510.

362. Nevertheless, as with regards to civil servants, the main principle is that those who started work before the entry into force of Act No. 5510, provisions of Act No. 5434 on Pension Fund shall apply. Also, for those who receive pensions, invalidity pensions, survivors' pensions, Act No. 5434 shall be applicable. Some of

268. *See supra* paras 69–72.
269. *See infra* paras 474–475.
270. *See supra* para. 86.

those provisions, which enable contributors to the Pension Fund to keep their advantageous positions, raise doubts about the unification aimed at by the Reform. Therefore, Act No. 5510 applies only to civil servants who acquired this status for the first time after the entry into force of the Act (Trans. Article 4 of Act No. 5510).

Chapter 2. Invalidity Insurance

363. Invalidity as a social risk is regulated under a separate heading along with other long-term insurance branches, old age and survivors. Since healthcare services are excluded from the cover of social insurances, the invalidity pension is the main service offered to insurance holders.[271] There exist three sub-groups due to the temporal application rules. The legal status of those who started work under Act No. 5510 will mainly be examined below.

§1. Conditions

364. Article 25 of Act No. 5510 sets out conditions for entitlement to invalidity pensions. First, the insured person must be an invalid within the sense of Article 25, second, he/she must have paid a certain amount in contributions for invalidity insurance, and lastly must have left employment and applied to the Social Security Institution.[272]

I. Invalidity

A. Those Who Are Subjected to Article 4/I, a and 4/I, b

365. Article 25 defines an 'invalid' as an insured person whose loss of capacity for work or earning capacity in his/her profession is at least 60%. Act No. 5510 brings amelioration in respect to the degree of invalidity compared to the previous system. An insured person, either wage earner or the self-employed, is considered an invalid if he/she has lost at least 60% of his/her capacity to work. The reason for the loss carries no importance. The reason may be either directly related to work or not. Furthermore, the negligence of the insured person does not affect the allocation of pensions.[273]

366. If the insured loses at least 60% of his/her earning power in his/her occupation as a result of an industrial accident or occupational disease, this invalidity shall also fall under the scope of invalidity insurance. In the case of industrial accidents and occupational diseases, not only the loss of capacity to work but also at

271. For general evaluation of the reform, *see* N. Caniklioğlu, '5510 Sayılı Kanuna Göre Malullük Aylığı', *Sicil Der.*(Eylül, 2006), pp. 145–159; L. Akın, '5510 Sayılı Yasa'nın Maluliyet Düzenlemelerinin Değerlendirilmesi', *Sicil Der.*(Mart, 2008), pp. 132–143.

272. *See* A. Güzel/A.R. Okur/N. Caniklioğlu, n. 7, pp. 434–449; C. Tuncay/Ö. Ekmekçi, n. 7, pp. 444–453; F. Uşan, n. 28, pp. 199–205; A.N. Sözer, n. 70, pp. 258–271; Y. Alper, n. 7, pp. 279–283; K. Arıcı, n. 7, pp. 353–360; R. Korkusuz/S. Uğur, n.83, pp. 349–352; N. Caniklioğlu, 'Malullük Aylığı', pp. 146–155; L. Akın, 'Malulliyet Düzenlemelerinin Değerlendirilmesi', pp. 136–137; The same author, *Sosyal Güvenlik Hukukunda Bağımlı Çalışanların Maluliyeti* (Ankara, 2007), pp. 146–155.

273. A. Güzel/A.R. Okur./N. Caniklioğlu n. 7, p. 435; F. Uşan, n. 28, p. 201; N. Caniklioğlu, 'Malullük Sigortası', p. 147.

least 60% loss of earning power in his/her occupation shall result in granting the invalidity pension. Therefore, an insurance holder who has not lost his/her earning power in his/her occupation shall be considered invalid, even if he/she has the capacity to work. For example, a model whose face was burned off may have the capacity to work, but surely has lost her earning power in her occupation. While determining the earning power, the occupation in which the insured person is working is taken as a basis. If the permanent incapacity to work is over 10%, the insured employee is also entitled to a permanent incapacity pension from the insurance for industrial accidents and occupational diseases. If the invalidity is 60% or more, he/she will also benefit from an invalidity pension. In such cases, the total amount of the higher sum, either invalidity pension or permanent incapacity allowance, is paid, plus half of the lower amount.

367. Whether the degree of loss has attained 60% of a person's ability to work is determined by the Regulation of Determination Loss Ratio in Earning Capacity and Capacity to Work.[274] The potential for finding a job in the labour market is not taken into account under the Turkish system [275] (Article 25/1 of Act No. 5510).

368. The loss of the ability to work is evaluated from a medical point of view. The loss of capacity to work or the earning power of insurance holders must be determined by medical reports issued by the health boards of service providers authorized by the Institution (Article 25/1 of Act No. 5510).

B. Those Who Are Subjected to Article 4/I, c

369. With regard to civil servants, for those who have acquired civil servant status before the entry into force of Act No. 5510, provisions of Act 5434 will be applicable, unless there is no contradictory provision (Trans. Article 4/4 of Act No. 5510). For this group, three kinds of invalidity exist: ordinary invalidity, job invalidity and military veterans. For civil servants who have acquired the civil servant status after the entry into force of Act No. 5510, there exist two kinds of invalidity: ordinary invalidity and job invalidity. Military veterans are regulated as a subsection of job invalidity.

370. A civil servant insurance holder who has lost at least 60% of the capacity to work, shall benefit from the invalidity insurance, which may be called as ordinary invalidity. In addition, civil servants who have lost their earning power in their occupation at a degree that they cannot further perform their duties shall be considered invalid. Unlike wage earners and self-employed persons, the Act does not require that the loss of earning power in the occupation must result from an industrial accident or occupational disease. Thus, whatever the reason, if a civil servant has lost his/her capacity to perform his/her duty, he/she will benefit from invalidity

274. OJ, 11 Oct. 2008, No. 27021.
275. N. Caniklioğlu, 'Malullük Sigortası', p. 148; A. Güzel/A.R. Okur/N. Caniklioğlu, n. 7, p. 437; C. Tuncay/Ö. Ekmekçi, n. 7, pp. 449–450.

insurance. However, if an invalid insurance holder prefers, he/she shall be assigned to another position appropriate to his/her invalidity and will be deemed to have resigned (Article 25/4 of Act No. 5510).

371. If an insured civil servant suffers from a sickness to a degree as to not to be able to carry out his/her duties and if the sickness lasts longer than the periods fixed, the insurance holder may be considered as suffering from either ordinary invalidity or job invalidity in accordance with the nature and reasons for the invalidity (Article 25/6 of Act No. 5510). The length of the period which results in invalidity because of sickness is fixed by personal statuses applicable to the insurance holder. In the absence of such specific regulation, Act No. 657 will find the place of application. Therefore, if the sickness requires a long-lasting treatment such as cancer, tuberculosis or mental illnesses, the civil servant is entitled to a sick leave up to eighteen months. If the civil servant suffers from sickness other than those requiring long-lasting treatment, he/she is entitled to a sick leave up to twelve months, during which the insurance holder receives the full amount of his/her salary. If such sickness is repeated within one year, the first and second sickness periods shall be cumulated. If at the end of the sick leave, the sickness of an insured civil servant still continues, the sick leave shall be extended up to eighteen or twelve months. At the end of this extension, the insured civil servant will be subjected to provisions of invalidity insurance.[276]

372. Job invalidity is defined in a very similar manner to the definition in Act No. 5434 on Pension Fund. Job invalidity includes cases similar to industrial accidents and others.[277] If the invalidity occurs due to the job or occurred while the civil servant is performing his/her duty, while performing tasks belonging to another public entity, or performing any activity with the aim of protecting the interest of the public entity to which the insured is associated, and the loss of capacity to work reaches 60%, such an invalidity is considered job invalidity. Furthermore, invalidities arising from accidents occurring in the workplaces or in vehicles provided by the employer while on the way to and from work are also considered as job invalidity (Article 47 of Act No. 5510).[278]

373. The Act excludes certain circumstances under which the invalidity occurred from the cover of invalidity insurance such as: if the invalidity is caused by abusing stupefacient substances, spirits or any kind of substances; acting in violation of an act, regulation or order; committing prohibited actions, committing suicide and conducts with the purpose of deriving benefits or harming oneself or others (Article 47/2 of Act No. 5510). In these cases, if the participant loses the invalid job status, he/she may be deemed to be ordinarily invalid.[279]

276. A.N. Sözer, n. 70, pp. 263–264.
277. L. Akın, 'Malullüyet Düzenlenmelerinin Değerlendirilmesi', p. 137; A. Güzel/A.R. Okur/N. Caniklioğlu n. 7, pp. 461–463; C. Tuncay/Ö. Ekmekçi, n. 7, pp. 456–457; A.N. Sözer, n. 70, pp. 284–290.
278. *See also* L. Akın, '5754 Sayılı Yasa Sonrasında Yeni Malullük Sigortası', in *Prof. Dr. Ali Güzel'e Armağan, II* (Istanbul, 2010), pp. 886–892.
279. L. Akın, 'Malullüyet Düzenlemelerinin Değerlendirilmesi', p. 138; A.N. Sözer, n. 70, pp. 290–291.

374. Military veterans are regulated under a special subsection of job invalidity. This invalidity occurs while engaged in military activities. Civilian or military personnel of the Turkish Armed Forces are the principal group covered by this insurance branch.

375. The loss of capacity to work or loss of earning power of insurance holders must be confirmed by a report of the Medical Health Board of the Institution, unlike wage earners and Self-Employed persons who only need medical reports issued by health boards of service providers authorized by the Institution (Article 25/1 of Act No. 5510).

II. Invalidity Must Occur after Having Started Work

376. Second, the invalidity must occur after the insured has started working for the first time. If the disabled person suffers a disease or defect to a degree which requires considering him/her as an invalid before beginning work, under Act No. 5510, he/she cannot benefit from invalidity insurance (Article 25/2 of Act No. 5510). The very first day on which the person started working as an insurance holder must be taken into consideration.[280] Those who suffer from loss of capacity to work of less than 60% before starting to work could only receive benefits under old-age insurance, which is quite difficult. However, the insured may suffer from a disease or defect while starting work if the disability increases, he/she may benefit from invalidity insurance. Only the fact that the disability degree is lower than the required one is sufficient.[281] With regard to civil servants, if the loss of earning capacity in his/her job is found out before his/her appointment, the civil servant cannot benefit from insurance for job invalidity (Article 25/II of Act No. 5510).

III. Contribution Payment and the Length of Insured Period

377. Lastly, the insurance relationship between the Institution and the insured person must have continued for a specified time. According to Article 26/II, b of Act No. 5510, he/she must have been insured for a total period of ten years[282] and his contributions for invalidity, old age and survivors' insurance have been notified, at least, for 1,800 days Since the Act refers to the notification of contributions, for those who are subjected to Article 4/I, a, the non-payment of contributions by the employer does not prevent the entitlement for an invalidity pension. If the person concerned is in need of permanent attendance by another person, the notification of

---

280. A. Güzel/A.R. Okur/N. Caniklioğlu, n. 7, p. 440; C. Tuncay/Ö. Ekmekçi, n. 7, p. 451.
281. Court of Cass., 10th Ch., 25.6.2001, 4606/4920, cited and evaluated by S. Başterzi, 'Sosyal Sigorta Türleri', in *Yargıtayın İş Hukukuna İlişkin Kararlarının Değerlendirilmesi 2001*(Ankara, 2003), pp. 347–351; A. Güzel/A.R. Okur/N. Caniklioğlu, n. 7, p. 440; C. Tuncay/Ö. Ekmekçi, n. 7, p. 451; F. Uşan, n. 28, p. 204; A.N. Sözer, n. 70, p. 259.
282. For the concept 'insured period', *see infra* paras 468–470.

contributions for invalidity, old age and survivors' insurance for at least 1,800 days is sufficient to receive an invalid pension. There is no requirement with respect to the insured period.

378. The period of insured status to be taken into consideration for the purposes of invalidity, old age and survivors' insurance is the period between the date of commencement and the date on which the insured person submits a written claim for pension. The insured period commences on the date on which the insured person entered into employment. There is no need that the insurance holder works during that period without any interruption.[283] Therefore, for example, an insurance holder who has been working for five years and who has paid contributions for 1,800 days suffers from invalidity, he/she should wait for five more years to receive benefits from invalidity insurance, as he/she has not completed the ten-year period as an insurance holder. Also, if an insurance holder starts work before the age of 18, the days for which contribution is paid shall be taken into account; however, the years before the age of 18 are not appraised as insured. Thus, an insurance holder, who started to work at the age of 15 and lost his/her working capacity at the rate of 60% because of an accident at the age of 26, he/she must wait until ten years period is completed (28 years old) to receive the invalidity pension. The unfair nature of the regulation is highlighted by many authors.[284]

379. As regards the notification of contributions for at least 1,800 days, it is not necessary that all contributions have been notified to the Social Security Institution. Contributions paid to the Pension Fund and Bağ-Kur were also taken into account in the calculation of the 1,800 days. The amount of contribution for invalidity, old age and survivors' insurance is 20% of the income of the insured (22% for mining workers working underground). In fact, the notification of contribution days is sufficient to get benefits, while the Act does not require the effective payment, at least for wage earners.[285]

However, for self-employed persons, the Act requires an additional condition: those who are subjected to Article 4/I, b must be out of all kinds of debts related to contribution payment including contributions for universal health insurance to benefit from invalidity pension (Article 26/2 of Act No. 5510).

IV. Written Request

380. In order to be granted a pension, the insured must have left work and submitted a written claim for a pension. The Institution does not allocate pensions automatically without the written claim of the insured person (Article 26/2, c Act No.

283. A. Güzel/A.R. Okur/N. Caniklioğlu, n. 7, p. 446; C. Tuncay/Ö. Ekmekçi, n. 7, pp. 452–453.
284. Critics about ten-year requirement, *see*, N. Caniklioğlu, 'Malullük Aylığı', pp. 152–153; L. Akın, 'Mallullüyet Düzenlemelerinin Değerlendirilmesi', pp. 139–140; A. Güzel/A.R. Okur/N. Caniklioğlu, n. 7, pp. 444–445; C. Tuncay/Ö. Ekmekçi, n. 7, pp. 452–453.
285. N. Caniklioğlu, 'Malullük Aylığı', p. 153; A. Güzel/A.R. Okur/N. Caniklioğlu, n. 7, p. 444; C. Tuncay/Ö. Ekmekçi, n. 7, p. 452; A.N. Sözer, n. 70, p. 268.

5510). The self-employed persons must transfer their workplaces or close them up. The Institution grants pension upon written request of the concerned insurance holder.

§2. Type of Benefits

I. Invalidity Pension

381. The most important benefit granted under the framework of insurance for invalidity is pensions which aim to guarantee the income level of invalids.

The payment of the pension starts from the date of the written claim. However, if required health reports are not ready, the payment commences from the month following the date of the report. For those who are subject to Article 4/I, c, the payment of pension commences the month following the date they quit their job because of their invalidity (Article 27/2 of Act No. 5510).

II. Lump-Sum Payment

382. Invalids who have not fulfilled the required conditions to receive an invalidity pension may ask for lump-sum payments.

III. Retirement Gratuity

383. For civil servants, Act No. 5434 on the Pension Fund provides a special payment. Not only in the case of retirement but also participants who receive ordinary or job invalidity pensions are entitled to receive that indemnity called a retirement gratuity. It is similar to the severance payment for wage earners. Although certain amendments were inserted, Act No. 5510 maintains this benefit for civil servants, the details of which will be examined below.[286]

IV. Healthcare Services and Rehabilitation

384. Before the reform, those who received an invalidity pension and their dependants also benefited from healthcare. However, healthcare services are provided by universal health insurance under the new system. Nevertheless, invalidity pension receivers and their dependants are considered universal health insurance holders and receive healthcare services without being obliged to pay health insurance contributions.

286. *See infra* paras 418–419.

385. While receiving an invalidity pension, if the possibility exists that the working capacity of the insured person may be improved by occupational rehabilitation, rehabilitation services are provided under the invalidity insurance. Like healthcare services, rehabilitation services are also provided under the universal health insurance under the new system.

§3. AMOUNT OF BENEFITS

386. The calculation of average annual earnings is the same as for old-age pensions, and the details will be examined below.[287] The Act provided detailed transition provisions about the calculation of periods before the entry into force of Act No. 5510. Basically, for wage earners, the periods before the entry into force of Act No. 5510 is calculated according to principles in force at that time. For the Self-Employed persons, past periods are taken into account according to principles provided in Articles 27 and 33 of Act No. 5510 (Trans. Article 2 of Act No. 5510).

387. For those who started work after the entry into force of Act No. 5510, pursuant to Article 27 of Act No. 5510, if the number of contribution paid days is less than 9,000 days, the invalidity pension shall be calculated over 9,000 days, and if the number of contribution paid days is 9,000 days or more, the invalidity pension shall be calculated over the exact amount of contribution paid days. If the insured person needs the constant care of another person, the rate is raised by ten points. Nevertheless, with regard to those who are subjected to Article 4/I, a, mainly wage earners, 7,200 days instead of 9,000 days will apply, because 7,200 days of contribution payment is sufficient for wage earners to receive an old-age pension. Therefore, differences exist between wage earners and self-employed persons in terms of not only the conditions to receive benefits but also the amount and calculation method of the invalidity pension. Overall, the pension rate is reduced by Act No. 5510 compared to that of the previous system. Considering the small amount of pensions, if reducing the number of contributions paid days is in favour of insurance holders, reflecting such criteria to the amount of pensions will result in a reduction in pension amounts.[288]

388. Invalidity pension is paid as long as the insured person is considered an invalid. Therefore, the change in the state of health which qualified him/her to benefit from invalidity pensions affects the amount of the pension. These changes may lead to an increase or decrease or end of payments. Thus, a re-examination may be requested, either by the insured person or by the Institution. In addition, the insured person has the right to claim that the permanent attendance of another person is needed (Article 94/2 of Act No. 5510).

287. *See infra* paras 423–425.
288. For details, *see* N. Caniklioğlu, 'Malullük Aylığı', pp. 156–157; A. Güzel/A.R. Okur/N. Caniklioğlu, n. 7, p. 450.

389. The Institution may, at any time, request that the insured person drawing an invalidity pension submit to a control examination. If the insured person fails, without an acceptable excuse, to submit to the control examination, the invalidity pension is terminated at the beginning of the month following the date set for the re-examination. However, if the insured person submits to re-examination within three months following this due date and it is revealed that the invalidity continues, awarded pensions continue to be paid, including those previously cancelled from the time of termination. If the insured person submits to re-examination after three months, the pension resumes starting from the date of the report (Article 94/VI, VII of Act No. 5510).

390. If the insured person resumes working while drawing pensions, the pension is suppressed (Article 27/3 of Act No. 5510). All kinds of work are regulated by Act No. 5510, as well as work subject to foreign legislation. Before the reform, self-employment, working under group insurance, as well as work relations abroad, did not cause the termination of pensions. However, due to the reform, any kind of work relation, either performed in Turkey or abroad, shall cause the termination of pension payments.[289] Nevertheless, if such an invalid person quit the new work and requested for invalidity pension, the invalidity pension may be re-calculated and re-granted, if the invalidity degree has been kept upon the results of control examinations (Article 27/3 of Act No. 5510).

289. N. Caniklioğlu, 'Malullük Aylığı', p. 158; A. Güzel/A.R. Okur/N. Caniklioğlu, n. 7, p. 458; C. Tuncay/Ö. Ekmekçi, n. 7, p. 456; F. Uşan, n. 28, pp. 205–206; A.N. Sözer, n. 70, pp. 277–278.

Chapter 3. Old-Age Insurance

391. The old-age insurance system is one of the most debated topics under the Turkish Social Security Law. Old-age insurance was introduced into the legal system by Act No. 5417 in 1950. Since then, the system has been changed several times. Since the beginning of the 1990s, in order to resolve problems of the social security system, a need for reform has been stated by different groups. Act No. 4447, which came into force on the 1 January 2000, brought many fundamental changes to what had previously been done for a fifty-year period as regards the calculation of contributions, the retirement age, the decrease in pension allocation ratio, etc. However, Act No. 4447 has not returned satisfactory results in meeting the budget deficits of social security institutions. Therefore, in July 2004 and again in April 2005, the government announced a new reform proposal for the social security system. The provisions of the new act, No. 5510, which govern old-age insurance, are the most debated ones. Therefore, many provision annulled by the Constitutional Court are related to the civil servants' pension system.[290] Following the annulation by the Constitutional Court, many amendments have been adopted.[291] The Constitutional Court refused the unconstitutionality claim about these amendments.[292]

§1. Conditions

392. Article 28 of Act No. 5510 sets out conditions for entitlement to old-age pensions. First, the insured person must have paid a certain amount of long-term insurances, completed the required age and the required number of insured years, and lastly, must have left employment and applied to the Social Security Institution.[293] It should be underlined that like other long-term insurance branches, there exist three sub-groups because of the temporal application of Act No. 5510.

---

290. Cons. Court., 15 Dec. 2006, 111/112; OJ, 30 Dec. 2006, 5.M, No. 26392; for evaluations about this jurisprudence *see* A.R. Okur/H. Ergin, 'Tek Çatı Tek Yasadan, Tek ÇatıÇok Yasaya', *İşveren Der*.(Aralık, 2006); Y. Alper, 'İptal Bir Fırsata Dönüştürülmelidir', 2, *Çimento İşveren Der.*(Mart, 2007), pp. 4–19; K. Arıcı, 'Sosyal Sigortalar ve Genel Sağlık Sigortası Kanununun Memurlar ve Diğer Kamu Görevlileri Yönünden Anayasaya Aykırılığı Sorunu', 3, *TİSK Akademi*(2007), pp. 14–24; H. Ergin, 'İptalle Gelen Sorun: Reformdan Geriye Ne Kaldı? Anayasa Mahkemesinin 15.12.2006 Tarihli Kararına İlişkin Bir Değerlendirme, 3, *TİSK Akademi*(2007), pp. 26–63; U. Araslı, 'Anayasa Mahkemesi İptal Kararı ve Sosyal Güvenlikte Gelinen Son Durum', *Sicil*(Mart, 2007), pp. 125–129; C. Erbaş, 'Sosyal Güvenlik Kurumunun Tarihi Gelişimi ve 5510 Sayılı Yasanın Anayasa Mahkemesi'nce İptali Karşısında Yeniden Yapılan FırsatıÜzerine Düşünceler', *Sicil Der.*(Mart, 2007), pp. 135–139; S. Yorgun, '5510 Sayılı Kanun, Anayasa Mahkemesinin İptal Kararı ve Çatırdayan Norm ve Standart Birliği', 4, *TİSK Akademi*(2007/II), pp. 126–145.
291. Act No. 5754 of 17 Apr. 2008, OJ, 8 May 2008, No. 26870.
292. Cons. Court., 30 Mar. 2011, 2008/56, 2011/58, OJ, 28 Dec. 2011, No. 28156.
293. *See* A. Güzel/A.R. Okur/N. Caniklioğlu, n. 7, pp. 476–506; C. Tuncay/Ö. Ekmekçi, n. 7, pp. 364–484; F. Uşan, n. 28, pp. 207–222; A.N. Sözer, n. 70, pp. 354–392; Y. Alper, n. 7, pp. 294–302; M. Şakar, n. 7, pp. 242–249; K. Arıcı, n. 7, pp. 365–370; S. Başterzi, '5510 Sayılı Yasaya Göre Yaşlılık Aylığına Hak Kazanma Koşulları – Önceki Mevzuatla Karşılaştırmalı Bir Değerlendirme', *Prof. Dr. Sarper Süzek'e Armağan, C. II*(Istanbul, 2011), pp. 2203–2242; R. Korkusuz/S. Uğur, n. 83, pp. 357–363.

I. Age and Contribution Payment

393. To be entitled to old-age pensions, Act No. 5510 established a system based on three variables: the age of the insured person; the duration of the insured period; and the number of days that the insured person paid contributions. These variables attracted such important political concern that different governments brought several amendments which either extended or restricted conditions enabling the granting of old-age pensions.[294]

394. The age of retirement has been used as an important political device to gain mass support for political parties. Therefore, different governments have interfered with the system enabling the insured to receive old-age pensions by reducing the age limit or inserting a third way where, without an age requirement, only the fact of having completed certain premium days and insured periods was considered sufficient. Such a third way was abolished by Act No. 4447 dated 25 August 1999.[295] However, the Constitutional Court annulled certain provisions of Act No. 4447 on the basis that the transition period brought by the new amendments did not satisfy the criteria that social security regulations must be reasonable, fair and proportional.[296] However, since the absence of legal regulation resulting from the annulment has the effect of damaging public order and such absence is against the public interest, the annulment would, therefore, come into effect six months later.[297] The new act, No. 4759, came into effect on 1 June 2002[298] but took the date of 23 May 2002 to regulate the transition period. The retirement regime has been changed, at last, by the entry into force of Act No. 5510.[299]

395. Due to many legislative amendments, there currently exist three different systems in force to which insurance holders are subject to with respect to their entry date to the social insurance system: conditions applicable to those who had the insured status for the first time before 8 September 1999; conditions applicable to those who had the insured status for the first time between 8 September 1999–30 April 2008; and conditions applicable to those who had insured status after 30 April 2008. The last group is the only one to which Act No. 5510 is applicable.

A. Those Who Have Started to Work First Before 8 September 1999

396. By Act 4447 dated 1999, the transitory Article 81 was included in the abrogated Act No. 506 on Social Insurances providing a transition period with respect to conditions to get old-age insurance for wage earners. Before the implementation of

294. *See* F. Başterzi, *Yaşlılık Sigortası* (Ankara, 2006), pp. 107–148; A.N. Sözer, n. 7, pp. 356–359.
295. OJ, 8 Sep. 1999, No. 23810.
296. Cons. Court, 23 Feb. 2001, 1999/42, 2001/41, OJ, 23 Nov. 2001, No. 24592.
297. Six months period was completed on the 23 May 2002.
298. Act No. 4759, OJ, 1 Jun. 2002, No. 24772.
299. About transitory provisions of Act No. 5510, *see* H. Ergin, 'Geçiş Hükümleri', in *Yeni Sosyal Güvenlik Sistemi* (Istanbul, 2010), pp. 79 et seq.

Act No. 4447, there was no minimum age requirement to receive an old-age pension. Therefore, an insurance holder who had completed the required contribution payment and the length of the insured period, twenty years for women and twenty-five years for men, could ask for an old-age pension. Thus, insurance holders could start receiving old-age pensions at the age of 38. The sustainability of such a system was out of the question. Therefore, by Act No. 4447, the legislator inserted the minimum age requirement to the system with a transition period. Pursuant to the annulment by the Constitutional Court, Act No. 4759 implemented another transition period which was also criticized.[300]

Therefore, reserving transitory rules, in principle, wage earners who had insured status before 8 September 1999, must have completed:

- 3,600 contribution days and must have completed the fifteen years of insurance period and reached the age of 50, if female, and the age of 55, if male;
- 5,000 days and must have completed the age of 50, if female, and the age of 55, if male;
- 5,000 days and must have completed an insurance period of twenty years, if female, or twenty-five years, if male, to receive the old-age pension.

397. Self-employed persons, reserving specific transitory rules in terms of age and insurance period, must have paid twenty years of contribution payments, if female, and twenty-five years of contribution payments, if male, without any minimum age requirement.[301] Insurance holders are also entitled to get a partial pension if they have fulfilled fifteen years of contribution payment and completed the age of 50, if female, and 55, if male.

398. For civil servants, reserving specific transitory rules in terms of age and insurance period, twenty years of the insurance period, if female, and twenty-five years of the insurance period, if male, have been required.

B. Those Who Have Started to Work First Between 8 September 1999–30 April 2008

399. For those who acquired insured status between 8 September 1999 and 30 April 2008, shall be subject to provisions of abrogated Act No. 506 (Trans. Article 9 of Act No. 5510). Therefore, in order to be entitled to an old-age pension, the insured person must, first of all, have notified contributions under the invalidity, old age and survivors insurance branch, for a minimum period of:

- 7,000 days and must have completed the age of 58 if the insured is female, and the age of 60, if male.

---

300. OJ, 1 Jun. 2002, No. 24772; for critics, *see* A. Güzel/A.R. Okur/N. Caniklioğlu, n. 7, pp. 488489.
301. A. Güzel/A.R. Okur/N. Caniklioğlu, n. 7, p. 478; C. Tuncay/Ö. Ekmekçi, n. 7, p. 475; A.N. Sözer, n. 70, p. 369.

– 4,500 days and must have completed an insurance period of twenty-five years and the age of 58, if female, or the age of 60, if male.[302]

400. Self-employed persons who have started work for the very first time between 8 September 1999 and 30 April 2008, shall be entitled to receive a full old-age pension, if:

– The insured must have completed the age of 58 if the insured is female, and the age of 60, if male.
– The insured person must have paid contributions for, at least, full twenty-five years (Trans. Article 9/2 of Act No. 5510).

The Act provides less heavy conditions to get partial pension that the fulfilment of fifteen years of contribution payment and the completion of the age of 60, if female, and 62, if male (Trans. Article 9/2 of Act No. 5510).[303]

401. For civil servants who acquired the insured status during 8 September 1999–30 April 2008, to receive the full amount of pension, female participants must have reached the age of 58, male participants the age of 60, and both must have paid contributions for twenty-five years (9,000 days). If they have reached the age of 61 and have given fifteen years of contribution payments, they are also entitled to receive partial pension payments (Trans. Article 9/3 of Act No. 5510).[304]

C. Those Who Have Started to Work First under Act No. 5510

402. The new Act, No. 5510, unifies all those who are subjected to Article 4/I, a, b and c also, brings changes to this system which is far from being established. The Act increases both the age requirements and the number of days for which contributions must have been paid. Faced with strong opposition, the age of retirement is 58 for women, and 60 for men and will remain the same until 2036. After 2036, the Act envisages a gradual transition to a retirement age of 65 for both men and women in 2048.

403. The number of contribution paid days was the breaking point for the unified system. Under Act No. 5510, not only the retirement age but also the number of paid contribution days has been increased. According to Act No. 5510, the insurance holder must have paid 9,000 days of contribution for the invalidity, old age and survivors' insurance branch. A total of 9,000 days would not bring any change for contributors to the Pension Fund and self-employed persons. However, as regards wage earners, such a regulation would have created considerable difficulties regarding eligibility for old-age pensions. Considering the number of non-registered

302. A. Güzel/A.R. Okur/N. Caniklioğlu, n. 7, pp. 478–479; C. Tuncay/Ö. Ekmekçi, n. 7, pp. 476–480; A.N. Sözer, n. 70, pp. 359–363.
303. A. Güzel/A.R. Okur/N. Caniklioğlu, n. 7, p. 483; A.N. Sözer, n. 70, p. 369.
304. A.N. Sözer, n. 70, pp. 373–374.

employees in Turkey, 9,000 days, which equals twenty-five years of regular contribution payments, seemed to be quite a high level for entitlement to old-age pensions. In addition, the unemployment rate in Turkey and flexible employment forms becoming more and more extensive caused worry that a considerable number of people would find themselves without any income guarantee in the future because of this increase.[305] Thus, Act No. 5754[306] reduced the number of contribution payment days for wage earners. Therefore, those who are subjected to Article 4/I, a and who started work after 30 April 2008, are entitled to receive old-age pension by the contemplation of 7,200 days of contributions for long-term insurance branches. It should be underlined that the notification of contribution days is sufficient to get benefits, while the Act does not require the effective payment, at least for wage earners.[307]

404. A facilitating option still exists. The Act provides a facilitating option while increasing the age limit by reducing the number of days for contribution payment. Insurance holders may receive an old-age pension under the condition of having 5,400 days of long-term insurance contributions and having completed three years added to the age limit (Article 28/3 of Act No. 5510). Nevertheless, the increased age cannot pass beyond the age of 65.

405. The Act provides another requirement for self-employed persons that the insurance holder must have settled all contribution and contribution-related debts due to his/her own insurance holdership including those for universal health insurance to the Institution (Article 28/9 of Act No. 5510).

D. Special Conditions for Certain Groups

406. For certain occupations, due to their working conditions, different entitlement conditions for receiving pensions are required. Not only the number of days is reduced but also the calculation of their insured periods is different from that of other groups. It should be underlined that, also for these groups, different transitory rules are valid with respect to their entry date to the social security system, after that, the details are out of the scope of this work.[308]

407. Therefore, for those who acquired insured status for the very first time under Act No. 5510, special conditions are as follows:

---

305. Y. Alper, 'Türk Emeklilik Sisteminde Reform', *Mercek*(Ocak, 2005), p. 115; N. Caniklioğlu, 'Yaşlılık Sigortasının Yeniden Yapılandırılmasının Esasları', pp. 199–200; A.R. Okur, 'Uzun Dönemli Sigorta Dalları', pp. 111–112.
306. OJ, 8 May 2008, No. 26870.
307. For details, *see* A. Güzel/A.R. Okur/N. Caniklioğlu, n. 7, pp. 479–481; C. Tuncay/Ö. Ekmekçi, n. 7, pp. 480–483; F. Uşan, n. 28, pp. 216–222; A.N. Sözer, n. 70, pp. 379–381.
308. For details, *see* A. Güzel/A.R. Okur/N. Caniklioğlu, n. 7, pp. 491–501; C. Tuncay/Ö. Ekmekçi, n. 7, pp. 485–497; A.N. Sözer, n. 70, pp. 384–390.

(a) Workers who are employed in underground workplaces of mines (Article 28/6 of Act No. 5510), if they have been permanently in underground labour for at least twenty years with insured status, have already paid contributions for invalidity, old age and survivors' insurance for at least 7,200 days and have reached the age of 55, are awarded an old-age pension. If the insurance holder is subjected to Article 4/I, c, the number of contribution paid days shall be 9,000 (Trans. Article 9 of Act No. 5510).

(b) Insured persons suffering invalidity before starting work for the first time as an insurance holder are not entitled to receive benefits from invalidity insurance. However, to be entitled to an old-age pension, they profit from better conditions. A minimum insured period of fifteen years and at least 3,960 days, for which the contributions have been paid, are sufficient to receive old-age benefits. There is no age requirement with regard to these insurance holders (Article 28/4 of Act No. 5510).

(c) Considering the difficulty in finding employment for invalid persons, the Act provides special conditions for those whose invalidity is more than 40% but less than 60%, the degree required to get benefits from invalidity insurance. Pursuant to Article 28/5, a and b, if the insurance holder's loss of working capacity is:
  - Between 50% and 59%, they are entitled to receive an old-age pension, if they have completed sixteen years of the insured period and paid contributions for 4,320 days.
  - Between 40% and 49%, they are entitled to receive an old-age pension, if they have been insured for at least eighteen years and paid 4,680 days of contributions.

(d) Those found to be prematurely aged (Article 28/7 of Act No. 5510) are entitled to an old-age pension if they have completed the age of 55 and have paid contributions for at least 7,200 days. Persons, who have completed the age of 55 but before reaching the retirement age become as aged as persons who have biologically reached this age and lost their capacity to work to the same degree as biologically aged persons are considered prematurely aged. The Health Board of the Institution evaluated the medical reports submitted by service providers to set prematurely aged status.

(e) Act No. 5510 provides a new right for female insurance holders. Considering the insufficient care facilities for disabled children, the legislator provides a facilitative retirement option for women who have a child who is in need of permanent care (Article 28/8 of Act No. 5510). However, the way chosen by the legislator is quite complicated: One-fourth of the number of contribution paid days after the enactment of Act No. 5510 shall be added to the total number of contribution paid days, and also these added years shall be deducted from the retirement age limit. Only female insurance holders can benefit from this opportunity.

II. Termination of the Work Relation

408. Due to Article 28/8 of Act No. 5510, in order to benefit from old-age pensions, the insured employee must terminate the work relation which is on the basis of social insurance relationship and submit a written request to the Institution. Likewise, civil servants must take the approval of the authority for retirement procedures. If the insured person applies for a pension before terminating the contract, the pensions will be paid following the date of termination.[309] However, the Act does not require self-employed persons to close down their independent activity. They should only declare their intention whether they will close their work or not. The reason for such differences arises from the opportunity given to the self-employed persons to receive old-age pension and work at the same time.[310]

III. Written Request

409. To be awarded an old-age pension, the insured person must submit a written claim. Without a written claim, the Institution does not, in principle, automatically grant pensions. For wage earners and self-employed persons, there is no mandatory retirement system.

410. However, for civil servants, the general mandatory retirement age is 65. However, for certain occupations, such as university academic personnel, judges and public prosecutors, ambassadors, officers, police, etc., the Act fixes mandatory ages other than 65 (Article 40 of Act No. 5434). For example, for university professors, the retirement age is 67. In addition, under certain circumstances, even if the contributor does not wish so, the public entity to which he/she has been appointed may, if need be, retire him/her on its own authority in certain cases. In these cases, there is no need for a written request.

IV. Special Conditions for Certain Public Officers

411. Act No. 5510, as under the previous system, provides special rules about old-age pension of certain public officers. Presidents of the Republic, who resigned from office for any reason, shall be entitled to receive an old-age pension upon written request. The amount of the pension is 40% of the monthly allowance paid to the President. If the President of the Republic is entitled to receive an old-age pension pursuant to other provisions of Act No. 5510, he/she shall be granted the pension of the amount which is highest (Article 43/1, 2 of Act No. 5510).

412. Presidents of the Turkish Grand National Assembly or Prime Ministers who resign from office for any reason shall be entitled to an old-age pension upon their request. This opportunity is extended to non-parliamentary ministers and members

---

309. *See, as example,* Court of Cass., 10th Ch., 17 Apr. 1979, 1130/3402, *YKD*(Kasım, 1979), p. 1601.
310. A. Güzel/A.R. Okur/N. Caniklioğlu, n. 7, p. 503; A.N. Sözer, n. 70, p. 390.

of the National Assembly under the condition that they have completed two years of service in these positions.[311] The amount of the old-age pension is 75% of the pension payable to the President of the Republic. If they are also entitled to receive an old-age pension pursuant to the above-mentioned provisions, the pension amount, which is the highest shall be granted (Article 43/3 of Act No. 5510).

413. As we mentioned above, for civil servants, Act No. 5434 states three kinds of retirement: voluntary retirement, forced retirement and mandatory retirement due to age. Although the new act, No. 5510, subjects conditions for entitlement to voluntary retirement to the same provisions as old-age insurance, it also contains some specific provisions (Articles 43, 44, 45, 46, 48 and 49 of Act No. 5510) with respect to old-age pensions for certain groups of civil servants.

414. A public entity may retire a civil servant, under certain circumstances, even if he/she does not wish to do so, on its own authority. Such persons are determined as follows:

- Civil servants who have reached the age limit, if they have completed the 5,400 days of contribution paid days.
- Civil servants for whom there is a lack of position in the public entity pursuant to special statutes, if they have completed 9,000 days of contribution paid days, are retired mandatorily. However, they are still entitled to receive an old-age pension (Article 44/I, a and b of Act No. 5510).

415. In addition, if their public entity considers it necessary, army officers and military officers who have been sentenced to the punishment due to moral defects, inadequacy or a black mark on their records because of insubordination or military court decisions, the public entity may retire him/her on its own authority. In addition, civil servants other than army officers and military officers may also be retired on the public entity's own authority, if it is considered necessary because of disorderly conduct or inadequacy. They shall only receive an old-age pension if they satisfy the conditions mentioned in Article 28 (Article 44/2 of Act No. 5510).

§2. Types of Benefits

I. Old-Age Pension

416. The main benefit allocated to insurance holders by the old-age insurance is surely monthly old-age pension.

The payment of pension starts from the beginning of the month following the date of the written request for wage earners and self-employed persons. For civil servants, pensions are allocated from the beginning of the month following the day on which they have no further connection with the public entity upon the approval of the retirement (Article 30/1 of Act No. 5510).

311. Act No. 6270 of 17 Jan. 2012, OJ, 26 Jan. 2012, No. 28185.

II. Lump-Sum Payment

417. If the insured person left employment without being entitled to receive an old-age pension, contributions paid for invalidity, old age and survivors may be refunded. Before the reform, a specific lump-sum payment from which only insured females could benefit was granted. An insured female quitting work in the year immediately following marriage or getting married within one year of leaving employment might have requested a refund of paid contributions (Supp. 1 of Act No. 506). However, since married women could always go back to working life after marriage, Act No. 5510 revoked such an option.[312]

418. Article 31 lists the conditions as follows:[313] First of all, only wage earners and Self-Employed persons benefited from this opportunity. For those who are subjected to Article 4/I, c, those who have started work after the entry into force of Act No. 5510 may receive a lump-sum payment.

Second, the insured person is not to be entitled to invalidity or old-age pension. If the insurance holder is entitled to a pension, he/she cannot receive a lump-sum payment.

Third, the insurance holder must satisfy the condition of age, but not the contribution days' requirement and the required insured period. Thus, a female insured person must have completed the age of 58 and 60 if male.

Lastly, the insured must have left employment and must request the lump-sum payment with a written claim. If the insurance holder works for more than one work, he/she must have left all of them.

419. The amount of the lump-sum payment is the total amount of paid contributions for the invalidity, old age and survivors' insurance branches. The paid contributions for each calendar year are to be updated until the calendar year of the insured's pension claim is submitted. Although the Act sets no time limitation on such a demand, many authors argued that the statute of limitations to ask for such a refund must be ten years.[314]

III. Retirement Gratuity

420. Participants, who receive retirement are entitled to receive a special indemnity, called a retirement gratuity. It is similar to the severance payment for wage earners. Although certain amendments were inserted, Act No. 5510 maintains this benefit for civil servants. For those who have started work before the entry into force of Act No. 5510, there exist different periods, in respect, of the eligibility conditions.[315]

312. A. Güzel/A.R. Okur/N. Caniklioğlu, n. 7, p. 570; A.N. Sözer, n. 70, p. 406.
313. A. Güzel/A.R. Okur/N. Caniklioğlu, n. 7, pp. 571–572; A.N. Sözer, n. 70, pp. 408409.
314. M. Çenberci, n. 80, p. 395; A.Güzel/A.R. Okur/N. Caniklioğlu, n. 7, p. 572; C. Tuncay/Ö. Ekmekçi, n. 7, p. 505.
315. For details, *see* A.N. Sözer, n. 70, pp. 411419.

421. For those who started work first under Act No. 5510, the retirement gratuity is paid under the following circumstances (Supp. Article 82 of Act No. 5434):

- If the whole service period has been under Article 4/I, c of Act No. 5510.
- If the insurance holder has worked under different social security regimes, he/she has worked as subjected to Article 4/I, c at the time of the request for a pension.
- If the insurance holder is not working, which requires a compulsory insurance holdership at the time of the request for a pension, with respect to, long-term insurance branches, the last work must be subjected to Article 4/I, c.
- If the insurance holder has received a lump-sum payment for old-age pensions, with respect to, long-term insurance branches, the last work should be subjected to Article 4/I, c.
- If the insurance holder has died while working as subjected to Article 4/I, c, survivors who receive the survivors' pension or a lump-sum payment.
- If the insurance holder has worked under Article 4/I, c but is not working at the time of death, the survivors who receive survivors pension or a lump-sum payment.
- If the insurance holders have received an old-age pension or a lump-sum payment after they have been voluntary insurance holders following the compulsory work subjected to Article 4/I, c.

IV. Healthcare Benefits

422. Before the reform, since healthcare benefits were provided under the social insurance system, those who received an old-age pension and their dependants also benefited from healthcare. However, healthcare services are provided by universal health insurance under the new system. Nevertheless, old-age pension receivers and their dependants are considered as universal health insurance holders and receive healthcare services without being obliged to pay any health insurance contributions (Article 60/I, f of Act No. 5510).

§3. Amount of Benefits

I. Calculation of Pensions

423. Since 1 January 2000, the system of calculating old-age pensions has been changed. Before, the calculation was made according to indicator tables and coefficients. Since 2000, the amount of old-age pension is calculated on the basis of the pension allocation ratio and average annual income. Act No. 5510 brings considerable changes to the calculation method for pensions. Therefore, there exist three different calculation methods: for periods before 1 January 2000, between 1 January 2000–1 October 2008 and 1 October 2008.[316] Basically, for wage earners and

316. For calculation of pensions for different periods, *see* F. Başterzi, n. 294, pp. 257–309.

self-employed persons, if they have started work before the entry into force of Act No. 5510, the old-age pensions are calculated according to a mix of rules arising from abrogated acts and Act No. 5510.

424. For those who are subjected to Article 4/I, a, b or if they started working under Act No. 5510, to Article 4/I, c, the old-age pension shall be computed by multiplication of the average monthly income by the pension allocation rate (Article 29/1 of Act No. 5510). The status of the insured's annual income, on which contributions are based, would be updated on the date on which the pension is requested. This amount will be divided by the number of days for which the contributions were paid. The average monthly income is thirty times that of the determined daily income.

*425. The a*nnual average income for five or ten years' periods was replaced by the average annual income calculated over the whole insured period by the reform. The income taken as a basis for contributions for each calendar year is to be updated until the calendar year of the insured's pension claim is submitted. The amount of income for each calendar year is to be increased according to the increase ratio calculated on the basis of the urban consumer prices and gross national product. The division of the sum of annual increased incomes by the total number of days for which contributions paid gives the daily income of the insured (Article 29/II of Act No. 5510).

426. The pension allocation ratio is the sum of ratios of 2% for every 360 days of the initial days of the total days of contribution payment of the insured. However, the pension ratio cannot exceed 90% (Article 29/III of Act No. 5510). Under this new system, an insurance holder who has regularly paid contributions for 9,000 days will receive approximately 50% of his/her earning as a pension. The amount is insufficient. In fact, since 2000, every reform has an effect of reducing pensions.[317]

427. The amount of pension awarded under this Act is not to be less than 35% of the monthly sum of the average monthly income. If the insurance holder has a dependent spouse or child, the pension amount cannot be less than 40% of the average monthly income (Article 55/III of Act No. 5510). Although such amount is also low, nevertheless, such a minimum limit is quite meaningful.[318] The amount of old-age pension shall be regularly increased two times, in January and July, in a year. The increase rate is determined according to the exchange rate of the last six months' urban consumer prices announced by the Turkish Statistical Institute.

428. Unlike wage earners and the self-employed persons, the method of indicators and coefficient remains in force for civil servants who acquired this status before the entry into force of Act No. 5510. While calculating retirement pensions, indicator tables fixed in Article 43 of Act No. 657, Civil Servants are used. To the

317. For criticism, *see* N. Caniklioğlu, 'Yeniden Yapılandırılma Esasları', pp. 207–208.
318. A. Güzel/A.R. Okur/N. Caniklioğlu, n. 7, p. 655.

amount of indicator, certain other payments, such as additional indicators, seniority payments and floor payments, are added. The method of calculation consists of complicated mathematical computations.

429. For civil servants, who entered to the system before the entry into force of Act No. 5510, the ratio of pension allocation is 75%. The ratio is computed on the basis of twenty-five actual service years. For those who have service periods of more than twenty-five years, the ratio is increased at the ratio of 1% for each complete year. Nevertheless, the amount of pension cannot be more than 100% of the amount of monthly income. For each year below twenty-five years, it is decreased by 1% for each complete year (Article 41 of Act No. 5434). Retirement pensions for those who requested it while still employed start following the month in which the participant's salary is terminated.

II. Calculation of Retirement Gratuity

430. While calculating the retirement gratuity, whole periods passed under Article 4/I, a and 4/I, c in public entities are taken into account. The amount of the gratuity is calculated pursuant to provisions of Act No. 5434.

431. For civil servants, who have started work before the entry into force of Act No. 5510, all participants, who receive retirement pensions or a lump-sum payment, are entitled to receive a retirement gratuity. The amount of gratuity is a month of salary for each year of service. While calculating the gratuity, services exceeding thirty years are not taken into account. However, the Constitutional Court annulled this provision referring to the rule of law, the right to social security and the right to equality.[319]

319. Cons. Court, 25 Dec. 2014, 2013/111, 2014/195, OJ, 7 Jan. 2015, No. 29229.

Chapter 4. Survivors' Insurance

432. To support, a family explains the risk of death as a social risk. The social insurance system protects not only insurance holders, but also their dependants.[320] With respect to the temporal scope of application of Act No. 5510, those who are granted survivors' pensions before the entry into force of Act No. 5510 shall be subjected to either abrogated acts or Act No. 5510. Abrogated acts shall apply in the cases of suspension, deduction, increase and re-allocation of pensions due to status changes of the insurance holder. However, the increases in the amount of pensions shall be calculated according to the related provisions of Act No. 5510.[321]

§1. Conditions

433. Act No. 5510 introduces common and specific rules in order to be vested survivors' pension.

I. Common Conditions

434. First, the insured must have died. The reason for death is of no importance. However, if the death is due to an industrial accident or occupational disease, whether the provisions of survivors' insurance shall apply, is a matter of discussion. Certain authors argue that survivors' insurance provides benefits to survivors of the deceased insured except for those who lose their lives during an industrial accident or occupational disease.[322] However, the others argue for the applicability of the provisions of survivors insurance even if the death is due to an industrial accident or occupational disease.[323]

435. Second, the dead person must have been insured or must have maintained a relationship with the Institution. He/she may either have been working or drawing invalidity, job invalidity or old-age pension or have been entitled to receive these pensions upon written request (Article 32/2 b and c Act No. 5510). He/she may also have lost his/her life during a period in which the pension payment was suspended because employment was resumed while drawing a pension (Article 32/2, c of Act No. 5510).

---

320. A. Güzel/A.R. Okur/N. Caniklioğlu, n. 7, p. 578; C. Tuncay/Ö. Ekmekçi, n. 7, p. 510; A.N. Sözer, n. 70, pp. 43–44; Y. Alper, n. 7, pp. 314–319; F. Uşan, n. 28, p. 227; K. Arıcı, 'Sosyal Sigorta Sistemimizde Ölüm Sigortasından Ana-Babaya Sağlanan Sosyal Güvenlik Yardımları', *Kamu-İş Der.*(Ocak, 1999), p. 16.
321. A.N. Sözer, n. 70, p. 422.
322. M. Çenberci, n. 80, p. 396; C. Tuncay/Ö. Ekmekçi, n. 7, p. 511; C. Tuncay, '5510 Sayılı Kanun Açısından Ölüm Sigortası', in *Prof. Dr. Ali Güzel'e Armağan*, II (Istanbul, 2010), p. 1232; F. Uşan, n. 28, p. 228; A.N. Sözer, n. 70, p. 429.
323. A. Güzel/A.R. Okur/N. Caniklioğlu, n. 7, p. 578.

436. Third, the insured must have paid a certain amount of contributions. The number of paid contribution days is different for those who are subjected to Article 4/I, a and 4/I, b and c (Article 32/2 a of Act No. 5510):

- For the self-employed persons and civil servants, the insured person must have paid contributions for a total of at least 1,800 days. In addition, the self-employed insurance holder must have no outstanding debts related to contribution payments, including contributions for universal health insurance (Article 32/II of Act No. 5510). Nevertheless, the survivors have the right to pay the outstanding debts of the deceased insurance holder.[324]
- For wage earners, in addition to the above-mentioned contribution notification for a total of at least 1,800 days, Act No. 5510 provides a facilitating option: If the insured person has paid contribution for except all indebted periods, for a total of at least 900 days and been insured for at least five years, his/her survivors will be granted pension (Article 32/II, a of Act No. 5510). However, Act No. 5510 restricts wage earners from this right of indebting, in the sense that, survivors of a deceased wage-earner have no right to owe five years insured period.[325] For wage earners, since it is the employer who is charged with the payment of contributions, the notification of contribution days is sufficient to get benefits. This five-year period is not necessarily the five years immediately preceding the date of the death. Since these two requirements are cumulative, survivors of those who lost their lives before the completion of the five-year period cannot receive benefits, even if the number of contribution paid days is more than 900.[326]

The Soma mine disaster, an explosion at a coal mine in Soma, in Turkey on 13 May 2014, was Turkey's worst mine accident ever; 301 miners were killed. The second major accident came within six months in Ermenek. Unfortunately, mine accidents continue to happen. In order to prevent the public indignation, the legislator abolished the eligibility conditions related to contribution days and insured period. The survivors of those who have lost their lives in mine accidents happened between the dates of 13 May 2014 (the date of the Soma accident) and 28 October 2014 (the date of the Ermenek mine accident) are entitled to receive survivors' pension without being obliged to have any insurance contributions and insured period.[327] The deficient part of the number of contribution days is provided by the Ministry of Finance.[328]

437. If the insured period or the number of days for which contributions have been paid is incomplete, the Act grants certain possibilities to potential beneficiaries to remedy these deficiencies. As will be examined below, the insured person or his/her survivors have the right to owe social insurance contributions for non-insured

324. A.N. Sözer, n. 70, p. 441.
325. For critics about such difference, *see* A. Güzel/A.R. Okur/N. Caniklioğlu, n. 7, pp. 585–586; C. Tuncay, 'Ölüm Sigortası', p. 1233; A.N. Sözer, n. 70, p. 430, n. 2; M. Şakar, n. 7, p. 333.
326. A. Güzel/A.R. Okur/N. Caniklioğlu, n. 7, p. 584.
327. Act No. 6552, OJ, 11 Sep. 2014, No. 29116 (M).
328. A. Güzel/A.R. Okur/N. Caniklioğlu, n. 7, p. 584; C. Tuncay/Ö. Ekmekçi, n. 7, pp. 514–515.

periods.[329] Survivors may benefit from the right to owe social insurance contributions for periods passed under, for example, military service, services abroad or periods passed during a strike or lock-out.

438. Another way to make up incomplete contribution paid days or insured periods is by taking advantage of the right to restore. Thus, survivors may reimburse the lump-sum payment given to the insured by his/her insurance benefit source. In such cases, the Institution is obliged to take into account these periods while calculating survivors' pensions.[330]

439. Lastly, the survivors of the insured must submit a written request in order to draw a survivors' pension. The Institution does not award pensions automatically.

II. Specific Conditions

440. The personal field of application of survivors' insurance is restricted to the spouse, children and parents of the insured deceased. Conditions related to beneficiaries vary.

441. In order to consider the spouse among the beneficiaries, they must have been legally married. The sex of the spouse, male or female, has no bearing regarding the beneficiaries. However, an unmarried partner does not fall under cover of the insurance. For spouses, the only condition to keep the right to pension is not remarrying. However, if a widow or widower remarries, his/her pension is suppressed. But if this marriage ends in divorce, the pension payments will be resumed. Whether or not the widow or the widower works under insured or non-insured status, or draws a pension from social security institutions, does not affect the pension allocation.[331] In that case, only the amount of pension is reduced.

442. Children of the insured deceased also benefit from survivors' insurance. If the benefits are derived from the mother, the children do not necessarily have to have been born in wedlock. However, children deriving benefits from their fathers must have been born in wedlock. Acknowledged children, legitimized children, children recognized by a court decision and posthumous children benefit from survivors' pensions. In addition, adopted children are also under cover of the insurance. However, stepchildren do not receive survivors' pensions.

443. For sons and daughters, the Act states different conditions: For sons, children must be younger than 18 years. However, this is extended if he is receiving secondary education and has not yet completed the age of 20 or is receiving higher

329. *See infra* paras 470–477.
330. A. Güzel/A.R. Okur/N. Caniklioğlu, n. 7, pp. 588–589.
331. C. Tuncay, 'Ölüm Sigortası', pp. 1232–1233; A. Güzel/A.R. Okur/N. Caniklioğlu, n. 7, pp. 589–590; C. Tuncay/Ö. Ekmekçi, n. 7, p. 516; A.N. Sözer, n. 70, pp. 433–434.

education and has not yet completed the age of 25. By the fulfilment of this age, the pension shall be suspended. In addition, to receive a pension, children must not work, both abroad and be subject to Act No. 5510. In addition, they must not receive an income or pension due to their own work.

444. Daughters of the insured deceased draw survivors' pensions if they are not married or working, both abroad and as subject to Act No. 5510. Also, they must not receive income or pension due to their own work. For daughters, the Act has not introduced any age limit as it did for sons. Pensions of daughters are terminated on marriage or commencement of employment. However, if the marriage ends in divorce, the pension right will be reinstated. Nevertheless, if she is also entitled to a pension because of her husband, the higher one is paid. In the case of invalidity of a daughter, she will benefit from a survivors' pension, even though she is married (Article 34, 1, b, 2 of Act No. 5510).[332]

445. If the children of the insured deceased suffer an invalidity, have lost at least 60% of his/her capacity to work, he/she does not work, and he/she does not receive any pension derived from any employment of his/her own, subject to the Social Security Institution, the children will benefit from a survivors' pension, regardless of his/her age and his/her educational status (Article 34/I, b, 2 of Act No. 5510).

446. Parents of the insured deceased are also among the beneficiaries. Due to the restrictive wording of the Article, neither step-parents nor adoptive parents have the right to receive benefits.

447. In order for a pension to be awarded to parents, Article 34 requires two conditions: First, the total amount of pensions awarded to the spouse and children must be less than the amount of the insured's own pension. The Act gives priority to spouse and children. However, if parents are above the age of 65, there is no need for leftover share (Article 34/I, d of Act No. 5510). Second, parents must be dependent, which means the total income arising from all earnings and benefits must be less than the amount of minimum wage, as well as they do not receive other incomes or pensions than the allotted pension due to their other children.[333] In certain cases, for example, the son decided to attend university, the pension allocated to the parents may be terminated.

448. Provisions of abrogated Act No. 5434 will apply to civil servants who started work for the first time before the entry into force of Act No. 5510 (Trans. Article 4/V of Act No. 5510). Act No. 5434 calls survivors' pension 'widow/widower' or 'orphan pension'. Thus, survivors of civil servants who receive widow or orphan pension, before the entry into force of Act No. 5510, will receive these pensions, as long as, they fulfil the required conditions.

---

332. A. Güzel/A.R. Okur/N. Caniklioğlu, n. 7, pp. 590–591; C. Tuncay/Ö. Ekmekçi, n. 7, pp. 516518; A.N. Sözer, n. 70, pp. 434–435.
333. About this issue under Act No. 506 K. Arıcı, 'Ölüm Sigortasından Ana-Babaya Sağlanan Gelirler', pp. 20–22.

In order to award a widow's or orphan's pension, the death of the participant must have occurred under the circumstances set out in the Act (Article 66 of Act No. 5434). Certain examples are as follows:

- During a presidency or after leaving the presidency.
- Those who have at least ten years of actual service.
- Those who are entitled to retirement, ordinary, or job invalidity pensions.
- During surgery or treatment due to accidents or reasons arising from the nature of their position, etc.

449. Widow's or widower's pension is paid to the spouse of the deceased contributor. Even if the widow/widower works subject to the Social Security Institution, or receives income or pensions from the Institution, this does not prevent him/her from receiving benefits.

450. In order for orphan's pension to be awarded, the son of the participant must not have completed the age of 18. If he is receiving secondary education, the age limit is increased to 20 and in the case of higher education, to 25 (Article 74 of Act No. 5434). If the son suffers from a disease or disability where successful treatment is impossible, he is entitled to receive a pension, regardless of his age (Article 74/7 of Act No. 506).

For daughters, it is sufficient not to be married at the date of the insured's death. The Act does not require any other condition. However, if she marries afterwards, the pension is eliminated. In the case of divorce or death of her husband, the pension right is reinstituted (Article 75/1, 2 of Act No. 5434).

451. As regards parents of the deceased insured, the only condition regarding mothers being granted a survivors' pension is that she not be a contributor to the Fund on the date of death. Fathers must not be subject to the Pension Fund and must be in need and must have completed the age of 65. If the father in need also suffers invalidity preventing him from working, having completed the age of 65 is not necessary (Article 72/1 of Act No. 5434).

§2. Type of Benefits

I. Survivors' Pension

452. A survivors' pension is the principal benefit provided by survivors' insurance. The survivors' pension commences from the beginning of the month following the date on which the insurance holder is deceased or entitlement to such a pension occurred (Article 35/1, a, b of Act No. 5570). Each beneficiary must submit an individual written request.

453. Beneficiaries must apply to the Institution within five years following the death of the insured (Article 97 of Act No. 5510). Even if they fail to make this request within five years, a pension may still be awarded. However, in such cases, retroactive payment is not possible. Pensions are awarded from the beginning of the month following the date of the decease of the insurance holder or the date on which the dependent fulfilled the required conditions (Article 35/I of Act No. 5510).

II. Lump-Sum Payment

454. If none of the survivors of the deceased insured is entitled to a survivors' pension, the total amount of contributions for the invalidity, old age and survivors' insurance branches paid by both the deceased insured and his/her employer are to be refunded to the survivors proportionally (Article 36/1 of Act No. 5510). Insurance holders subjected to Article 4/I, a and b, as well as civil servants who started work for the first time under Act No. 5510 benefit from this opportunity.

455. Conditions entitling the receipt of lump-sum payments and survivors' pension are similar: As regards sons, they must not have completed the age of 18, or if receiving secondary education, the age of 20, or if receiving higher education, the age of 25. For daughters, the only condition is not to be married. It is not necessary to not be employed or be receiving a pension. Irrespective of age, disabled children, to the extent of being unable to work, benefit from lump-sum payments.

III. Marriage Assistance

456. In case of marriage, Act No. 5510, like previous acts, grants a specific aid for daughters drawing a survivors' pension. They shall receive, one time only, marriage assistance in an amount equal to the total amount of the pension over a period of two years. Until the end of these two years, she will not benefit from any other help if her marriage ends in divorce or the death of her husband (Article 37/I of Act No. 5510). If the daughter is invalid since the survivors' insurance is allocated, survivors' insurance shall not be suppressed by marriage, and she will not receive marriage assistance.[334]

IV. Funeral Assistance

457. Due to Article 37/III of Act No. 5510, in the case of the death of the insured, an allowance for funeral expenses is to be paid to the family of the insured. In order to benefit from funeral assistance, the insured must have died while drawing invalidity, job invalidity, old-age pensions or permanent incapacity allowance or died in an industrial accident or due to an occupational disease or while 360 days of long-term insurance contributions have been notified for himself/herself.[335]

---

334. A. Güzel/A.R. Okur/N. Caniklioğlu, n. 7, p. 653.
335. Critics for a requirement of contribution payment A. Güzel/A.R. Okur/N. Caniklioğlu, n. 7, p. 611.

Funeral assistance is allocated successively to the spouse, if not then to the children, if not then to the parents and if not then to the brother and sisters of the deceased insurance holder (Article 37/III of Act No. 5510).

458. Survivors of insurance holders subjected to Article 4/I, c also receive another benefit named death assistance. When assigned for the first time as a civil servant, he/she submits a notification to inform the public entity or the Institution about who should profit from death aid, in case of his/her death. If there exists no such notification, the spouse and children, on their absence parents, on their absence, brothers and sisters shall receive death aid. The amount of death aid is twice the highest salary of civil servants. In addition, funeral expenses of civil servants are met by their public entity (Supp. Act No. 4 of Act No. 5434). In that case, their survivors do not receive funeral assistance (Article 37/V of Act No. 5510).

V. Retirement Gratuity

459. If the civil servants entered into the system before the entry into force of Act No. 5510, and the participant dies before drawing his/her retirement gratuity, his/her survivors benefit from this gratuity at the same ratio as receiving a pension (Article 89 of Act No. 5434). Even if the civil servant is started work as subject to Article 4/I, c of Act No. 5510, dies while working under Article 4/I, c or dies after that his/her last work relation is subject to Article 4/I, c, his/her survivors benefit from his/her pension or lump-sum payment shall be paid as retirement gratuity by the Institution (Supp. Article 82/I, e of Act No. 5434).

VI. Healthcare

460. Survivors of the insured also benefited from healthcare under the previous system. However, by the reform, spouse, children and parents drawing a pension from the Institution, benefit from healthcare under universal healthcare insurance without paying health insurance contribution /Article 60/I, f of Act No. 5510).

§3. Amount of Benefits

I. Calculation of Pensions

461. A survivor's pension is computed on the same basis as old-age pensions. The amount of the pension varies according to the position held by the insured.

462. The insured died while drawing invalidity, job invalidity or old-age pension, his old-age or invalidity pension is the one to be distributed among the beneficiaries (Article 33/I, a of Act No. 5510). If the insured restarts working while drawing a pension and then dies, contributions paid days during this re-employment are also to be taken into account while calculating the survivor's pension. However, if the insured dies while paying the social security support pension, the insured's old-age pension is to be distributed among the beneficiaries. If the insured person dies while working, the old-age pension is calculated taking this into account.

463. In the computation of the amount of pension, the pension allocation rate will be calculated as though the insured had paid contributions for 9,000 days, even if the number of contribution paid days is less than 9,000. If the number of contribution paid days is more than 9,000, the pension allocation rate will be determined according to this number (Article 33/I, c of Act No. 5510). However, for those who are subject to Article 4/I, a, 7,200 days paid contribution is taken into account instead of 9,000 days. Therefore, if the number of contribution paid days for a wage earner is less than 7,200 days, pensions shall be computed over 7,200 days.

464. The pension, which is the basis of the survivors' pension is not to be less than 35% of the amount of average monthly income calculated on the lower limits. This amount shall not be less than 40% if the deceased insurance holder has a dependent spouse and children. (Article 55/III of Act No. 5510). If there is only one survivor, the pension of the survivor cannot be less than 80% of the minimum pension limit. If there are two survivors, the pension cannot be less than 90% of the minimum limit (Article 55/III of Act No. 5510). The upper limit of a pension is the amount payable to the insured person (Article 34/III of Act No. 5510).

465. How the pension shall be distributed among beneficiaries is also regulated by Article 34. If the spouse is the only beneficiary, she/he receives 75% of the pension under the condition that he/she does not work as subject to Act No. 5510 or does not receive any income or pension due to his/her own employment. If the spouse and children both benefit, the spouse is entitled to 50% of the pension. Likewise, if the spouse works as subject to Act No. 5510 or abroad, he/she is entitled to 50% of the pension (Article 34/I, a of Act No. 5510).

If only children exist as beneficiaries, the pension is to be divided among the children under the condition that each child receives at most 25% of the pension (Article 34/I, b of Act No. 5510).

Parents are entitled to a pension only if the total amount of pension awarded to the spouse and children is less than the amount of the pension of the insured person. In this case, the difference is paid in equal shares to the parents of the insured. However, each of their shares cannot exceed 25% of the insured person's pension (Article 34/I, d of Act No. 5510).

If only spouse and parents of the deceased insured are sharing the pension, 75% of the pension is to be allocated to the spouse. The rest is to be divided between the mother and father of the insured.

If the spouse, children and parents are all beneficiaries, the share of the spouse is 50%, the share of the single child 25% and the mother and father share the remaining 25%. If there are two or more children since the total amount of distributed pension cannot exceed the amount of old-age pension allocable to the insured, proportional reductions must be made (Article 34/III of Act No. 5510).

466. Since civil servants started work after the entry into force of Act No. 5510, they are subject the above-mentioned rules; to those who acquired the status before, Act No. 5434 will find a place of application. Pursuant to Article 68 of Act No. 5434, the basis for widow's and orphan's pension is the retirement, ordinary or job invalidity pension awarded or to be awarded to the participant. This pension is to be distributed among the beneficiaries at the rated fixed by the Act itself. The total of the rates cannot exceed the amount of the main pension. Thus, if necessary, a proportional reduction shall be made (Article 68/V of Act No. 5434).

If the spouse is childless, 75%, with children, 50% of the main pension is allocated. If there are the spouse and one child, the spouse receives 60% and the child 30% of the pension. If the spouse is also a participant or draws retirement, ordinary or job invalidity pensions, she/he is also entitled to receive 50% of the pension. This rule is quite advantageous when compared with the regulations governing pensions for wage earners and self-employed persons.

The share of the child and of each of the parents cannot exceed 25%. If there is no spouse, the spouse's share is added to the shares of the children and parents at equal rates. However, the total amount of pensions cannot exceed 50% of the main pension, if there is one person left, 80%, if there are two persons, and 100% if there are three persons (Article 68/VI of Act No. 5434).

II. Calculation of Lump-Sum Payment

467. The amount of the lump-sum payment is the total amount of paid contributions for the invalidity, old age and survivors insurance branches. The paid contributions for each calendar year are to be updated until the calendar year of the pension claim is submitted. The amount which will be reimbursed to shareholders is determined in terms of their share (Article 36 of Act No. 5510). If the deceased insured has no child, the spouse is entitled to receive 75% of the lump-sum payment. If he/she has children, the spouse benefits from 50%. A child's share cannot exceed 25%.

Chapter 5. Common Issues in Long-term Insurance Branches

§1. Insured Period

468. The insured period is a common condition for pension entitlement in all long-term insurance branches. Act No. 5510 requires a minimum insured period to receive old-age, survivors or invalidity pensions. The insured period starts from the date on which the insurance holder enters into the scope of long-term insurance branches for the first time. Whether the insurance holder starts work as subject to Act No. 5510 or other abrogated acts has no importance. The first working day under cover of long-term insurance branches is also the start of the insured period (Article 38/I of Act No. 5510). Those who benefit only from short-term insurance branches, such as industrial accidents and occupational diseases, do not enter into the long-term insurance branches; therefore, their insured period does not commence. The insured period ends up by a written request of the insurance holder for the pension. With respect to the survivors' insurance, the decease of the insurance holder ends the insured period (Article 38/III of Act No. 5510). For civil servants, the insured period is the period between the starting day of the insured status and the last day of the month in which the insurance holder is approved by a competent authority to be transferred to retirement from duty pursuant to Article 48 and his/her connection is terminated.

469. There is no need that the insurance holder works actively during the insured period. Thus, the insured period comprises the active working periods, as well as non-working periods. Therefore, the years insured are not equivalent to the number of days for which insurance contributions have been paid, that causes a duality under the current system: the number of paid contribution days and the length of the insured period are set as separate conditions for receiving pensions from long-term insurance branches. Periods which have not been registered may be fixed by a declaratory judgment.[336] In that case, premium days which are fixed by the Court's decision will be taken into account.

470. In addition, to prevent premature retirements, the insured period of persons who were insured under old age, invalidity and survivors' schemes before reaching the age of 18, commences on the date on which the insured person has completed the age of 18. Nevertheless, for those who are subject to Article 4/I, a, contributions paid before the age of 18 shall be taken into account while calculating contribution days.

§2. Indebted Periods

471. Not only active working time but also 'indebted periods' are taken into account, with respect to old age, invalidity and survivors' insurance branches. The

336. *See supra* paras 196–201.

insured employee may owe for periods for which due contributions were not paid. Thus, these periods are taken into consideration while determining the insured period and paid contribution days.[337]

472. The Act fixes the indebting possibility for specific cases. Thus, out of the below-mentioned periods, no indebting possibility exists:

- Confinement and maternity leave: Act No. 5510 recognizes two new periods which can be indebted by female insurance holders.[338] Whether confinements before the entry into force of Act No. 5510 can be owed was a debatable issue. Following conflicting jurisprudence, the Court of Cassation recognized the possibility to owe these periods even passed before the entry into force of Act No. 5510.[339] Another debated issue is whether confinements before the insured woman has acquired insured status for the very first time can be owed. Neither the Social Security Institution nor the Court of Cassation accepts the indebtment of confinement periods passed before the first insurance holdership.[340]

  As we mentioned above, during the eight weeks before and after the confinement, it is forbidden for female wage earners to work. Therefore, no contribution is paid. Likewise, six months of maternity leave is unpaid. Female civil servants receive their full salary during sixteen weeks of maternity leave. However, they are also able to ask for non-paid maternity leave of up to twenty-four months (Article 108/B of Act No. 656). The female insurance holders subjected to Article 4/I a and c may owe for these unpaid periods. There is no limit with regard to the number of confinements that can be owed. Therefore, women wage earners or civil servants may owe contributions for many periods.[341]

  The second opportunity recognized to female insurance holders is that they can owe up to two years following the confinement. Only wage earners were able to benefit from this opportunity.[342] Act No. 6652[343] extended this opportunity to Self-Employed or civil servant female insurance holders also. Pursuant to Article 41/I, a of Act No. 5510, the insurance holders must not work in any place during

337. *See also* A. Güzel/A.R. Okur/N. Caniklioğlu, n. 7, pp. 510–533; A.N. Sözer, n. 70, pp. 470–489; M. Şakar, n. 7, pp. 325–332.

338. *See also* H. Duygu Özer, 'Doğum Borçlanması', in *Prof. Dr. Ali Güzel'e Armağan, II* (Istanbul, 2010), pp. 1137–1157; E. Özkaraca, 'Doğum Borçlanması', 26, *Legal-İSGHD*(2010), pp. 501–524.

339. About this issue Court of Cass, 10th Ch., 25.02.2010, 2009/8312, K. 2010/2516 noted by E. Özkaraca, 'Doğum Borçlanması', 26, *Legal-İSGHD*(2010), pp. 503–524; also noted by K. Arıcı, '5510 Sayılı Kanun'un Yürürlük Tarihinden Önceki Dönemde Doğum Borçlanması Yapan Kadın Sigortalılar (4A)da Doğum Borçlanması Yapabilirler', *Sicil Der.*(Eylül, 2010), pp. 159–167; noted by C. Tuncay, 'Doğum İzni Borçlanması', 27, *Legal-İSGHD*(2010), pp. 1015–1023.

340. Court of Cass., Gen. Ass., 18.5.2011, 10-311/322, *Legal-İSGHD*(32/2011), pp. 1478–1489, for critics *see* S. Ocak, 'Sigorta Başlangıcından Önceki Doğumlar Nedeniyle Hizmet Borçlanması', *Legal-İSGHD*(2011/32), pp. 1493–1522; A.N. Sözer, n. 70, pp. 479–480.

341. D. Özer, 'Doğum Borçlanması', pp. 1149–1150; A. Güzel/A.R. Okur/N. Caniklioğlu, n. 7, p. 512.

342. For the view that such restriction is against the principle of equality, A. Güzel/A.R. Okur/N. Caniklioğlu, n. 7, p. 513; D. Özer, 'Doğum Borçlanması', p. 1150; E. Özkaraca, 'Doğum Borçlanması', p. 523.

343. OJ, 11 Sep. 2014, No. 29116 (Mük.).

this period, and her child must be alive. The women insurance holders can use this right three times. Therefore, they are enabled to owe these periods for up to six years.

- Military service: In addition, contributions due for time spent in military service periods may be owed under the existing system. Therefore, the period passed under compulsory military service may be taken into account in terms of the insured period and paid contribution days (Article 41/I, b of Act No. 5510). A period passed for a reserve officer could also be owed.
- Unpaid Leaves: For those who are subjected to Article 4/I, c of Act No. 5510, they may also owe for unpaid leave periods (Article 41/I, c of Act No. 5510).
- Periods during doctoral studies or special education in medicine, either passed in Turkey or abroad (Article 41/I, d of Act No. 5510) may be owed.
- Training period for lawyers could also be owed for long-term insurance branches (Article 41/I, e).
- For insurance holders who are arrested or placed under police custody for any offence and then acquitted, such periods may be owed (Article 41/I, f of Act No. 5510).
- Periods passed during strikes or lock-outs may also be owed following the end of the strike or lock-out (Article 41/I, g of Act No. 5510).
- Periods under voluntary assistantship for medical doctors may be owed. Voluntary assistantship exists only for foreign medics who are accepted on to an assistantship without a salary. If these medics have a Turkish nationality after their assistantship is completed, they may owe for these periods (Article 41/I, h of Act No. 5510).[344]
- Individuals who resign from their duties due to election laws, the unemployed terms between the date of resignation and the beginning of the month following the date of the election may be owed (Article 41/I, ı of Act No. 5510).
- Those who were part of a faculty or high school and participated in the Turkish Armed Forces or Security General Directorate may owe periods passed during their education (Article 41/I, j of Act No. 5510).
- Although part-time workers are compulsorily insured, the number of contribution paid days is less than thirty days in a month. The part-time insurance holder has the right to voluntarily pay his contributions for the rest of the month.[345] Nevertheless, voluntary insurance affects the future. Act No. 6111 brought a possibility for part-time workers to owe the non-working periods passed before. For those who work part-time have the right to owe contributions for the deficit days of the part-time worked months.
- Students who sent abroad to have education without being insured returned back after having accomplished their education and have completed their compulsory service may owe their periods of study abroad. The study periods before reaching the age of 18 shall not be taken into account.

473. To owe these periods, the insurance holder or right holders must give a written requirement. Only insurance holders or their dependants are entitled to that

344. A. Güzel/A.R. Okur/N. Caniklioğlu, n. 7, p. 518; A.N. Sözer, n. 70, pp. 474–476.
345. *See supra* paras 89–90.

right. Therefore, while requesting, the person must have been registered as an insurance holder under the system.[346] Whether actually he/she works does not carry importance.[347]

474. The insurance holder must pay the total amount of contributions within the utmost one month following the notification of their debt. An income level between the lower and upper limits of Act No. 5510 shall be chosen by the insurance holder. The contribution rate is 32% of this income level (Article 41/I of Act No. 5510). The non-payment of the debt within one month does not end the right; however, another request is required.

475. The service periods of Turkish citizens working abroad can cause a problem with respect to the social security rights of these persons. If there is an international agreement between the Turkish Republic and the country where the employee works, the service periods performed there will be counted. However, in the absence of such an agreement, their service periods could not be aggregated to their service periods in Turkey. With the aim of taking these periods into account, Act No. 2147 in 1978 dealt with the appraisal of Turkish citizens' services performed abroad with regards to social security.[348] This Act was replaced by Act No. 3201.[349]

476. According to this Act, Turkish citizens who worked abroad or who were housewives there may ask to be indebted for these periods. Having Turkish nationality on submission of this requirement is not sufficient to benefit from such a right. The insurance holders must have Turkish nationality during the whole period whilst they are abroad (Article 1 of Act No. 3201). To owe these periods, there is no requirement that insurance holders must come back to Turkey definitely.[350]

477. However, indebted periods are composed of worked periods which are approved by an appropriate certificate, unemployed periods up to one year and the whole or partial periods passed as a housewife. The periods before the age of 18 cannot be owed (Article 1 of Act No. 3201).

478. The insurance holder has the right to choose the level of contribution payment between the lower and upper limits of daily income fixed by Act No. 5510. The contribution amount is 32% of their daily income (Article 4/I of Act No. 3201).

346. For details, *see* S. Ocak, 'Hizmet Borçlanmalarında Talep Tarihindeki Statünün Borçlanılan Sürelere Etkisi', *Sicil Der.*(Aralık, 2010), pp. 153–168.
347. A. Güzel/A.R. Okur/N. Caniklioğlu, n. 7, p. 522.
348. OJ, 7 Jun. 1978, No. 16309.
349. OJ, 22 May 1985, No. 18761; for details, *see* H. Ergin, 'Yurtdışı Hizmet Borçlanmasında Son Gelişmeler', *Sicil Der.*(Aralık, 2009), pp. 163–167; A. Güzel/S. Ocak, 'Yurt Dışı Hizmet Borçlanmasına İlişkin Yeni Düzenlemeler ve Yargı Kararları Hakkında Genel Bir Değerlendirme', 12, *Legal-İSGHD*(2006), pp. 1310–1354; A.R. Okur, 'Yurt Dışı Hizmet Borçlanması ve Türk Vatandaşlığı Koşulu', 10, *Çalışma ve Toplum Der.*(2006/3), pp. 101–133.
350. Such a requirement is annulled by the Constitutional Court: Cons. Court, 12 Dec. 2002, 36/198, OJ, 25 Apr. 2003, No. 25089.

The amount of the debt must be paid within three months following its notification. In case of non-payment, a re-request is required. These indebted periods passed abroad can be counted as insured periods for the purposes of calculating invalidity, old age and survivors' pensions. The date of entry into the insurance system is also carried back as many as the number of indebted days. In determining the age limit, this entry date carries big importance.

§3. Increment of Actual Service Periods

479. With respect to certain occupations which are deemed to be particularly exhausting, such as underground work in mining or work at under the sea, actual service periods are increased by additional periods to enable the insured to acquire old-age pensions earlier. Act No. 5510 determines such occupations and additional periods in a new way compared to that of Act No. 506.[351]

480. Only wage earners and civil servants benefit from service period increments. The insurance holder must work actively at jobs and in workplaces fixed by the Act. Article 40 of Act No. 5510 also fixes the number of days corresponding to every 360 days of the service terms passed in these workplaces. Those works and workplaces, as well as the number of days, are determined under fifteen subcategories such as lead and arsenic work for 60 days, glass factories and workshops for 60 days, mercury production works industry for 90 days, cement factories for 60 days, coke factories and thermal power plants for 60 days, aluminium factories for 60 days, iron and steel factories for 90 days, casting factories for 60 days, acid-producing factories for 90 days, underground works for 180 days, works done with radioactive materials for 90 days, underwater or in pressurized conditions for 60 days, Turkish Armed forces for 90 days, police forces and National Intelligence Organization for 90 days, and fire departments and fire extinguishing works for 90 days, journalists and those who work in media for 90 days, press-card owners working at the news department of the Turkish Radio and Television Corporation for 90 days, the members of Turkish Parliament, vice-Presidents and ministers for 90 days(Article 40/II of Act No. 5510).

481. For every 360 days, these extra days shall be added to the paid contribution days of the insurance holders. Nevertheless, the maximum increment period cannot be more than five years for military forces, police forces, and for the Intelligent Institution, it is eight years (Article 40/III of Act No. 5510). Furthermore, half of these periods up to three years shall be discounted from the retirement age limit.

482. There also exist assumed service periods, which are only valid for civil servants. Officers, reserve officers, non-commissioned officers, specialist gendarme and officers benefit from assumed service periods. Assumed service periods are added to actual service periods, as with regards to, wars and military conflicts, as well as

351. For general evaluation, *see* H. Ergin, '5510 Sayılı Kanun'da Fiili Hizmet Süresi Zammı Uygulaması', *Sicil Der.*(Eylül, 2009), pp. 183–191.

flight and diving personnel. The assumed service periods cannot be more than three years. These periods are not taken into account while determining whether the insurance holder has satisfied the required conditions of age, insured period and the number of contribution paid days. In addition, assumed periods are not taken into account while calculating retirement gratuity.[352]

§4. Suppression and Re-allocation of Pensions

I. Resume to Work While Receiving Old-Age Pension

483. One of the most controversial issues of the reform was about re-employment while drawing a pension. The low amount of pensions forces pension holders to continue to work after their retirement. The premature retirement policy has been affected by this practice. In 1986, legislation permitted insured persons to benefit from old-age pensions while remaining employed. The principle was that if a person drawing an old-age pension was re-employed as an insured person, the old-age pension would be terminated from the date on which he/she began working. However, insurance holders had the right to continue drawing an old-age pension while working under the condition that the social security support contribution was deducted from their wage. The new Act No. 5510 maintains this opportunity with certain restrictions. However, new rules shall apply only to those who are insured for the first time after the entry into force of the Act.[353]

484. For those who are insured before the entry into force of Act No. 5510, the related provisions of abrogated acts shall find a place of application (Trans. Article 14/I of Act No. 5510).[354] If the insured wage earner submitted a written request, the pension would continue to be paid. However, a social security support contribution was deducted from the monthly income at a rate of 30% if the new employment is also subjected to Article 4/I, a, however, if the new work is subjected to Article 4/I, b, no support contribution is paid (Trans. Article 14/I, a of Act No. 5510). The right to work and receive pensions at the same time was also granted to Self-Employed insured persons. Social security support contribution at the rate of 15% is revoked by Act No. 6663.[355](Trans. Article 14/I, b of Act No. 5510). However, for civil servants, if the person drawing a pension resumes duties subject to Act No. 5434, the retirement pension was terminated following the month in which the appointment was made (Article 99 of Act No. 5434). The pension shall be re-allocated as from the date on which the retired civil servant quits this new job, without any need for

352. A. Güzel/A.R. Okur/N. Caniklioğlu, n. 7, p. 542; A.N. Sözer, n. 70, pp. 396397.
353. For details, *see* A.R. Okur, 'Çalışmanın Gelir ve Aylıklara Etkisi',in *Prof. Dr. Sarper Süzek'e Armağan, C. II*(Istanbul, 2011), pp. 2141–2179.
354. F. Başterzi, n. 294, pp. 337–355; Ş. Ertürk, 'Sosyal Güvenlik Destek Primi Ödeyerek Çalışanların Sağlık Yardımlarından Yararlanması', *Sicil Der.*(Mart, 2011), pp. 221–229; A.N. Sözer, n. 70, pp. 398–403.
355. OJ, 10 Feb. 2016, No. 29620.

a written requirement (Article 30/II of Act No. 5335).[356] Nevertheless, retired civil servants may also work as a wage earner or Self-Employed and receive pensions at the same time.

485. For those who are insured for the first time under Act No. 5510, a person drawing an old-age pension may be re-employed as an insured person, but then the old-age pension is suppressed from the date the employment begins (Article 30/III of Act No. 5510). To suppress a pension, it is not important whether the work is performed in Turkey or abroad. Following a definitive end to employment, the old-age pension will be re-calculated, taking into account the additional paid contributions.

486. However, for activities subject to Article 4/I, b, the Act makes an exemption: If those who receive an old-age pension, resume a Self-Employed activity subject to Article 4/I-b, they may ask for the non-termination of their old-age pension. In that case, they receive old-age pensions and work as subject to Article 4/I b of Act No. 5510 at the same time (Article 30/III, b of Act No. 5510). The legislator separates independent activities with regard to re-employment. Therefore, for those who are subjected to Article 4/I, b, mainly Self-Employed persons, may continue to carry out their activities and receive the old-age pension in the same period (Article 58/I, b of RSIP). In addition, retired wage earners and civil servants may also resume carrying on an independent activity and receiving their pensions. The duty to pay a social security support contribution is also abolished by Act No. 6663 (Article 30/II, b of Act No. 5510). In that case, those who are re-employed while receiving an old-age pension are not deemed insurance holders (Article 6/I, n of Act No. 5510). Therefore, if they have suffered from an industrial accident, they are not entitled to receive any benefits from industrial accidents and occupational diseases insurance branch.[357]

II. Suppression of Invalidity Pensions

487. If an insurance holder who receives invalidity pension starts working either in Turkey or abroad, his/her invalidity pension will be suppressed as of the payment period following his/her date of starting work (Article 27/III of Act No. 5510). Whether the new activity is subject to Article 4/I, a, b or c does not carry any importance. Unlike old-age pensions, the Act does not provide the possibility to work by paying social security contribution pension, even for those who are subjected to Article 4/I-b of Act No. 5510.

488. When such an insurance holder quits work and asks for a re-allocation of their invalidity pension, the invalidity pension will be re-calculated and re-allocated under the condition that he/she is subjected to medical control and it is proven that the invalidity persists (Article 27/III of Act No. 5510).

356. Adopted by Art. 2 of Act No. 6385 dated 10 Jan. 2013, OJ, 19 Jan. 2013, No. 28533; A.N. Sözer, n. 70, pp. 399–400.
357. A. Güzel/A.R. Okur/N. Caniklioğlu, n. 7, p. 568.

§5. ACCUMULATION RULES

489. Since under each insurance branch, different pensions are available for insured persons, the accumulation of different pensions is regulated by Article 54 of Act No. 5510 in the following manner:

- *Old-age pension and invalidity pension:* If an insured person is entitled to receive both old-age and invalidity pensions, he/she is awarded the higher of these two but if their amounts are equal, only the old-age pension (Article 54/I, a, 1 of Act No. 5510). Since the contribution is common for invalidity, old age and survivors insurance branches, only benefits from one branch are to be paid.[358]
- *Invalidity Pension and a lump-sum payment for old-age pension:* Act No. 5510 has no rule regarding the accumulation of lump-sum payment with invalidity pension. However, if the insured is entitled to receive an invalidity pension, as well as a lump-sum payment under old-age insurance, only an invalidity pension would be allocated.[359]
- *Invalidity, job invalidity or old-age pension and pension due to deceased spouse:* If the insured survivor is entitled to receive invalidity, job invalidity or old-age pension due to his/her own employment, and also survivors' pension due to his/her deceased spouse, both pensions shall be allocated, while two different contributions are paid (Article 54/I, a, 2 of Act No. 5510).
- *Children entitled to receive pensions due to both parents*: If children are entitled to receive pensions following the death of an insured mother and father, the full amount of the higher and one-half of the lower pension is allocated (Article 54/I, a, 3 of Act No. 5510). If the daughter of the deceased insured marries, her pension is terminated. In the event of the death of her husband, whichever pension is higher, the father's or the husband's is to be paid.
- *Parents entitled to receive pensions due to many children:* If the parents are entitled to receive a pension due to many children, among pensions, he/she is awarded the full amount of the highest and the one-half of the second-highest pension (Article 54/I, a, 5 of Act No. 5510).
- *Survivors' pension due to parents and due to spouse:* If the spouse or child is entitled to receive survivors' pension due to his/her parents, and due to his/her spouse, the Act grants the beneficiary the right to choose between the two pensions (Article 54/I, a, 6 of Act No. 5510).
- *Job invalidity pension and invalidity pension:* If the insurance holder, who receives job invalidity pension under Act No. 5510, resumes working and becomes re-insured and is allocated invalidity pension, he/she is awarded the higher of these two but if their amounts are equal, only the job invalidity pension, if he/she is entitled to receive job invalidity and old-age pensions at the same time, he/she will be allocated both pensions (Article 54/I, a, 6 of Act No. 5510).

358. M. Çenberci, n. 80, p. 621; A. Güzel/A.R. Okur, n. 7, p. 569; A.N. Sözer, n. 70, p. 491.
359. A. Güzel/A.R. Okur/N. Caniklioğlu, n. 7, p. 569.

- *The end of a marriage because of the death of the spouse:* If the spouse is entitled to receive a pension due to his/her first and second spouses, the Act grants the beneficiary spouse the right to choose between the two pensions (Article 54/I, a, 7 of Act No. 5510).

490. In the case of accumulation of short-term insurance benefits with long-term insurance benefits, the accumulation of pensions and allowances are as follows:

- *Pensions and allowance from insurance for industrial accidents and occupational diseases:* If the insured person is entitled to receive both old age or invalidity or job invalidity pensions and permanent incapacity allowances from the insurance branches for industrial accidents and occupational diseases, this person or his/her survivors is entitled to the full amount of the higher pension and one-half of the lower pension, as contributions for these insurance branches are separate. If their amounts are equal, the full amount of the permanent incapacity allowance and the one-half of the pension shall be allocated.
- *Survivors' pension and permanent incapacity allowance:* If the insurance holder is entitled to receive permanent incapacity allowance due to an industrial accident or occupational disease and survivors' pension due to his/her deceased spouse, the beneficiary will receive both the pensions (Article 54/I, b, 1 of Act No. 5510).
- *Allowances due to mother and father separately:* If the child receives death allowances from both mother and father, the beneficiary will receive the full amount of the higher allowance and one half of the lower allowance (Article 54/II, b, 2 of Act No. 5510).

§6. Coincidence and Aggregation of Different Social Security Regimes

491. Since the social insurance status of the insurance holder is a determinant factor in the entitlement conditions for benefits, if an insurance holder works under different statuses in the same period, the problem of designating certain periods under the juristic status as 4/I a, b or c is revealed as important.

I. Coincidence of Active Periods under Article 4/I a, b or c

492. The insurance holder may work being subject to different insurance statuses in the same period; such as a person may work with a contract of employment and carry out an independent activity at the same time. However, the principle of oneness is admitted in the social security system. Thus, if there is a period subject to different social insurance regimes, it should be determined which one has the priority.[360] According to Article 53/I of Act No. 5510, if the insurance holder works at

360. *See* A.N. Sözer/C. Saraç, 'Sosyal Sigorta İlişkisinde Çokluk: Sigortalılık Hallerinin, Tiplerinin ve Sürelerinin Birleşmesi', *Sicil Der.*(Aralık, 2008), pp. 152–159; M.H. Kahraman, '5510 Sayılı

the same time as being subject to Article 4/I a, b or c, his/her social insurance status will be determined pursuant to Article 4/I c of the Act. Therefore, if a person works as a civil servant and has a partnership in commercial cooperation, his/her insurance status shall be determined pursuant to Article 4/I, c of Act No. 5510. The absolute precedence is recognized to the civil servants' status. Even if the insurance holder has been registered as Self-Employed before, by the start of civil servant status, the status of 4/I b will be terminated and contributions will be paid according to Article 4/I c.

493. If the insurance holder works as a wage earner and carries out an independent activity at the same time, the insurance status will be determined pursuant to Article 4/I, a of Act No. 5510. Thus, the status of 4/I a will be predominant (Article 53/I of Act No. 5510).[361] Nevertheless, for periods which fall out of the scope of contribution payment under Article 4/I, a, the insurance holder may wish to be subjected to Article 4/I, b. Upon his/her written request, that insurance holder will pay contributions. In that case, he/she shall be subjected to both Article 4/I a and b. Those contribution paid periods shall be considered, with respect to, benefits provided by short-term and long-term insurance branches, as passed under item 4/I, a of Act No. 5510. However, with respect to industrial accidents or occupational diseases, as passed under item 4/I, b of Act No. 5510 (Article 53/I of Act No. 5510).

494. The Act restricts to be registered under item 4/I, a of Act No. 5510 for those who are subjected to Article 4/I, b. They shall not be registered as an employee in the company which belongs to them or of which they have a partnership (Article 53/II of Act No. 5510). The reason behind such an exemption lies on the different entitlement conditions for pensions. As examined above, wage earners are subjected to lighter conditions than Self-Employed persons in terms of receiving an old-age pension. Therefore, many insurance holders tried to register themselves as employees in their own companies. The legislator prevents such abuse by that exemption.[362]

II. Aggregation of Services Subjected to Different Social Security Regimes

495. The fragmented nature of the social security system also caused assessment problems for periods subjected to different social security regimes. Before the three institutions were unified, the question had been: under which institution were pensions to be allocated to the insured who has worked under different social security regimes over the course of his/her life? To solve this problem, by Act No. 228 in 1961, for the first time the aggregation of services was inserted into the system.

Kanunda Tanımlı Sosyal Sigorta Statüleri ve Çakşan Sigortalılık İlişkisi', *Prof. Dr. Ali Rıza Okur'a Armağan, Marmara Üniversitesi Hukuk Fakültesi Hukuk Araştırmaları Dergisi*C. 20, S. 1 (2014), pp. 875–893; F.B. Savaş Kutsal, n. 25, pp. 16–29.

361. This rule is adopted by an amendment made by Act No. 6111 of 13 Feb. 2011. Therefore, these principles will find place of application after 1 Mar. 2011. About new regulation, *see* M. Şakar, '4/b'liliğe Veda! (Ya da İsteyene Hem 4/a Hem 4/b! …)', *Sicil Der.*(Mart, 2011), pp. 215–220.

362. A. Güzel/A.R. Okur/N. Caniklioğlu, n. 7, p. 139.

This Act was later replaced by Act No. 2829.[363] In fact, the problem had arisen from the patchwork nature of the social security system: wage earners, Self-Employed persons and civil servants, each being governed by different regimes. By the unification of these three systems, the problem did not disappear. Although the institutional unification has been realized under the roof of the Social Security Institution, conditions to entitle long-term insurance benefits are not same for those who are subjected to Article 4/I, a (mainly wage earners), 4/I, b (mainly the Self-Employed persons) and 4/I, c (mainly civil servants). Therefore, the problem is not any more the aggregation of different service periods but is determining according to which the pension allocation is governed. This question is very much related to the entitlement conditions to receive a pension.

496. Periods to be aggregated are those passed as subjected to Article 4/I, a, 4/I, b and 4/I, c. Furthermore, through specific statutory regulations enacted from time to time, the insured has been given the right to be indebted, which means he/she may owe contributions for the periods during which strikes and lock-outs, military service, work abroad and restored periods occur. Such indebted periods may also be aggregated.

497. For those who acquired insurance holder status before the entry into force of Act No. 5510, the previous rules of the abrogated Act No. 2829 will be applied (Trans. Article 2/end of Act No. 5510): Within the last seven actual service years, the status under which the longest service period has passed is the status according to which the pension is allocated to beneficiaries. Thus, it must be determined under which status the longest service period was passed during a period of 360 x 7= 2,520 days. It must be noted that contributions must have been paid during these seven years. Thus, the meaning of 'year' here does not necessarily refer to the immediately previous seven years, but to the final seven-year period during which contributions were paid. If the duration of service periods are equal, the final social security regime is applicable to the payments of pensions.

498. For those who acquired insurance holder status for the first time under Act No. 5510, if they have worked as subject to different statuses of Act No. 5510, 4/I, a, b or c, the status having the longest period of service in the whole service period shall be dominant (Article 53/VI of Act No. 5510). Therefore, the conditions for pension allocation will be determined according to that status. For example, if an insurance holder has worked for ten years as a wage earner, but for the rest of his/her life was self-employed, his/her pension shall be granted according to the conditions for self-employed persons. If service periods are equal, the last insured status shall be taken into account (Article 53/VI of Act No. 5510).

499. In certain cases, the last regime to which the insured is subject to is to be applicable. In cases of forced retirement due to age, invalidity, survivors' pension,

363. OJ, 27 May 1983, No. 19059.

the appointment or election to certain tasks that the term of office is fixed by statutes, and in the case of a change of the insured's social insurance institution by statutory regulation, the last social security regime will be applicable.

500. In certain cases, the insured is entitled to receive retirement gratification or severance payment. If the final job in which the insured works is subject to Article 4/I, c, even if the old-age pension is allocated according to rules applicable to 4/I, a or 4/I, b than Article 4/I, c, the insured is entitled to receive a retirement gratuity for the periods for which the contributions were paid. If the insured was working under an employment contract, under certain conditions, he/she might receive a severance payment, even though his/her old-age pension is granted according to rules applicable to those subjected to Article 4/I, c.

Part V. Universal Health Insurance

Introduction

501. The fundamental change implemented by the reform is on the health insurance system. Before the reform, healthcare services were provided under the social insurance system. Thus, the basis for receiving these benefits depends upon membership in a specific social security institution. Each social security regulation had its own conditions under which healthcare services were received. Therefore, variation both in conditions for receiving healthcare benefits and in their amount and the quality existed among different groups. For those who were not covered by social insurance and who were out of the scope of social assistance and services, the system did not provide any healthcare. With respect to healthcare services, 85.9% of the population was under a social security system. Those not covered by those systems may have only received very limited social assistance after being granted a 'green card'. That system was far from providing satisfactory healthcare to the whole population. Therefore, the need for the unification of the health system has been stated several times by different groups. However, the path that the government has chosen in order to achieve that unification is a strongly debated issue in Turkey.

502. In different parts of the legislation, such as Act No. 5434 on the Pension Fund, Act No. 657 on Civil Servants, and Act No. 3359 on Healthcare Services, the establishment of universal health insurance was envisaged, and many drafts had been prepared before the enactment of Act No. 5510.[364] However, it took a long time for it to be implemented.

503. The Universal Health Insurance Draft, which was prepared according to the World Bank and IMF model, was replaced with another: the Draft Bill on Universal Health Insurance and then the Draft Bill on Social Insurance and Universal Health Insurance. In fact, these drafts overlapped with a Transformation in Health Programme carried out by the Ministry of Health.[365] Under this framework, 2004 witnessed a series of new acts, which either brought improvements to the existing

364. About the historical evaluation of healthcare services in Turkey, *see* A.R. Okur/H. Ergin, 'Türkiye'de Sağlık Reformunun Geçmişi ve Geleceği', in *Prof. Dr. Devrim Ulucan'a Armağan* (Istanbul, 2008), pp. 599–629; A. Güzel/A.R. Okur/ N. Caniklioğlu, n. 7, pp. 712–720.
365. Proposal for Reform in the Social Security System, 29 Jul. 2004, pp. 34–35.

system or re-structured it with this perspective.[366] On the one hand, the Ministry of Finance is empowered to privatize (sell) immovable properties, health institutions, belonging to the Ministry of Health.[367] On the other hand, all kinds of health institutions, movable and immovable properties, rights and duties belonging to ministries, their affiliated institutions, and other public institutions and entities, public establishments, in particular to the Social Insurance Institution have been transferred to the Ministry of Finance by Act No. 5283 of 6 January 2005.[368] Act No. 5283, which received the harsh criticism of social partners,[369] was brought before the Constitutional Court for the alleged incompatibility of its transfer methods with the Constitution. Although the Act has a very large scope, in practice, only hospitals belonging to the Social Insurance Institution and the public entity responsible for postal services were transferred to the Ministry of Health. Other health centres belonging to public institutions remained untouched.[370] Therefore, hospitals belonging to the Social Insurance Institution were transferred to the Ministry of Health. In addition, Act No. 5258, the Family Medicine Pilot Project, was implemented on 9 December 2004 as the first step towards Universal Health Insurance.[371]

As the last step, by the enactment of Act No. 5510, universal health insurance would have entered into force from 1 January 2007. However, implementation of such a fundamental change took time. Therefore, some part of the provisions of Act No. 5510 has entered into force on 1 July 2008 (Article 108/I, c of Act No. 5510); however, it was not until on 1 January 2012 that all provisions related to universal health insurance came into force.[372]

504. Act No. 5510 regulates 'universal health insurance' under a separate heading than other social insurance risks. The definition of the insurance holder, the commencement of the insured period, the registration of insured persons, and provided healthcare services are regulated in a different manner than other social insurance branches. By Act No. 5510, healthcare services were separated from monetary benefits granted according to insurance principles.

505. The Act describes universal health insurance as insurance which ensures the maintenance of an individual's health and finances the costs of expenditures

366. A.N. Sözer, 'Genel Sağlık Sigortası Kimin Yararına?', *Mercek*(Ocak, 2005), pp. 22–27.
367. Act No. 5220, OJ, 21 Jul. 2004, No. 25529.
368. OJ, 19 Jan. 2005, No. 25705.
369. *See* A.N. Sözer, 'Genel Sağlık Sigortası Kimin Yararına?', pp. 27–28.
370. A. Güzel/A.R. Okur, N. Caniklioğlu, n. 7, p. 719.
371. OJ, 9 Dec. 2004, No. 25665; *see* A. Güzel/A.R. Okur, N. Caniklioğlu, n. 7, pp. 718–719.
372. For general evaluation, *see* A.N. Sözer, 'Sosyal Sigortalar ve Genel Sağlık Sigortası Kanun Tasarısında Genel Sağlık Sigortasına İlişkin Düzenlemeler', 7, *Legal-İSGHD*(2005), pp. 1176–1190; The same author, Genel Sağlık Sigortası', in *Yeni Düzenlemeler Çerçevesinde Sosyal Güvenlik Mevzuatı* (Istanbul, 2007), pp. 134–147; A.R. Okur, 'Sosyal Güvenlik Reformu ve Genel Sağlık Sigortası', 12, *Legal-İSGHD*(2006), pp. 1286–1307; The same author, 'Genel Sağlık Sigortası', *Yeni Sosyal Güvenlik Sistemi* (Istanbul, 2010), pp. 111–125; H. Ergin, 'Genel Sağlık Sigortasında Gelinen Son Durum', *Sicil Der.*(Eylül, 2008), pp. 112–128; K. Arıcı, 'Türk Genel Sağlık Sigortası Sisteminin Yeterliliği Sorunu', *Sicil Der.*(Mart, 2009), pp. 148–156; For different dates for entry into force A.N. Sözer, *Türk Genel Sağlık Sigortası* (Istanbul, 2014), pp. 7–8.

occurred in case of illness (Article 3/8 of Act No. 5510). Not only is the treatment of illnesses under cover of health insurance, but it also covers preventive medicine.

506. Act No. 5510 recognizes the entire population residing in Turkey as insured for universal health insurance. Not only Turkish citizens and their dependants but also stateless persons and refugees, as well as foreigners who have resided in Turkey for longer than one year are under cover of the universal health insurance system (Article 60 of Act No. 5510). Act No. 5510 introduced universal healthcare insurance supported by the means principle. Thus, Beveridgean elements within the social security system have gained importance. Nevertheless, an insurance characteristic is still apparent in most aspects.[373]

507. The new system covers not only the entire population but also all health risks, whatever their cause. Unlike the previous system, health services provided in case of industrial accidents and occupational diseases, sickness, as well as maternity procedures, are unified under one insurance branch.

508. Health service providers are determined on three levels: first stage service provision is based on Family Medicine. The other stages would be determined by the Ministry of Health by concluding agreements with service providers. Universal health insurance does not provide any health service. Therefore, healthcare services are provided by outsourcing. The Institution makes agreements with service providers found in Turkey or abroad. Insurance holders and their dependants have the right to choose the one they prefer under the condition of respecting the transfer chain. Before the reform, the Social Insurance Institution provided healthcare services in its own hospitals and health institutions. However, for Self-Employed persons, healthcare was provided on the basis of agreements concluded between Bağ-Kur and service providers at an agreed price. Through the unification of the institutions, such a difference has disappeared. The reform movement aims to change the very fundamentals of the system through provisions that certain authors interpreted as indications that the system is to be privatized.[374]

373. K. Arıcı, 'Genel Sağlık Sigortası', p. 152.
374. A.N. Sözer, 'Genel Sağlık Sigortasına İlişkin Düzenlemeler', p. 1189.

Chapter 1. Field of Application

§1. Territorial Field of Application

509. The fundamental condition to get benefits from universal healthcare is that the person must reside in Turkey. In fact, there exists a double territorial limitation: the beneficiary has to reside in Turkey when applying for benefits, and these healthcare benefits must be provided in Turkey. There are a limited number of exceptions in these rules.

510. Article 63 states the principle that healthcare services shall be provided by service providers in Turkey. First of all, with respect to employees and public officers, if they have been assigned by their employer or public entity to temporary duties abroad, they will receive all necessary healthcare benefits abroad only in emergency cases. Therefore, if there is no emergency case, insurance holders do not have any health protection against sickness occurred whilst abroad. Considering that the length of temporary duty is less than six months, the postponement of treatment may cause more serious health problems.[375] The Act recognizes health protection only to insurance holders, but not their dependents, who also went abroad to accompany the insurance holder.[376] In addition, there is a considerable restriction: the Institution reimburses only the amount which would have been due if the treatment was received by service providers in Turkey. The rest of the amount shall be paid by employers or public entities (Article 66/III of Act No. 5510).

511. If an insurance holder, either an employee or public officer, is sent abroad on permanent duty, he/she enjoys healthcare services provided by service providers abroad. Permanent duty is described as duties which continue for more than six months. Like temporary duty, the Institution reimburses the expenses which would have been due if the treatment was provided in Turkey. The rest shall be paid by the employer.[377]

512. If an employee is working in the workplace of a Turkish employer in a foreign country with whom the Turkish Republic has no bilateral agreement, that employee shall be deemed to be a social insurance holder for short-term insurance branches, as well as for universal health insurance (Article 5/I g of Act No. 5510). Therefore, Turkish employees working for a Turkish employer abroad shall receive healthcare services abroad.

513. Only wage earners and civil servants have protection against health risks abroad. Although both groups are subjected to main principles, the conditions for

375. A.Güzel/A.R. Okur/N. Caniklioğlu, n. 7, p. 752; A.N. Sözer, *Genel Sağlık Sİgortası*, p. 266.
376. For critics, *see* A.Güzel/A.R. Okur/N. Caniklioğlu, n. 7, pp. 752753. Sözer argues that the dependants can also benefit from healthcare services in abroad: A.N. Sözer, *Genel Sağlık Sigortası*, n. 371, p. 267.
377. *See also* A.Güzel/A.R. Okur/N. Caniklioğlu, n. 7, p. 753.

civil servants have been clarified by supplementary Article 4, adopted by Act No. 6009.[378] However, Self-Employed insurance holders do not benefit from this protection.

514. The Act enables the Institution with the possibility to provide healthcare services for employees or public officers assigned with a permanent or temporary duty by insuring them in the concerned country, under the condition that the amount of insurance contribution does not exceed the amount of contribution paid to the Institution (Article 66/V of Act No. 5510).

515. Second, healthcare benefits must, in principle, be provided in Turkey. However, under certain conditions, insured employees residing in Turkey may also receive treatment abroad (Article 66/I, c of Act No. 5510). It must be proved that the required treatment is not available in Turkey upon the appropriate opinion of the Ministry of Health. Not only the treatment but also detailed examinations which are not possible to make in Turkey may be made abroad. Unlike those who are on temporary or permanent duty, there exists no ceiling for financed costs. To receive healthcare abroad, Act No. 5510 requires no extra contribution payment. Before the reform, at least 300 days of sickness insurance contribution has to have been paid for the insured person during the year proceeding the date on which the sickness or invalidity was diagnosed.

516. It was a debatable issue whether the dependants or pension or income owners may receive treatment abroad under Act No. 506. The Supreme Court ruled that in cases of urgent and vital situations if the dependants of an insured could not receive the necessary treatment in Turkey, the Social Security Institution is to provide the treatment abroad.[379] However, a supplement to Article 32, Act No. 506 stated clearly that the insured worker was the only beneficiary of treatment abroad. After this amendment, the validity of the Supreme Court ruling was questionable. By a supplement brought by Act No. 5264 issued on 2 December 2004, dependants of the insured were entitled to have treatment abroad. The spouse of the insured, who is not working under cover of the Social Security Institution or receiving pensions or income and children and parents who are under the insured's duty of care, are considered dependants of the insured. Act No. 5510 makes no difference among insurance holders and dependants as regards to receiving healthcare benefits.

378. OJ, 1 Aug. 2010, No. 27659.
379. Court of Cass., 10th Ch., 19.9.1980, 4823/5124, noted by C. Tuncay, *İHU* 1981/II, SSK. 32 (No.3).

§2. Personal Field of Application

I. Universal Health Insurance Holders

517. Act No. 5510 provides two types of insurance holdership: social insurance holders and universal health insurance holders. Article 60 of Act No. 5510 lists universal health insurance holders.[380] For an act adopted with a claim of having universal coverage, just mentioning exemptions should be preferred than listing all those who are covered by the system.[381] In contrast, the Act enumerates different groups which are included and excluded in a casuistic way. Such a method raises doubts with regard to those who are not specifically mentioned. Such a listing method renders the personal scope of health insurance quite complicated, that, in certain cases, even makes doubtful the universal nature of the insurance system.

518. The Act not only differentiates social insurance holders from universal health insurance holders but also ramifies health insurance holders into sub-groups that are each subject to different registration processes; for one part, an automatic registration without the need to notify is provided. For others, they should be registered upon when a notification is made. The personal scope of universal health insurance holder may be divided into two sub-groups: Those who have social insurance holdership either compulsorily or voluntarily and those who fall fully or partly out of the social insurance system.

519. Those who are compulsory social insurance holders are also deemed to be universal health insurance holders: those who are subject to Article 4/I, a (mainly employees), Article 4/I, b (mainly Self-Employed persons) and 4/I, c (mainly public civil servants). Their universal health insurance holder status begins with the date of notification to the social insurance system. There is no other notification needed to get health insurance holdership (Article 61/1, a of Act No. 5510). By the notification to the Social Security Institution, they are deemed to have universal health insurance holder status.

520. Those who have voluntarily insured are also deemed to be universal health insurance holders without additional notification to the system (Article 60/I, a of Act No. 5510).

521. Regarding those who have no social insurance holder status, there exist five sub-groups:

The first group consists of different parts of society, who have no job and live with very limited financial resources. For those who are mentioned in Article 60/I, c in addition to the condition of residing in Turkey, the Act requires that these persons must not be considered among the dependants of a universal health insurance

380. *See* A.Güzel/A.R. Okur/N. Caniklioğlu, n. 7, pp. 723724; C. Tuncay/Ö. Ekmekçi, n. 7, pp. 552–563; A.N. Sözer, *Genel Sağlık Sigortası*, pp. 113143.

381. A.R. Okur, 'Sosyal Güvenlik Reformu ve Genel Sağlık Sigortası', 12, *Legal-İSGHD*(2006), p. 1291.

holder. If he/she is a dependent of an insurance holder, he/she will get benefits through the main insurance holder. The cover of Article 60/I, c are listed below:

- Citizens whose domestic income per capita is less than one-third of the amount of the minimum wage and children who have Turkish nationality and have not completed the age of 18 if they are not a universal health insurance holder without being examined by a means test or have any dependants. The domestic income per capita of an individual is examined by a 'means test' that involves all expenses, movable and immovable properties and rights to be taken into calculation. The family, in the sense of this item, consists of a spouse, not married children and parents living in the same household (Article 60/V of Act No. 5510). Those whose income is less than one-third of the amount of the minimum wage receive healthcare services without paying any contribution to the system.

  Before the reform, those citizens benefited from the 'green card' provided under abrogated Act No. 3816, on State Provision of Medical Care to Indigent Citizens through the Granting of 'Green Cards'. Under this Act, the state was under an obligation to pay the health expenses of poor citizens. Act No. 3816 covered Turkish citizens who were not covered by any social security institution and whose monthly income or income share in the family was less than one-third of the amount of the minimum wage (after tax and social insurance contribution shares are deducted) and who resided in Turkey (Article 2 of Act No. 3816). 'Green card' holders benefited from healthcare services without paying any contribution before the reform. As of 1 January 2012, green card holders are deemed to have universal health insurance status automatically.[382] The medical expenses of those who receive silicosis pension and his/her spouse and children shall be met without requiring a means test (Trans. Article 1 of Act No. 2022).

  If the concerned person has had no green card and lost his income capacity after the entry into force of Act No. 5510, his/her insurance holder status begins with the date of registration by the Social Security Institution (Article 61/I, b of Act No. 5510).

  Victims of violence in the family and their children had difficulties in accessing healthcare. Therefore, Act No. 6284[383] enables protected persons who are under the protective cautionary decisions taken within the scope of Act 6284 on the Protection of Family and Prevention of Violence[384] to receive health insurance benefits. If the protected persons are not under the scope of the health insurance holders or of his/her dependant or if they have not fulfilled the conditions to receive health insurance benefits, they are deemed to be health insurance holders without being examined by a means test (Article 60/IX of Act No. 5510).
- Children who had graduated but were unemployed were obliged to be examined by a means test and were deemed to be health insurance holders. Thus, children's

382. For the cover of green card and health contributions for poor groups, *see* O. Karadeniz, '*Extension of Health Services Coverage for Needy in Turkey: From Social Assistance to General Health Insurance*', 2 J. Soc. Sec. (2012) pp. 103–123.
383. Act No. 6284, OJ, 29 May 2013, No. 28661.
384. For the English version of Act No. 6284, http://ilo.org/dyn/natlex/docs/SERIAL/91822/106656/F-1918776246/Non-official%20translation%20-%20Law%20to%20protect%20famil.pdf.

health insurance contributions were met by their families, which caused complaints. Act No. 6663[385] provides a facility that the children who have graduated are deemed to be general health insurance holders under the status of 60/I, c (whatever their domestic income) for two years, following the graduation date until the age of 20 (secondary education), 25 (higher education). Stateless and persons who have/apply for international protection: If they reside in Turkey, stateless and persons having international protection are also considered as universal health insurance holders (Article 60/I, c, 2 of Act No. 5510).

- Those who receive pensions pursuant to Act No. 2022 of 1 July 1976 on Granting of Pensions to Persons over 65 and Indigents: According to Act No. 2022, Turkish citizens of 65 years of age or over or who are handicapped or invalid may request assistance if they are in need. If their application is accepted, they receive a monthly pension, as well as healthcare services in state hospitals. The right to health services was granted equally to the spouses of income recipients. By Act No. 5510, these persons are considered universal health insurance holders as soon as they are entitled to receive the monthly pension (Article 61/1, b of Act No. 5510). If they lose their monthly pensions under Act No. 2022, their universal health insurance holdership under Article 60/I, c, 3 of Act will also end.
- Those who receive 'pension of honour' pursuant to Act No. 1005 (Article 60/I, c, 4 of Act No. 5510): According to Act No. 1005, those who have been granted the Independence Medal receive a 'pension of honour'. Those who receive that pension are deemed to have universal health insurance holdership, as from the date that pension is allocated (Article 61/1, b of Act No. 5510).
- Those who receive pensions pursuant to Act No. 3292 (Article 60/I, c, 5 of Act No. 5510): Act No. 3292 allocates a pension to those who have served the country with assiduity and success. Those who receive this pension are also deemed to be universal health insurance holders, as from the date that such pension is allocated.
- Those who receive a pension pursuant to Act No. 2330 (Article 60/I,c,6 of Act No. 5510): Act No. 2330 grants compensation in grants and pensions to the survivors of those who lost their lives in service aiming to protect the safety and security in peacetime or to prevent or trace and investigate smuggling. Pension receivers are also considered as universal health insurance holders.
- Those who benefit gratuitously from protection, care and rehabilitation services provided under Act. No. 2828 on Social Services and the Institution for the Protection of Children and children having Turkish nationality, who have lost both parents and not have completed the age of 18 (Article 60/I, c, 7 of Act No. 5510): Although Act No. 2828 covers every individual, the indigent, infants, disabled and aged persons are given priority. They are also deemed to be universal health insurance holders, and healthcare services are provided under Act No. 5510.
- Military veterans receiving a pension and those who receive a pension under Act No. 3713 on Struggling Against Terrorism (Article 60/I, c, 8 of Act No. 5510): Act No. 3713 includes provisions aiming to protect those struggling against terrorism. If they die or become disabled in the line of duty, they or their widows

385. Act No. 6663, OJ, 10 Feb. 2016, No. 29620.

and orphans will receive benefits. Those persons are also deemed to have universal health insurance as from the date that they are allocated the pension or benefit.

- Village guards appointed pursuant to Article 74/II of Act No. 442 or temporary village guards who receive a pension according to supplementary Article 16 of Act No. 442: Those village guards are also deemed to have universal health insurance holder status (Article 60/I, c, 9 of Act No. 5510).
- Those who receive a pension pursuant to Act No. 5774 (Article 60/I, c, 10 of Act No. 5510): Act No. 5774 allocates a pension to successful sportsmen and their families in case of their death. They are deemed to have universal health insurance holder status as from the date that the pensions are allocated.

522. On condition of reciprocity, foreigners who have a residential permit in Turkey are considered as universal health insurance holders, unless they are insured by another social security system abroad (Article 60/I, d of Act No. 5510). In addition, if a foreign person has been residing in Turkey for a period of less than one year, such a person is not covered by the health insurance system, neither as an insurance holder nor as his/her dependant (Article 60/III of Act No. 5510). Regulation on Universal Health Insurance Procedures requires having a residential permit for at least one year without interruption to have health insurance holder status (Article 6/IX of RUHIP). Therefore, foreigners who reside in Turkey for a shorter period are not insured against health risks. As of the date that the foreign person has completed one-year residing period, he/she is deemed to be a universal health insurance holder. The foreign person is registered upon an entrance request within one month pursuant to the end of one year. If a foreign married couple is in consideration, they have the right to determine who will be the insurance holder and who will be the dependant (Article 60/IV of Act No. 5510). Nevertheless, if a foreigner is working under a contract of employment or as a Self-Employed person, he/she shall be deemed to be an insurance holder because of his/her compulsory social insurance relation pursuant to Article 60/I, a.

523. Those who receive unemployment allowance or payments in case of short-time working periods or tradesmen and guilt fund allowances[386] are also covered by universal health insurance (Article 60/I, e of Act No. 5510). Unemployed persons or employees working reduced time are deemed to be insurance holders as of the date that they benefit from unemployment, guaranteed payments or guilt allowances. The Turkish Employment Institution notifies the Institution about them within one month following the allocation of allowances (Article 61/1, d of Act No. 5510).

524. Those who receive pensions or an allowance pursuant to Act No. 5510 or any other act are also covered by health insurance (Article 60/I, f of Act No. 5510). The insurance holdership starts from the date of receiving the pension or allowance.

386. Act No. 6824, OJ, 8 Mar. 2017, No. 30001, this rule will entry into force on 1 Jan. 2018.

Like working people, there is no need to notify the Institution separately. If a person enjoys several statuses, like pension receiver, as well as working under a contract of employment, other insurance holder statuses than item f will be superseded.

525. According to Article 60/I, g, all citizens who fall out of the scope of the above-mentioned paragraphs and who do not have any health insurance from any other country are deemed to have health insurance. This last subsection gives the universal characteristic to the system. However, this is a misleading interpretation, as even Act No. 5510 leaves certain Turkish citizens and their dependants off the cover of universal health insurance, the details of which will be examined below. For example, unemployed persons who do not receive unemployment benefits are within this group.

526. As of the date that those persons lost their insurance holder status pursuant to the above-mentioned subsections, they shall be registered by the Institution on its own initiative. Before an amendment made by Act No. 6111 of 13 February 2011, the Act imposed a notification duty of their statuses to those citizens, and non-compliance was sanctioned with a fine. Nevertheless, considering the financial difficulty of these people, the notification duty was removed. If both spouses are health insurance holders according to Article 60/I, g, they have the right to determine who will be the main insurance holder and who will be the dependant.

527. Such a listing method runs the risk of forgetting certain groups. Thus, new groups are added to the Act, by amendments such as those made by Act No. 6111 of 13 February 2011, Act No. 6486 of 21 May 2013, Act No. 6494 of 27 June 2013, Act No. 6663 of 29 January 2016 and Decree-law No. 681 of 2 January 2017:

- The first group is international students. Students who have Turkish nationality receive, in principle, healthcare services through their parents. However, there was no clarity regarding international students. Foreign students who continue higher education pursuant to Act No. 2547 on Higher Education, during their education, become health insurance holders if they make a request within three months following their first registration. They are under an obligation to pay health insurance contribution to the amount of thirty times the lower limit of the minimum daily earnings. If international students do not make such a request, they are not held as health insurance holders.
- Apprentices, candidate apprentices, vocational education students, students working part-time in universities, participants to vocational trainings organized by the Turkish Employment Institution, trainees of vocational or technical secondary or higher education, technical or secondary school students who have vocational training or field education are deemed to be health insurance holders, unless they are considered dependants.
- Another group which has reached health security by this amendment of February 2011 is trainee solicitors. Pursuant to Act No. 1136, to be a solicitor, one year of training is mandatory. Unless trainees are dependants or universal health insurance holders pursuant to another subsection of Act No. 5510, trainee solicitors are

deemed to be health insurance holders during their training time. Their contributions are paid by the Bar Association (Article 60/VIII of Act No. 5510).

- Faced with the difficulties arising from the required contribution payment, the legislator envisages different methods to cover certain part-time workers under the scope of universal health insurance. Thus, drivers of commercial taxis or other inner-city transportation vehicles and artists, if they work for less than ten days in a month under a contract of employment and if they pay contributions for thirty days, they are deemed to be health insurance holders (Supp. Article 6 of Act No. 5510). Such a condition of paying contributions to get insurance holder status is quite unusual in the system.

  According to Act No. 4769 on the Training Centres of Prisons and Detention Houses, the personnel who will work on prisons and detention houses are obliged to take pre-job training. The pre-job training continues for at least five months. Those pre-job trainees are deemed to be health insurance holders during their training time (Article 60/X of Act No. 5510). Their health insurance contributions to the amount of thirty times the lower limits of the minimum daily earnings are paid by the Ministry of Justice. Their dependants also benefit from health insurance.
- Those who do compulsory military service or who are cadets at the school of reserve officers were out of the scope of health insurance unless they are income taxpayers because of their commercial activities or shareholders of commercial companies (Article 8/a, 1 of RUHIP). By Decree-law No. 681, those who do compulsory military service, cadets and candidate cadets at the school of reserve officers, military school students and guest military personnel and their families who came to Turkey under the frame of an international military training and education treaty fall under the scope of universal health insurance, if the treaty contains a clause providing the responsibility of the host country (Article 60/XII-XIV of Act No. 5510).

528. In addition to Act No. 5510, Regulation of Universal Health Insurance Registration, Contribution and Benefit Owners clarifies the health insurance holder status of certain groups such as those who work with a contract of employment in public entity workplaces, employees during the suspension of their employment contract, Turkish employees working in the workplace of a Turkish employer in a foreign country with whom the Turkish Republic has no bilateral agreement, and insurance holders' daughters who have received marriage assistance and who are not dependant on their spouses or who are divorced within a period of two years (Article 6 of RUHIRCB).

529. Act No. 5510 exempts certain groups from the scope of short- and long-term social insurance branches (Article 6 of Act No. 5510): the spouse of an employer who works gratis in the workplace; those who live together in the same dwelling and are relatives; domestic servants and maids; students engaged in vocational training, in manufacturing and production work in official schools established for arts and crafts; sick or disabled persons who are undergoing a course of occupational rehabilitation; those who work in agricultural or forestry works with a contract of employment for temporary works; those who are below the age of 18; those who work temporarily in agricultural and forestry works with a contract of employment and those who are self-employed; however, their monthly income is lower than the amount fixed by the Act.[387] With respect to their health insurance holder status, first of all, it should be checked whether they are a dependant of another health insurance holder. If that is the case, they are not deemed to be a health insurance holders. However, if they are not a dependant of an insurance holder, they, themselves, shall have the health insured status (Article 60/II of Act No. 5510).

II. Dependants

530. The Act also confers the right to receive health benefits on the dependants of insurance holders. Family members of insurance holders receive healthcare services through the insurance of the main insurance holder, if they, themselves, are not deemed to be an insurance holder, due to their own work or status. Before the reform, the dependants of the insured employees received the same healthcare services as the insured. However, unlike insured employees and their dependants, the extent of healthcare provided to those who receive incomes or pensions, and to their dependants, was restricted. Due to the reform, all differences regarding the cover of health insurance were removed.

531. In order to be qualified as a dependant,[388] first of all, the health insurance holder must be eligible to have dependants; thus, Act No. 5510 exempts dependency status from certain insurance holders.

532. Those who are not eligible to have dependants are mentioned below:

(1) Apprentices, candidate apprentices and vocational training students benefit from insurance for industrial accidents and occupational diseases and sickness insurance. However, with respect to healthcare services, if they are a dependant of a health insurance holder, they receive healthcare services as a dependant, if not, they are deemed to be a universal health insurance holder (Article 5/I, b of Act No. 5510). Even in that case, apprentices cannot have dependants:
   - Citizens whose domestic income per capita is less than one-third of the amount of the minimum wage.
   - Heimatlos persons and refugees.
   - Those who receive benefits pursuant to Act No. 2828 on Social Services.
   - Foreign students in universities.
   - Trainee solicitors are deemed to be universal health insurance holders, but they cannot have dependants in the system.

---

387. *See supra* para. 86.
388. *See* A.Güzel/A.R. Okur/N. Caniklioğlu, n. 7, pp. 727–734; C. Tuncay/Ö. Ekmekçi, n. 7, pp. 564–566; A.N. Sözer, *Genel Sağlık Sigortası*, pp. 143–153.

533. Second, to be qualified as a dependant, the concerned person must not be an insurance holder due to his/her work or under cover of voluntary insurance. Likewise, those who receive pensions or allowances due to his/her own work are not considered as dependants. Therefore, to receive healthcare services through the insured status of someone else, the concerned person should not have any insurance protection.

534. Lastly, the scope of dependants is determined by the Act: Spouses, infants and parents. With respect to spouses, the Act requires no other condition than those mentioned above. Children must not be over the age of 18, or over the age of 20 if receiving secondary education, or over the age of 25 if receiving higher education. There is no age limit with respect to infants who are invalid unless they are not married (Article 3/I, 10, b of Act No. 5510). Regarding children, the condition of not being married was brought to the system first by Act No. 5510.[389]

535. In order to qualify parents as dependants, it must be proven by the criteria developed by the Institution that the livelihood is provided by the insurance holder. Regulation on the Universal Health Insurance Procedures envisages that the amount of income derived from every profit and rent must be less than the net amount of the minimum wage, and the mother and father must not receive healthcare through their other children to consider them as a dependant.[390]

III. Universal Nature and Those Who Are Not Covered by Health Insurance

536. Considering its name, one might assume that health insurance covers every individual residing in Turkey. Article 60/I, g supports such an assumption, while it envisages that all citizens who fall out of the scope of the above-mentioned paragraphs and who do not have any health insurance from any other country are deemed to be health insurance holders. Nevertheless, that is not the case. Certain groups are exempted from the status of being both health insurance holders and being dependants of someone else. Those who fall totally out of the scope of provisions of universal health insurance are listed below (Article 60/III of Act No. 5510):

> Foreign nationals who are sent to Turkey for a period, not more than three months and for work to be done on behalf of, and on account of an undertaking whose headquarters are located abroad and who documents their insured status in their own country, fall out of the scope of the provisions related to health insurance.

389. H. Ergin, 'Genel Sağlık Sigortasında Gelinen Son Durum', p. 114.
390. Ergin argues for a conflict between Act No. 5510 and the Regulation, H. Ergin, 'Genel Sağlık Sigortasında Gelinen Son Durum', p. 114.

- Turkish citizens, having another state's nationality or having a permanent residence permit are recruited with an administrative contract in representative offices abroad fall out of the scope of health insurance if they are proved to be insured pursuant to the norms of that country. Convicts and detainees fall out of the scope of health insurance provisions.
- Although foreigners who work under a contract of employment in Turkey are compulsorily subjected to all social insurance branches if they have resided in Turkey for less than one year, they do not fall into the cover of health insurance.
- Save for the exemption provided for by bilateral agreements, those who are granted pensions or allowances pursuant to the abrogated Acts No. 2147 or 3201 if they reside abroad, they are not deemed to be health insurance holders.

537. There also exist groups which are exempted from the cover of health insurance by special acts. Members of the National Assembly, ministers and their dependants are excluded from the scope of health insurance by Act No. 3671 (Article 105 of Act No. 5510).[391]

391. F. Uşan, n. 28, p. 274; H. Ergin, 'Genel Sağlık Sigortasında Gelinen Son Durum', p. 115.

Chapter 2. Contributions for Universal Health Insurance

§1. Calculation Base

538. For those who are compulsory social insurance holders, those who are subjected to Article 4/1, a, b or c and those who are voluntarily insured, the calculation basis is the same as the one valid for the long-term and short-term insurances.[392]

539. The calculation basis means only with regard to those who only have the status of universal health insurance.[393] The Act determines for each sub-group a different calculation basis (Article 80/4 of Act No. 5510):

- For persons with limited financial resources (Article 60/I, c and XII, XIII, XIV of Act No. 5510),[394] the calculation basis is the minimum wage.
- For foreign nationals (Article 60/I, d of Act No. 5510), the calculation basis is thirty days amount of two times of the upper limit for the daily income.
- For those who received unemployment and reduced working time allowances (Article 60/I, e of Act No. 5510), the calculation basis is the lower limit of the daily income.
- For those who are subjected to Article 60/I, g, which covers those who fall out of all of the other groups of Article 60, the calculation basis is thirty days amount of the lower limit for the daily income. The health insurance was entered into force in 2012. The amount of contributions had been determined according to the results of the means test. Nevertheless, quite a big part of the health insurance holders abstained from having that test and did not pay their contributions. In order to collect more contributions, the contribution amount is fixed by a legislative amendment.[395] Therefore, for those who are subjected to Article 60/I, g, there exists a fixed rate of contribution, thirty days amount of the lower limit for the daily income, whatever the amount of their real income is. However, if the insurance holder requests a means test and his/her domestic income per capita is less than one-third of the amount of the minimum wage, the difference shall be reimbursed or deducted from future payments without any legal interest.

§2. Calculation Rate

540. The contribution amount of the insurance holder, covered by short and long-term insurance branches, is 12.5% of whatever income amount is set as the basis for the contribution for social insurances. A total of 5% of that imputes on the insurance holder and 7.5% on the employer, of the earnings based for contribution.

---

392. *See supra* paras 104–111.
393. F. Uşan, n. 28, p. 278.
394. *See supra* para. 519.
395. Act No. 6824, OJ, 8 Mar. 2017.

For employees and civil servants, employers are responsible to collect and deliver the contribution to the Institution. Self-Employed persons are responsible for their own contributions.

541. Nevertheless, if the insurance holder is subjected only to universal health insurance, the contribution amount is 12% of the contribution basis. A total of 12% of the contribution rate is also valid for those who receive unemployment or reduced working time allowances (Article 60/I, e of Act No. 6610), individuals who receive work loss compensation in privatized companies and voluntary insured insurance holders.

542. In addition, the state is under an obligation to contribute to the Institution at a rate of one-fourth of universal health insurance collections (Article 81/2 of Act No. 5510).

Chapter 3. Benefits

543. Since monetary aids are provided under the cover of social insurances, the health insurance satisfies the need for healthcare. Before the reform, the Institution had its own hospitals. In principle, the Institution provided healthcare given in kind, both goods and services. Except for treatments abroad, the system was not based on the remuneration of expenses incurred by the insured. However, under Act No. 5510, the Social Insurance Institution does finance healthcare service under the frame of health insurance through service providers.[396] In addition to healthcare, certain allowances are provided by the universal health insurance.

§1. Care Provided

I. Type of Benefits

A. Healthcare

544. Before the reform, the cover of healthcare services varied in accordance with the insurance holder status; whether he/she was an employee, Self-Employed or a civil officer, he/she is an insurance holder or a dependant. Healthcare services offered to workers in the agricultural sectors were restricted to a medical examination and clinical and laboratory examinations, however, dental prostheses were excluded. By Act No. 5510, all such differences were revoked. The new system defines the universal health insurance holder and dependant in quite a broad manner than just stating that everyone receives the same healthcare service.[397] If one talks about the unification of the system, it is the case for the health insurance system, but not for social insurances.

1. Preventive Healthcare

545. Preventive healthcare services are one of the most important items that were brought in by the reform. With an aim to ensure that health insurance holders and dependants stay healthy, the Social Security Institution finances preventive healthcare services (Article 63/I, a of Act No. 5510). Such preventive measures may prevent the illness of a person or may help to diagnose sicknesses at an early stage. All kinds of preventive measures, both person-oriented and environment-oriented, are included by Act No. 5510.[398] The Act defines the extent of preventive measures in a broad manner and gives discretionary powers to the Institution to determine the content of preventive services.

---

396. About the organizational structure of the universal health insurance, *see* A.N. Sözer, 'Genel Sağlık Sigortasının Organizasyonu', in *Osman Güven Çankaya'ya Armağan* (Ankara, 2010), pp. 431–449.
397. For details, *see* A.N. Sözer, *Genel Sağlık Sigortası*, pp. 216–254.
398. A. Güzel/A.R. Okur/N. Caniklioğlu, n. 7, p. 744.

2. Healthcare Services in the Case of Diagnosis and Treatment

546. In case of the sickness of an insurance holder or his/her dependant, healthcare services will be provided to ensure the recovery of the insurance holder. In addition, since only monetary aids are given under the social insurance system, in case of an industrial accident or occupational disease, healthcare is provided by health insurance to recover or decrease working incapacity.

547. Healthcare services which will be financed by the Institution are as follows (Article 63/I, b of Act No. 5510):

- Medical examination and clinical and laboratory examinations as necessary for diagnosis and treatment.
- Other diagnostic methods, such as x-ray examination, tomography, medical sonography.
- Medical treatments and operations.
- Patient follow-up and rehabilitation service.
- Healthcare services for organ, tissue and stem cell transfer.
- Cell treatment.
- Emergency healthcare services.
- Medical care treatments, such as physical therapy or massage, to be applied by health professionals upon the receipt of a medicine.

Healthcare services may be given both on an inpatient and outpatient basis.

3. Healthcare Services in Case of Maternity

548. In the case of maternity, maternity insurance meets the financial loss of the insurance holder. However, medical care is provided by universal health insurance. All female health insurance holders and the wife of an insurance holder as a dependant receive healthcare benefits on an inpatient or outpatient basis.

549. Due to maternity, all financed healthcare services are as follows (Article 63/I, c of Act No. 5510):

- Medical examination and clinical and laboratory examinations as necessary for diagnosis and treatment.
- Confinement and other diagnostic methods, such as x-ray examination, tomography, medical sonography.
- Medical treatments and operations.
- Patient follow-up.
- Uterus discharge.
- Medical sterilization and emergency healthcare.
- Medical care treatments, such as physical therapy or massage, to be applied by health professionals upon the receipt of a medicine.

4. Oral and Dental Examination

550. Dental healthcare services may be provided either on an inpatient or outpatient basis. Oral and dental examination services cover the clinical examination required for the diagnosis of mouth and teeth diseases upon the request of a dentist, laboratory examination and analysis and other diagnostic methods, medical operations and treatments to be applied based on the diagnosis, tooth extraction, conservative tooth treatment and channel treatment, patient follow-up, denture applications, emergency healthcare services for oral and dental diseases, and orthodontic dental treatment of individuals under the age of 18 up to the amount fixed by healthcare insurance (Article 63/I, d of Act No. 5510). Before the reform, benefits for dental prostheses were governed by special regulation that 20% of the cost of prostheses and other devices were to be paid by the insurance holder. It is widely welcomed that Act No. 5510 revoked such a participation rate; however, it is criticized that the orthodontic dental treatment is only provided for those who are under the age of 18.[399]

5. Auxiliary Reproduction Methods

551. In Parliament, an amendment was adopted with the aim of financing auxiliary reproduction methods under certain conditions. In order to get these benefits, in addition to having health insurance holdership, there exist other conditions: First of all, the couple must be married (Article 63/I, e of Act No. 5510). Second, it should be proven that if the health insurance holder is female then herself, if male, then his wife, cannot have a child via normal medical methods, and it is possible to have a child via auxiliary reproduction methods pursuant to medical examinations carried out by the health boards of service providers authorized by the Institution. In addition, the fact that no result is obtained from other treatment methods within the previous three years shall be documented by authorized health boards. Lastly, she must be older than the age of 23 and younger than the age of 39. Not every medical centre has the authorization to carry out these treatments; therefore, the medical centre must have a contract with the Institution (Article 63/I, e of Act No. 5510).[400]

552. Even though all the conditions are satisfied, the Act restricts the number of trials to three. However, the Court of Cassation, referring to the sacred nature of human life, ruled that the Institution should pay the expenses if using auxiliary reproduction methods is compulsory.[401] In the case, the plaintiff was obliged to have another child, such as in it will make it possible to transfer stem cell to his/her brother who suffers from Miyelodisplastik Sendrom, or otherwise, which could turn into leukaemia. Such a decision ruled out under the abrogated Act No. 506, which

399. A.R. Okur, 'Genel Sağlık Sigortası', p. 1294; A. Güzel/A.R. Okur/N. Caniklioğlu, n. 7, pp. 748–749; C. Tuncay/Ö. Ekmekçi, n. 7, pp. 574–575.
400. For details, *see* S. Ocak, 'Genel Sağlık Sigortasında Prim Koşulu', pp. 1088–1093.
401. Court of Cass., 10th Ch., 27.10.2009, 5150/16257, 26, *Legal-İSGHD*(2010), pp. 822–823.

provides any support to auxiliary reproduction methods, has been welcomed by authors.[402] We believe that the Supreme Court will also maintain this approach under Act No. 5510.

6. Medical Expenses

553. In addition to hospitalization, pharmaceuticals and other treatment material are provided by the Institution. The Institution meets all medical expenses related to the diagnosis and treatment of the above-mentioned health services, such as blood and blood products, bone marrow, vaccines, medications, orthosis, prosthesis, medical equipment and tools, medical equipment for personal use, medical consumables and medical consumables having treating capacity. The Institution not only finances the provided services, but it also finances the planting, maintenance until the end of the guaranteed period and repair and replacement services (Article 63/I, f of Act No. 5510).

554. However, the Act enables the Social Security Institution with an extended authorization to determine what kind of healthcare services and medical expenses shall be financed. Pursuant to Article 63/2 of Act No. 5510, the Institution is authorized by asking the opinion of the Ministry of Health to fix the types, amounts and using periods, payment principles and terms of healthcare services. Such a large authorization weakens healthcare protection, while the Institution has all the authority to determine what kind of healthcare services shall be financed or not. Therefore, many conflicts related to the reimbursement of expenses arise between insurance holders and the Institution. The Court of Cassation controls the discretionary powers of the Institution by ruling that experts must determine the necessity of medical equipment to protect or heal the health of the insurance holder, and curative feature of this equipment should be proven. One can observe that the Court of Cassation always refers to the sacred nature of human life with regard to conflicts related to health insurance. According to the Court, the welfare state is under an obligation to provide healthcare services, and the right to live healthy tolerates any condition that each person shall benefit from healthcare services. For this reason, in cases of an emergency, requiring certain conditions and procedures to get health services is not acceptable.[403]

7. Healthcare Services Not Financed by the Universal Health Insurance

555. The Act determines that certain healthcare services fall out of the cover of health insurance. Unlike the above-mentioned authority granted to the Institution to

402. C. Tuncay/Ö. Ekmekçi, n. 7, pp. 575–576.

403. Court of Cass., Assembly General, 4 Mar. 2009, 10-34/104 and 10th Ch., 7 Apr. 2009, 2008/1070, 2009/6616; 7.4.2009, 2007/12650, 2009/6615 cited and noted by Ö. Ekmekçi, 'Sosyal Sigortaların Genel Hükümleri ve Türleri', in *Yargıtayın İş Hukuku ve Sosyal Güvenlik Hukuku Kararlarının Değerlendirilmesi 2009* (Ankara, 2011), pp. 360–365.

determine what kind of healthcare services and medical expenses shall be financed, the Act itself excludes treatments as follows (Article 64 of Act No. 5510):

- Any kind of healthcare service for aesthetic purposes and orthodontic treatments for aesthetic purposes are not financed by health insurance. However, if such treatment is required to ensure the integrity of the body and was caused due to an industrial accident or occupational disease, sickness, accidents or congenital reasons, healthcare services fall into the cover of health insurance.
- Healthcare services not permitted or licensed by the Ministry of Health and also services which are not admitted as medical healthcare by the Ministry of Health, such as alternative medicines, are not covered.
- Chronic diseases suffered by foreign nationals or their dependants if such diseases have occurred before the date of their being universal health insurance holders fall out of the cover of universal health insurance.

B. Travel, Accommodation and Food Expenses

556. It may be required that the health insurance holder or his/her dependant need to be transferred to another health institute out of the residing area of the insurance holder. The receiver of the healthcare may also need to be accompanied (Article 65/I of Act No. 5510). Therefore, the Institution meets the transportation expenses for the going and coming back of the insurance holder and his/her companion, limited to one person and daily allowances, if the transfer is required by a medic or a dentist. If the treatment is given on an inpatient basis, the Institution meets only the daily allowances for travelling days. The patient may be directed to either an institution in Turkey or a health institution abroad if the above-mentioned required conditions are satisfied.

557. If the insurance holder or his/her dependant is hospitalized and a medic or dentist prescribes that it is a medical necessity to have company, the Institution will pay for the accommodation and food expenses of the companion, limited to one person (Article 65/II of Act No. 5510).

558. The Commission of Pricing Healthcare Services determines the amount of travel, accommodation and food expenses and daily allowances (Article 65/III of Act No. 5510). These expenses are financed by short- and long-term insurance branches.

II. Amount of Benefits

559. Except for provisions about co-payment, the Institution pays all necessary costs of treatment and drugs. If one of the aims of healthcare services is to enable the insured to regain the capacity to work, it is evident that healthcare is about continuing until a cure has been achieved. However, until 1991, the Act had put a maximum limit of eighteen months on the duration of treatment. However, the

Constitutional Court held that such a limitation of 'up to 18 months' is in conflict with the Constitution and annulled this restriction. Article 10 of the Constitution refers to the principle of equality, Article 17 about the right to life, Article 56 about healthcare services and Article 60 about the right to social security were the articles on which the legal argumentation was based. The Constitutional Court considered the right to social security as a fundamental right and underlined its firm relationship with the right to life. Article 65 of the Constitution, which allows restrictions on the extent of economic and social duties of the state due to 'the capacity of financial resources', does not apply to healthcare benefits.[404] Therefore, healthcare benefits, including providing, replacing and repairing prostheses, continue as long as the treatment is considered necessary. By the reform, it is stated that even if the sick insurance holder loses the required conditions to be a universal health insurance holder, healthcare services will be maintained until he/she has recovered from his/her illness (Article 63/III of Act No. 5510).

560. Furthermore, for treatments abroad, before the reform, the duration of treatment abroad could not exceed two years. One meets with a similar restriction not under Act No. 5510 but under the Regulation on Universal Health Insurance Implementation. Pursuant to Article 32/V, the length of medical treatment abroad is fixed by the medical report for up to six months. The duration may be extended by the medical reports for up to six months upon the opinion of the service provided and the approval of the Institution. The upper limit of two years is removed from the Regulation.

561. The temporal cover of health insurance is another issue to be solved. The problem is whether insurance holders will lose their protection whenever they lose their status as an insurance holder. The end of the work activity, the basis of the social insurance relation, also means, in general terms, the end of the social insurance relationship. Nevertheless, with respect to sickness and maternity insurance branches, special provisions have been adopted. First of all, the insurance holder continues to receive benefits during the ten days following the end of the working status basis of the insured status. Compulsory insurance holders, mainly wage earners, Self-Employed persons and civil servants, receive healthcare and medical treatment for sickness occurring within ten days following the date of losing insured status (Article 67/IV of Act No. 5510). However, if they have a compulsorily insured status for ninety days within the year immediately preceding the date of losing insured status, they and their dependants will receive benefits from health insurance during the following ninety days. Therefore, those who are subjected to Article 4/1, b and c continue to receive health benefits even for a limited time after losing their insured status.

562. It is well-known that for employees, contributions are deducted from their monthly wages. Therefore, during periods that an employee does not receive a wage, his/her contributions are also not paid, which may cause a problem with

404. Cons. Court, 17.1.1991, 1990/27, 1991/2, OJ, 19.8.1991, No. 20965, Judgment and notes by A. Güzel/Ş. Gökçeoğlu, *İHD*(Nisan-Haziran, 1993), pp. 283–298.

respect to receiving healthcare benefits. Act No. 5510 clarifies that during annual paid holidays, sixteen weeks of confinement period in which it is prohibited to employ a female, six months of non-paid leave after confinement and other leaves mentioned in labour acts, an insured employee maintains his/her status of having universal health insurance. Therefore, they continue to receive healthcare services. In addition, for non-paid leave up to one month in one calendar year, insurance holders maintain their status, if their employer documents such leave (Article 67/V of Act No. 5510). The insurance holder is deemed to have lost his/her insured status starting from the tenth day following the end of such status. Similarly, if an employer declares a lock-out, the insured status will be lost in a similar way.

563. Likewise, civil servants who benefit from non-paid leave right up to one year shall, during this period, maintain their insured status. At the end of one year, they benefit from healthcare services, without being obliged to pay contributions for thirty days.

Chapter 4. Conditions

564. In order to receive healthcare services, the universal health insurance holder is to have paid contributions for universal health insurance, paid a contribution fee and applied in accordance with due procedure. Although Act No. 5510 envisages a uniform and universal health insurance system, certain differences between insured persons are still maintained; for example, wage earners must pay at least thirty days of universal health insurance contribution (Article 67/I, a of Act No. 5510). But in addition to that condition, for Self-Employed persons and their dependants, the insured person must not have a contribution and contribution-related debt for more than sixty days (Article 67/I, b of Act No. 5510). Voluntarily insured insurance holders must have paid all short-term and long-term insurance contributions to the Institution, including the contribution for universal health insurance (Article 67/I, c of Act No. 5510).[405]

§1. Minimum Contribution Payment

I. Thirty Days of Contribution Payment

565. Act No. 5510 requires, in principle, thirty days of universal health insurance contribution days within the one year preceding the date on which the insured person or his/her dependant has applied to a service provider. It is not possible for insurance holders to pay off in lump-sum their contribution for thirty days. Thirty days must be completed to receive healthcare service (Article 16/IV of RUHIRCB).[406] However, if the dependant of an insurance holder loses his/her status of dependant and becomes an insurance holder herself/himself, it is not required for them to pay thirty days of contribution to get healthcare benefits (Article 67/II of Act No. 5510).

566. One year starts from the day on which the insured person applies to a service provider.[407] While calculating one year, certain periods are not taken into account (Article 67/II of Act No. 5510):

- For any reason, the service period of the insurance holder passed as the military.
- Period of arrest which did not conclude in conviction.
- Period during which the insurance holder suffers from an incapacity to work and receives temporary incapacity allowance from insurance for industrial accidents and occupational disease, sickness and maternity.
- Period during which the insurance holder participates in a strike or his/her employer goes for a lock-out.

---

405. For details, *see* A.N. Sözer, 'Genel Sağlık Sigortası Edimlerinden Yararlanmada Prim Koşulu', *Sicil Der.*(Mart, 2009), pp. 159–173; S. Ocak, 'Genel Sağlık Sigortasında Prim Koşulu', in *Prof. Dr. Ali Güzel'e Armağan, II* (Istanbul, 2010), pp. 1070–1124.
406. F. Uşan, n. 28, p. 283.
407. For details, *see* S. Ocak, *Genel Sağlık Sigortasında Prim Koşulu*, pp. 1079–1082.

567. For certain persons, the Act removes the minimum contribution day waiting duty. [408] Individuals under the age of 18 and those who are medically on a dependent condition for someone else are not obliged to pay contributions to receive healthcare services (Article 67/I of Act No. 5510).

568. Also, in certain circumstances, contribution day waiting are not required.[409] In the case of a traffic accident, emergency case, industrial accidents and occupational diseases, victims may receive healthcare benefits, although they have not had thirty days of contributions (Article 67/I of Act No. 5510):

- As examined below, to get allowances from insurance for industrial accidents, there is no contribution payment requirement. Therefore, victims of industrial accidents or occupational diseases receive healthcare services without any other requirement. With respect to traffic accidents, which are a considerable problem in Turkey, the legislator has adopted a new amendment to Act No. 2918 on Traffic on Highways[410] that the Social Security Institution shall meet all expenses of healthcare services provided by all hospitals belonging to private or public entities, as well as universities, as of 25 February 2011.
- In emergency cases, only services related to an emergency situation are provided. Pursuant to Article 27 of Regulation of General Health Insurance Implementation, emergency cases are circumstances, such as sickness, accident, injury or similar situations, which develop suddenly and which require medical intervention in the first twenty-four hours following the case. The absence of a sudden medical intervention or a transfer to another health institution risks the loss of life or bodily integrity.
- With respect to contagious diseases, a notification obligation exists; however, the insurance holder receives healthcare regardless of contribution payments.
- Healthcare services provided in case of maternity are also exempted from contribution payments (Article 16/II, e of RUHIRCB).
- To receive healthcare benefits in case of natural disasters and wars, as well as strikes and lock-outs, insurance holders and their dependants are not to pay any contribution payment (Articles 67/I of Act No. 5510).
- In addition, insurance holders who have no job and live with very limited financial resources (Article 60/I, c of Act No. 5510), insurance holders who receive a pension or income (Article 60/I, f of Act No. 5510), soldiers and military personnel under the framework of international training treaties (60/XII, XIII,XIV of Act No. 5510) benefit from health services without being obliged to pay health insurance contributions for thirty days.

---

408. S. Ocak, *Genel Sağlık Sigortasında Prim Koşulu*, pp. 1076–1077; A.N. Sözer, *Genel Sağlık Sigortası*, pp. 278–281.
409. A.N. Sözer, *Genel Sağlık Sigortası*, pp. 282–299.
410. Act No. 6111 of 13 Feb. 2011, OJ, 25 Feb. 2011, No. 27857.

II. Special Contribution Requirement: Auxiliary Reproduction Methods

569. In addition to the above-mentioned particular conditions, to receive treatment of auxiliary reproduction methods, the concerned person must be an insurance holder or his dependant at least for five years and have at least 900 days of contribution (Article 63/I, e, 5 of Act No. 5510). Such a minimum insured period requirement exists for long-term insurance branches. To receive such treatment, if the requirement for long contribution paid days are understandable, a requirement for the minimum insured period is questionable.[411]

III. Not Having Contribution Debt and Receiving Benefits

570. In addition to contribution payments for thirty days, the Act requires for certain insurance holders to have no outstanding contribution and contribution-related debt for more than sixty days to the Social Security Institution (Article 67/I, b of Act No. 5510).[412] Those are mainly Self-Employed persons who are subjected to Article 4/1-b and all citizens who do not fall into the mentioned groups of Article 60 and who do not benefit from any health insurance abroad (Article 60/I, g of Act No. 5510). For example, unemployed persons who have a monthly income for which the amount is more than the amount of one-third of that of the minimum wages and their dependants. Unlike enjoying monetary rights under cover of sickness insurance wherein the self-employed insurance holder must be out of all kinds of debts related to contribution payments, self-employed insurance holders must not have any contribution or contribution-related debt for more than sixty days.[413] Therefore, even if the insurance holder has non-paid contribution debts, if the total amount is less than contributions for sixty days, the insurance holder shall receive healthcare services, but not temporary incapacity allowance under sickness insurance.

571. In addition to contribution payment for thirty days, Article 67/I, c rules that voluntarily insured insurance holders and foreign nationals who have been residing in Turkey for more than one year and their dependants must be out of all kinds of debts related to contribution payments to receive healthcare services.[414] It is not important whether debts are related to universal health insurance or not.[415] Foreign students who continue higher education in Turkey are also considered as universal health insurance holders. They must also be out of any debts related to contributions to get their benefits. In addition, they are subject to another condition that all health insurance contributions belonging to one semester must be paid in a lump-sum by their universities within the one month starting from the beginning of the

411. S. Ocak, *Genel Sağlık Sigortasında Prim Koşulu*, p. 1088.
412. For details, *see* S. Ocak, *Genel Sağlık Sigortasında Prim Koşulu*, pp. 1083–1085.
413. F. Uşan, n. 28, p. 284.
414. For details, *see* S. Ocak, *Genel Sağlık Sigortasında Prim Koşulu*, pp. 1085–1087; A.N. Sözer, n. 405, pp. 301–304.
415. A.N. Sözer, 'Prim Koşulu', p. 167; S. Ocak, *Genel Sağlık Sigortasında Prim Koşulu*, p. 1086.

semester (Article 67/I, d of Act No. 5510). It is hard to understand the justification for such a lump-sum payment regarding foreign students.

§2. Identifying Identity and Service Levels

572. Faced with the false identity declarations to receive healthcare services, identity identification becomes a condition to enjoy insurance benefits (Article 67/III of Act No. 5510). Health service providers are obliged to require insurance holders and their dependants to present an identity card, driver's license, marriage certificate, passport or photographed health card document issued by the Institution and check whether or not these cards belong to someone else (Article 71/I of Act No. 5510). In emergency cases, an identity card is presented when the emergency is solved. If the insurance holder refrains from presenting one of these mentioned identity cards, he/she shall not benefit from any healthcare service.

573. The Act rules that it is prohibited for universal health insurance holders and their dependants to make another person receive healthcare services in his/her own name and to obtain unjust benefit from the Institution. It is obvious that such behaviours are prohibited. However, the legislator needed to underline that fact and sanctioned these conducts: the Institution has the right to collect two times of the amount of the suffered damages with legal interest from persons involved collectively and jointly (Article 71/II of Act No. 5510). Also, the Criminal Code applies to this situation.

574. Service levels and the transfer chain is another condition to be satisfied to receive health services (Article 70/II of Act No. 5510). Healthcare service providers have been cascaded into three levels by the Ministry of Health. Family medicines are on the first level.[416]

575. In principle, insurance holders should not make any other payment than the contribution fees. Nevertheless, there exist three exceptions that service providers belonging to public administrations may also charge insurance holders with an extra fee: hotel services which are above the standards fixed by the Institution and provided to insurance holders; health services provided by academics in university hospitals are charged with an extra fee. In addition, extraordinary health services, which cover services having no vital importance and services with alternative treatment method, may also be charged with an extra fee. The concept needs to be described clearly.[417] These extra fees shall not be more than three times of the service prices fixed by the Healthcare Service Pricing Commission (Article 73/IV of Act No. 5510). Such an extra fee practice endangers the insurance function, while health receivers may meet with unexpected fees at the end of their treatment. In addition,

416. For details, *see* A. Güzel/A.R. Okur/N. Caniklioğlu, n. 7, pp. 768771; C. Tuncay/Ö. Ekmekçi, n. 7, pp. 596–604; A.N. Sözer, *Genel Sağlık Sigortası*, pp. 256–259.
417. A. Güzel/A.R. Okur/N. Caniklioğlu, n. 7, p. 773, n. 142; C. Tuncay/Ö. Ekmekçi, n. 7, p. 609.

faced with strong criticism from private service providers, the Act enables contracted private service providers to ask for extra payment from service receivers (Article 73/II of Act No. 5510). The Institution fixes the amount of extra fees up to a ceiling fixed by the Council of Ministers. The Act determines for what kind of services an extra fee could be required. In addition to emergency cases, intensive care, cancer treatment, healthcare services provided to a new-born child, organ and stem cell transfer, health services given to operations for anomalies in confinement, dialysis and cardiovascular surgery cannot be charged with extra fee payment.[418]

§3. Contribution Fee

576. With an aim to discourage wasteful drug use and to prevent their abused and unnecessary applications, as well as to create certain a self-control conscience, a contribution fee practice is maintained by Act No. 5510.[419] If those aims could be found reasonable, the amount of contribution fee should not have a dissuasive effect to receive healthcare benefits.[420]

577. Except for healthcare services and insurance holders specified by the Act itself, health service receivers are to contribute to the service costs. Before the entry into force of Act No. 5510, the Court of the Constitution annulled the contribution fee provisions with regard to civil servants.[421] However, the legislator re-adopted similar provisions and also charged civil servants with contribution fee duties.

578. The amount of the contribution fee varies in accordance with the service received. If the medical or oral treatment is given on an outpatient basis in the state-run hospitals, the contribution fee is TRY 6, less than EUR 1 in 2018, and that amount is re-valued each year. The Institution has the authority to fix the contribution amount in accordance with the level and qualities of service providers (Article 68/II of Act No. 5510).

579. The Institution is authorized to fix the contribution rate between 10% and 20% of the amounts of orthosis and prosthesis, as well as pharmaceutical drugs given in outpatient treatment. While determining the contribution rate, the Institution takes into consideration the vital importance of healthcare services, the income level of insurance holders, and the reduction of unnecessary use. The amount of contribution fee charged for orthosis and prosthesis cannot be more than 75% of the minimum wage on the date on which the health service is provided (Article 68/III of Act No. 5510).

418. For details, *see* A.N. Sözer, *Genel Sağlık Sigortası*,pp. 319–325, fn. 28.
419. For details, *see* S. Ocak, 'Sağlık Hizmetlerinde Katılım Payı Uygulaması', *Sicil Der.*(Aralık, 2009), pp. 181–197; A.N. Sözer, *Genel Sağlık Sigortası*, pp. 306–314.
420. C. Tuncay/Ö. Ekmekçi, n. 7, p. 592.
421. Cons. Court., 15.12.2006, 111/112, OJ, 30.12.2006, No. 26392 (Mük.).

580. For healthcare services provided on an inpatient basis, the health service receiver is obliged to pay a contribution fee up to the amount of 1% of the service cost in accordance with the sickness groups fixed by the Institution (Article 68/I of Act No. 5510). The amount of contribution fee for each insurance holder shall not be more than one-fourth of the minimum wage for each hospitalized treatment, and the total amount cannot be more than the amount of the minimum wage for each calendar year.

581. With regard to auxiliary reproduction treatments, the contribution fee rate is 30% of the costs in the first trial and 25% of the costs in the second trial. Unlike other cases, there is no upper limit for the amount of contribution payment. However, the Act provides one exemption: if the auxiliary reproduction methods are used in the treatment of a sickness, while another treatment is not possible, there is no contribution fee charge (Article 68/IV of Act No. 5510).

582. Contribution fees are deducted, for income or pension owners, from their incomes or pensions and for working insurance holders from their wages and salaries. The Institution is authorized to determine the payment procedures for contribution fees and to collect fees via drug stores and other institutions. Contracted service providers receive their due after contribution fees paid by insurance holders are deducted. Contribution fees paid by poor persons, stateless persons, refugees and those who receive pensions pursuant to Act No. 2022 are reimbursed upon their request.

583. However, under certain conditions, no contribution obligation exists. According to Article 69 of Act No. 5510, for healthcare services provided in case of industrial accidents and occupational diseases or in case of military drills and manoeuvres, as well as in case of natural disasters and war, service receivers do not pay contribution fees. Likewise, family medicine treatments and personal preventive healthcare services are exempted from contribution fee payment. In addition, there is no contribution fee for treatment of certain chronic diseases determined by the Institution, like orthosis and prosthesis which have vital importance and organ, tissue and stem cell transfer if it is proven by a medical report. Control examinations are also out of contribution fees.

584. In addition to certain health services, the Act lists certain groups who are exempted from contribution fee payment. Those who have been granted the Independence Medal and their spouses (Article 60/I, c, 4 of Act No. 5510), those who receive a pension because they have served the country with assiduity and success (Article 60/I, c, 5 of Act No. 5510), those who receive pensions, because they are survivors of those who lost their lives in service aiming to protect the safety and security in peacetime or to prevent or trace and investigate smuggling (Article 60/I, c, 6 of Act No. 5510), those who benefit gratuitously from protection, care and rehabilitation services, children without parents and below the age of 18 (Article 60/I, c, 7 of Act No. 5510), military veterans receiving a pension and also those who receive a pension under Act No. 3713 on Struggling Against Terrorism (Article 60/I, c, 8 of Act No. 5510), cadets attending military academies, faculties and upper high schools (Article 4/4, d of Act No. 5510), cadets attending police academies, faculties and upper high schools (Article 4/4, e of Act No. 5510) and cadets attending Academy of Gendarmerie and Coast Guard, faculties and upper high schools(Article 4/IV, f of Act No. 5510) are exempted from contribution fee payments. In addition, invalids who receive a pension pursuant to Act No. 3713 and soldiers who receive job invalidity pension do not pay any contribution fee. Every orthoses and prostheses and other treatment devices based on medical reports are provided without applying any restriction (Article 69/I, f of Act No. 5510).

§4. Recovery Rights of the Social Security Institution

585. Act No. 5510 envisages the legal responsibility of the employer in case of failure of certain other duties. The employer is obliged to ensure all necessary medical care immediately to an employee required by the victim's state of health until the Institution can take appropriate action, in cases of industrial accidents or occupational diseases. The Institution reimburses to the employer these expenses if documented, up to the amount fixed by the Healthcare Pricing Commission (Article 76/I of Act No. 5510). However, because of negligence or delay in providing care, if the treatment of the insured person is extended or if the victim remains disabled or if the degree of disability is increased, the employer is to refund to the Institution all expenses as a result of these failures (Article 76/II of Act No. 5510). Such responsibility arises from the culpa of the employer in providing the necessary healthcare to insured employees. The extent of the responsibility is limited with the culpa degree of the employer.[422]

586. For certain jobs and for certain groups of employees, the employer is also under an obligation to ask for a medical report which shows the suitability of the health conditions of an insurance holder, before appointing him/her to a job. If the employer employs the health insurance holder without requiring a due medical report or appoints him/her to a job which is not appropriate for his/her health condition without taking into account the health report, the health insurance holder may fall ill, because of such a failure. In that case, the employer is under an obligation to reimburse all healthcare expenses paid by the Institution. Unlike, the abovementioned responsibility, in that case, the failure of the employer constitutes itself a fault. Therefore, the employer shall be responsible for all expenses without any reduction.[423]

587. In addition, the insurance holder employee may get sick while working. In that case, in order to resume work, the insured employee is again obliged to obtain a report, stating that treatment has been completed and the insured employee has regained the capacity to work. Without receipt of this document, if the employer allows the insured employee to work without requiring such a report and the

422. C. Tuncay/Ö. Ekmekçi, n. 7, p. 612.
423. C. Tuncay/Ö. Ekmekçi, n. 7, p. 612.

employee falls ill for the second time, the employer is to refund all healthcare expenses paid by the Institution (Article 76/III of Act No. 5510).

588. The negligence of an employer which lies on the ground of industrial accidents or occupational diseases is another legal basis for the Institution's recovery right. If the industrial accident or occupational disease is the result of an intentional act of an employer or an employer conducts contrary to legislation concerning the protection of employees' health and safety, the employer is under an obligation to refund the healthcare expenses paid by the Institution. Like liability in insurance for industrial accidents, this is a culpa responsibility of the employer. While determining the extent of the responsibility, the principle of unavoidability is taken into account.[424]

589. Not only the employer but also the health insurance holder is responsible against the Institution for certain expenses arising from his/her own fault. The insurance holder should also take care of himself/herself during the recovery period. Therefore, if the insurance holder works in another job without taking a medical report stating that his/her treatment is over and he/she can work again, the insurance holder shall be responsible for healthcare expenses paid by the Institution, because of his/her sickness (Article 76/III of Act No. 5510). The fact of working in another job is sufficient to be liable for the expenses of repeated sickness.

590. The Institution shall also refund its expenses from third persons who caused the health problems of the insurance holder or his/her dependants with an intentional act or offensive conduct. The failure of a duty assigned by law or negligent conduct of a third person may also cause the health problems of the insurance holder or the extension of his/her treatment (Article 76/V of Act No. 5510). The degree of culpa of the third person shall be determinant in fixing his/her responsibility.

424. A. Güzel/A.R. Okur/N. Caniklioğlu, n. 7, p. 776; C. Tuncay/Ö. Ekmekçi, n. 7, p. 613.

Part VI. Unemployment Insurance

591. Unemployment is the final social risk against which protection is provided. The first studies of this subject started in 1959 with a report prepared by ILO experts. Since then, despite many draft bills (about thirty), it was only in 1999, with Act No. 4447, that unemployment insurance became a part of the system. One of the main reasons for such a delay was the absence of a job security system in Turkey. Following the enactment of unemployment insurance, job security was introduced into the system with Act No. 4773 dated 15 August 2002. Provisions of that Act have been replaced by LA No. 4857 issued on 22 May 2003.

592. Unlike other social insurance branches, unemployment insurance is administered not only by another Act separate from Act No. 5510, Social Insurances and Universal Health Insurance Act but also by a separate institution, the Turkish Employment Institution (İş-Kur) founded by Act No. 4904 dated 25 June 2003, pursuant to the annulment of Decree-law No. 617 by the Constitutional Court.[425]

593. Taking the nature of the unemployment risk into account, the aim of the Act is to provide benefits and services in the case of unemployment of insured employees (Article 46 of Act No. 4447). In addition to monetary help, job placement and vocational training are among the benefits available under Act No. 4447.

§1. Field of Application

I. Territorial Field of Application

594. Act No. 4447 does not include any clear provision regarding the territorial field of application. Its territorial field of application coincides with the personal field of application of Article 4/I, a of Act No. 5510.

595. As regards employees, who are sent on missions abroad, Act No. 4447 clearly states that their rights and duties continue as long as they perform their services abroad. After they return to the country, under the condition that they have fulfilled the required conditions, they benefit from services provided by unemployment insurance (Article 48/end of Act No. 4447).

425. Cons. Court, 31 Oct. 2000, 63/36, OJ, 8 Nov. 2000, No. 24224.

II. Personal Field of Application

596. Article 47/ I, d defined 'insured' under unemployment insurance as those, who work under a contract of employment at workplaces covered by the Act and who have paid unemployment insurance premiums. The first group consists of wage earners covered by Act No. 5510. Therefore, while determining the personal field of application, conditions required by Act No. 5510 are taken into consideration.[426] Not only workers under cover of Act No. 4857, LA, but also Act No. 854, Maritime Labour Law, and Act No. 5953, Labour Management Relations in the Press, fall under the scope of the unemployment insurance. Although Act No. 4447 refers to Article 4/I, a of Act No. 5510, there are different groups, stated in Article 4/II, which are not employed with a contract of employment, nevertheless, subjected to the social insurance regime of wage earners. The unemployment insurance covers only those who are employed with a contract of employment. Therefore, performing artists and musicians, rural security guards, prostitutes, masters in the courses fall under cover of unemployment insurance, only if they work with an employment contract.

By Act No. 6111, part-time workers are enabled to complete their contributions for non-contribution paid days of the month, including contributions for unemployment insurance. Thus, for the periods they do not work, they have the possibility to complete their non-contribution paid days as voluntary insurance holders. In that case, they may also benefit from unemployment insurance allowances (Article 46/II of Act No. 4447). Likewise, performing artists and drivers may benefit from this opportunity to complete their contributions by themselves (Supp. Article 6 of Act No. 5510). If they wish, they may also pay contributions for unemployment insurance and get benefits in the unemployed periods (Article 46/II of Act No. 4447).

597. The second group is composed of wage earners insured under the bank and insurance companies' funds.

598. Finally, foreign employees who are covered by bilateral agreements based on the principle of reciprocity also fell under the scope of Act No. 4447. Before an amendment made by Act No. 5754 of 2008, to enable foreign employees to be entitled to benefits of unemployment insurance, there had to be a bilateral agreement between the Turkish Republic and the country in which the foreign employee had a citizenship tie. However, under Act No. 4958 dated in 2000, foreigners who work in Turkey were covered by the social insurance system without any further conditions being set. Article 4/II of Act No. 5510 states clearly that foreigners who work with a contract of employment fall under cover of the personal scope of Act No. 5510. Therefore, foreigners will benefit from unemployment insurance without requiring a bilateral social security agreement.[427]

---

426. *See supra* paras 76–81.
427. A. Güzel/A.R. Okur/N. Caniklioğlu, n. 7, pp. 673–674; C. Tuncay/Ö. Ekmekçi, n. 7, p. 626; F. Uşan, n. 28, p. 346; *See* Ö Bal Bektaş, *İşsizlik Sigortası* (Ankara, 2016), pp. 126–130; comp. A.N. Sözer, n. 70, p. 499, n. 4.

599. Furthermore, those who work while drawing old-age pensions, either paying social security support contributions or not, are excluded from the scope of the Act.

600. Those who fall out of the scope of unemployment insurance are enumerated as follows (Article 46/III of Act No. 4447):

- Those who are subjected to Article 4/I, b, mainly Self-Employed persons, and Article 4/I, c, mainly civil servants.
- Those who are subjected to Article 4/II of Act No. 5510, unless they work with a contract of employment.
- Those who are subjected to Article 4/III of Act No. 5510, jockeys and trainers.
- Those who are subjected to Articles 5, 6 or transitory 13 of Act No. 5510.[428]

601. Although the legal status of civil servants is different, Act No. 4447 clearly states that civil servants and public employees who are employed under an administrative contract are not covered by unemployment insurance benefits. Since civil servants do not work with an employment contract, whether it was necessary to include such a clear provision seems doubtful.

§2. Benefits

I. Type of Benefits

602. Benefits provided by unemployment insurance are unemployment allowances, wage payments from the Wage Guarantee Fund, payment of contributions due to Act No. 5510, job placement and vocational training.

A. *Unemployment Allowances*

603. In order to make up for the loss of income in case of unemployment, the Act provides unemployment allowances to insured unemployed persons. The duration of payment of unemployment benefits is fixed in accordance with contribution payments. Those, who have notified contributions for 120 days continuously and that too within the last three years, receive benefits up to:

- 180 days, if they have worked as insured and have notified contributions for 600 days.
- 240 days, if they have worked as insured and have notified contributions for 900 days.
- 300 days of unemployment if they have worked as insured and have notified contributions for 1,080 days (Article 50/ II of Act No. 4447).

428. *See supra* para. 85.

B. Wage Payments from Wage Guarantee Fund

604. The establishment of a Wage Guarantee Fund was provided by Article 33 of LA with an aim to harmonizing Turkish law with Directive 80/987 relating to the protection of employees on the insolvency of their employer. By an amendment made by Act No. 5763[429] of 15 May 2008, the regulations on the Wage Guarantee Fund were transferred to supplementary Article 1 of Act No. 4447. If the employer of the insurance holder is unable to pay due to the declaration of the composition of debts, receiving an instrument of incapacity or bankruptcy, the insurance holder may require Wage Guarantee Fund to pay three months of non-paid wages arising from the contract of employment (Supp. Article 1 of Act No. 4447).

The income of the Fund consists of 1% of the amount of the annual total of employers' contributions for unemployment insurance and earnings (Supp. Article 1/II of Act No. 4447 and Article 6 of Regulation on Wage Guarantee Fund[430]).

C. Shorter Working Times and Temporary Unemployment Allowances

605. Under certain conditions, employers are empowered to temporarily suspend the activities of the workplace. Loss of wages is met by unemployment benefits at that time. Due to supplementary Article 22 of Act No. 4447, the employer who temporarily shortens the weekly working time in the workplace or who temporarily suspends work wholly or partially in the workplace due to a general, regional or sectoral economic crisis or force majeure must communicate this matter to the Turkish Employment Institution. The acceptability of such a request is decided by the Ministry of Labour and Social Security. Subject to the approval of the Ministry, the work is suspended, or shorter working hours are applied for at the workplace for at least four weeks. Shorter working hours cannot be instituted for a period longer than three months or anyway longer than the length of the force majeure (Supp. Article 2/I of Act No. 4447). Nevertheless, due to the severe economic crisis, shorter working hours practice was extended up to six months, and its amount was increased by 50% in 2008, 2009 and 2010 (Trans. Article 9 of Act No. 4447).

D. Contribution Payments Due to Act No. 5510

606. Before the reform, contributions of the unemployed insured for sickness and maternity insurance were paid by the Unemployment Insurance Fund. Although the payment of contributions for sickness and maternity insurance was welcomed, the absence of similar payments for long-term insurance branches, especially considering long insurance premium requirements had been criticized.[431] By the reform, unemployed insurance holders are deemed to be universal health insurance

429. OJ, 26 May 2008, No. 26887.
430. OJ, 28 Jun. 2009, No. 27272.
431. A. Güzel/A.R. Okur, n. 7, p. 697.

holders pursuant to Article 60/I, e of Act No. 5510. Unemployed or those working in shorter working hours will be notified to the Social Security Institution by the Turkish Employment Institution. The Institution is responsible for the payments of the universal health insurance contributions, but not for the contributions for long-term insurance branches.[432] In addition, if they are not under cover of another health insurance holder, the Turkish Employment Institution is also responsible for health insurance contributions of participants to vocational training organized by the Turkish Employment Institution.

E. Job Placement and Vocational Training

607. Job placement is one of the fundamental missions of the Employment Institution. The Institution is also under the obligation to provide vocational training and improvement and development of vocational education. If the unemployed insured refuses an offer for vocational training without just reason, unemployment benefits are terminated (Article 52/ I, a of Act No. 4447).

F. Unpaid Leave Allowances

608. By Act No. 6663, parental leave is introduced to the system.[433] Workers may prefer to work for half of the maximum weekly hours per week and use the rest of their time to bring up their children. The length of unpaid leave is 60 days for the first child, 120 days for the second child and 180 days for the third child. The Wage Guarantee Fund will meet the loss of wage during this period. In order to be entitled to receive such allowances, at least 600 days of contributions should have been notified within three years, which precede the date of confinement or adoption.

II. Amount of Benefits

A. Unemployment Allowances

609. The amount of the daily allowance is 40% of the average daily earnings computed on the basis of the last four month's income (Article 50/ I of Act No. 4447). The Act also sets an upper limit on this amount with the aim of making unemployment insurance less attractive. The unemployment benefit cannot exceed 80% of the gross amount of the monthly minimum wage. However, the Act in no way considers the level of income of the insured while working on his/ her familial obligations. Therefore, the amount of unemployment insurance benefit is far from enabling the insured to continue at his/ her level of standard of living during the period of unemployment.

---

432. A. Güzel/A.R. Okur/N. Caniklioğlu, n. 7, pp. 696–697; C. Tuncay/Ö. Ekmekçi, n. 7, pp. 656–657.
433. *See supra* para. 340.

610. Unemployment benefits are paid on a monthly basis. If the insured resumes working while payments continue and becomes unemployed without fulfilling the required conditions, he/she will receive the rest of the payments. However, if the insured re-satisfies the conditions, unemployment benefits will be paid according to these new conditions (Article 50/ IV of Act No. 4447).

B. Wage Payments

611. The Wage Guarantee Fund is responsible for a maximum of three months of non-paid wages of the insurance holder. Wages are paid on the basic wage. The daily amount of guaranteed wage cannot exceed the upper limit of the daily income basis for contributions (Supp. Article 1 of Act No. 4447, Article 9/1, 3 of RWGF). In addition, wages must belong to the periods before the economic difficulties. Severance payments and other indemnities cannot be claimed from the Fund.

C. Shorter Working Times and Temporary Unemployment Allowances

612. During shorter working hours, employees are paid daily shorter working hours allowance. The daily amount of benefit payment for working shorter is 60% of the gross amount of the average daily income calculated over twelve months' income-based for contribution (Supp. Article 2/IV of Act No. 5510). However, the amount of shorter working hours allowance cannot exceed 150% of the monthly minimum wage.

D. Contribution Payments

613. Contributions for universal health insurance are paid as long as unemployment benefits continue to be paid. The amount of contributions is 12% of the daily income basis for contributions (Article 81/I, f of Act No. 5510).

E. Unpaid Leave Allowance

614. The worker will receive half of his/her real wage in return for his/her work from the employer. With respect to the half-wage loss, the Employment Institution will grant an allowance. The daily amount of allowance is the gross amount of the daily minimum wage (Supp. Article 5/I of Act No. 4447). Thus, the worker will carry the loss arising from the difference between the daily wage and the gross amount of the minimum wage.

III. Suspension or Suppression of Unemployment Benefits

615. The Act defines the situations where unemployment payments to unemployed insured persons are to be suspended or suppressed as follows (Article 52/I of Act No. 4447):

- A refusal by the unemployed insured of an offer of employment suitable to his/her profession, close to the wage and working conditions of his/her previous employment and performed in the municipality where the insured resides will cause the termination of benefits. If the unemployed refuses such an offer on the part of the Institution without just reason, unemployment allowance payments will cease.
- Working in return for money or drawing an old-age pension from the Social Security Institution also results in termination of unemployment benefits. If the second part of the provision is clear, it is not the case for the first part. Whether every gainful activity is to be assessed under this subparagraph is equivocal. Every activity permanent in nature with the aim of earning a living should cause the termination of contribution payment. Therefore, precarious jobs with low income do not prevent the payment of unemployment benefits.[434]
- A refusal, without just reason, of an offer for training, with the aim of professional improvement, acquiring a profession or vocational training, will cause the suspension of payments. Or despite acceptance, if such a vocational training is given up, the unemployment benefit will be suspended.
- A failure to respond to or to present necessary documents to the Institution when called upon will also result in the suspension of allowance payments.

616. In the last two cases, the unemployment benefits will also be suspended. On removal of these deficiencies, benefit payment will be resumed (Article 52/II of Act No. 4447).

617. While receiving unemployment allowances, if the insured unemployed is entitled to receive temporary incapacity allowances from sickness or maternity insurance, the payment of unemployment allowances ceases for as long as the other payment continues (Article 52/3 of Act No. 4447). Likewise, if the insurance holder is called to arms, except compulsory military service, the payment of allowances shall be ceased.

§3. CONDITIONS

618. The conditions under which unemployment allowances and temporary shorter working time allowances are received are the same.[435]

434. C. Tuncay/Ö. Ekmekçi, n. 7, p. 643; A.N. Sözer, n. 70, p. 511, note 5; Ö. Bal Baktaş, n. 472, pp. 174–175.

435. *See*, for details, A. Güzel/A.R. Okur/N. Caniklioğlu, n. 7, pp. 680–689; C. Tuncay/Ö. Ekmekçi, n.

I. Involuntary Employment

619. The main condition for entitlement to unemployment insurance allowance is being involuntarily unemployed. Article 51 of the Act determines the nature of contract termination in a detailed manner.

620. The termination of the contract of employment from the employer's side by giving a period of notice: The employer has the right to terminate the contract of employment for an indefinite period by giving notice, within such a period, at any time. For employees who are covered by job security, the employer must additionally have a valid reason to terminate the contract.[436] In all these cases, the termination of the contract is considered to be involuntary.

621. The termination of the contract of employment by the employee with just reason: Under the Turkish LA, contracts, both for definite or indefinite periods, may be terminated either by the employee or by the employer without giving a notice period if a just reason exits.[437] Just reasons which enable the employee to break the contract are listed under three subtitles (Article 24 of LA): for reasons of health; for immoral, dishonourable or malicious conduct or other similar behaviours of the employer; and for force majeure. In these three cases, the employee is entitled to break the contract, whether for a definite or indefinite period, before its expiry or without giving notice periods. In such cases of termination, he/she is entitled to benefit from unemployment insurance.

Under Article 14/ II of the Maritime Labour Act No. 854, just reasons are as follows: the non-payment of the wage of the employee; all kinds of misconduct by the employer or the employer's representatives towards the employee, regarding statutory regulations, contract of employment or other working conditions; misconduct of the employer in the area of maritime customs and morals or a ship remaining in port or at anchor for more than thirty days, for whatever reason, enable the employee to terminate the contract without need to give a period of notice.

622. The termination of the contract by an employee by giving notice periods prevents entitlement to unemployment insurance. However, unlike LA No. 4857 and Maritime Labour Act No. 818, Act No. 4447 empowers a journalist to receive benefits from unemployment insurance in cases where the journalist terminates the contract by respecting the one-month notice period. In addition, journalists may break their contracts without waiting for the expiry of notice periods, in cases where a journal's or periodical's character or direction has changed in a manner which contravenes the moral beliefs of the journalist or sullies his/ her reputation.

7, pp. 634–640; F. Uşan, n. 28, pp. 348–351; A.N. Sözer, n. 70, pp. 503–508; Ö. Bal Bektaş, n. 478, pp. 138–199.

436. *See* T. Dereli, n. 91, paras 389–394.

437. *See* T. Dereli, n. 91, paras 411–419.

623. The termination of the contract of employment by the employer with a just reason: Article 51/I, c of Act No. 4447 gives the right to be entitled to unemployment benefits, even if it is the employer who terminates the contract with a just reason. If the employer breaks the contract for reasons of health or force majeure (Article 25/ I, III of LA), the employee receives unemployment benefits.[438]

However, if the contract is terminated with the just reason for immoral, dishonourable or malicious conduct or other similar behaviours on the part of the employee, he/she cannot profit from unemployment insurance (Article 25/ II of LA).

624. The termination of the contract of employment for a definite period because of the expiry of time: With the expiration of the time period defined by the contract, a contract for a definite period ends automatically. Such an end is also evaluated as involuntary employment.

625. As regards employees who do not fall under the personal scope of application of Labour Acts s Nos 4857, 854 and 5953, employment contracts must be terminated according to the provisions of the collective agreement or related provisions of the new Turkish Code of Obligations (Article 430 of TCO) parallel to Article 51/a, b, c, d, e of Act No. 4447.

626. Act No. 4447 also gives space to the termination of the contract of employment because of transfer or closing down of the workplace or a change in the quality of the workplace. While the termination of the contract in such cases is also among those cases mentioned above, it does not seem necessary to include such regulations in the Act.

627. Being unemployed under Act No. 4046, privatization also enables to receive benefits from unemployment insurance.

628. In order to receive unemployment insurance, the insurance holder must be employed; thus, the contract of employment must be terminated. If the contract of employment is suspended because of strike or lock-out or other legal duties, the unemployment benefits are not paid while the contract of employment is in force (Article 51/end of Act No. 4447).

II. Not Drawing Old-Age Pension or Income from Social Security Institution

629. In the first version of the Act, the strict wording prohibited any kind of income or pension drawn from social security institutions, either because of the insured's own work or in the capacity of a beneficiary. However, by an amendment, this provision took the form of 'not drawing an old-age pension or income' from

438. *See* T. Dereli, n. 91, paras 414–415.

the Social Security Institution. Therefore, drawing pensions other than old-age ones does not prevent the entitlement to unemployment benefits.

III. Unemployment Contribution Payment

630. In order to be entitled to unemployment benefits, the insured must have worked as insured and at least 600 days his contributions for unemployment insurance should have been notified within the three years which precede the termination of employment. In addition, the insured must have worked and made contributions continuously during the 120 days before leaving work should have notified (Article 51 of Act No. 4447). This last condition relating to the work for 120 days continuously has been criticized since such a requirement is against social security principles.[439] The Employment Institution excluded some periods from the calculation of 120 days by a Communique.[440] While calculating 120 days, time passed under strike or lock-out or the period that an insurance holder suffers an illness or disciplinary punishment, the period of unpaid leave, the period of arrest not concluded in conviction, the periods of suspension or interruption of the work due to incidents which affect general life, economic crisis or force majeure will not be counted. Even if the employment contract continues, the time passed under these periods is not counted within 120 days.

IV. Application to the Institution

631. Before an amendment made by Act 5763,[441] the insured unemployed had to submit his/her written request personally to the Institution within thirty days following the termination of the contract of employment. Arguing on this provision, the Court of Cassation disapproved the submission of a request by the lawyer of the unemployed insurance holder, while the Act states clearly that the submission should occur by the insurance holder himself/herself.[442] However, as a result of the amendment, the electronic submission of the request has become possible.

632. If the insured delays submitting the request to the Institution, except in cases of force majeure, the period delayed is deducted from the total period for which benefits are entitled (Article 48/V of Act No. 4447). The employer is also charged with the duty of informing the Institution. The employer is to issue three copies of a certificate, one submitted to the Institution, another to the unemployed insured and the third to be kept by the employer (Article 51 of Act No. 4447).

439. A. Güzel/A.R. Okur/N. Caniklioğlu, n. 7, pp. 688689;Y. Alper, n. 7, p. 393; S.A. Limoncuoğlu, 'İşsizlik Sigortası ve Uygulama Sorunları', *Sicil Der.*(Haziran 2012), p. 91; Ö. Bal Bektaş, n. 478, p. 180.

440. Communique N. 3 of the Turkish Employment Institution, OJ, 30 Jan. 2002, No. 24656.

441. Act No. 5763 of 15 May 2008, OJ, 26 May 2008, No. 26887.

442. Court of Cass., Gen. Ass., 6.5.2006, 10-243/271, cited and noted by Ö. Ekmekçi, 'Sosyal Sigortaların Genel hükümleri ve Türleri', in *Yargıtayın İş Hukukuna İlişkin kararlarının değerlendirilmesi 2006* (Ankara, 2009), pp. 302–303; S.A. Limoncuoğlu, *İşsizlik Sigortası*, p. 92.

633. Although the Act contains no such express clause, the ratio of the Act necessitates that the insured must be available for the labour market in order to receive unemployment insurance benefits. Certain provisions include implicit indications of this principle. It is up to the insured to prove himself/herself available for employment.[443]

§4. ADMINISTRATION

634. Like other social insurance relationships, unemployment insurance is compulsory in nature. Hence, the rights and obligations of insured persons and of their employers are effective, starting from the date on which the insured resumes work. The statutory provisions of the Act have a mandatory character (Article 48/ III of Act No. 4447). Due to the second paragraph of Article 48, workplaces and employees notified to the Social Security Institution will also be deemed to be notified to the Employment Institution. Therefore, there is no need to register employees and workplaces separately with the Institution.

635. The Turkish Employment Institution is responsible for the administration of unemployment insurance considering its firm relationship with labour markets, vocational training and job placement. However, in order to prevent duplication of contribution payment to different organizations, it is the Social Security Institution, which is charged with collecting contributions for unemployment insurance.[444]

636. The main financial source is contributions. When determining the contribution rates, for the very first time, the state is charged with the duty of participating in contributions payments in Turkey. The contribution rate of the employee is 1%, that of the employer is 2% and of the state is 1%. Voluntary insurance holders must also pay employer's share, thus 3%. The contribution amounts are to be computed at the income level, which is the basis for calculating other insurance contributions.[445] After having collected contributions, the Social Security Institution will transfer them to the Unemployment Insurance Fund by the fifteenth of the month following the month contributions are collected (Article 49/ VII of Act No. 4447). The state contribution is received by the Employment Institution from the Treasury. The Treasury must transfer the required amount within fifteen days following the request (Article 49/end of Act No. 4447).

443. C. Tuncay, *İşsizlik Sigortası*, pp. 47–49; A.N. Sözer, n. 70, p. 507.
444. For further information about the organization of the unemployment insurance *see* Y. Alper, 'İşsizlik Sigortasının Örgütlenmesi, Yönetimi ve Finansmanı: Türkiye Uygulaması', in *Arbeits- und Sozialrechtliche Probleme der Arbeitslosigkeit, İşsizliğin İş Hukuku ve Sosyal Güvenlik Açısından Sorunları*(Ankara, 2003), pp. 99–119; Ö. Bal Bektaş, n. 478, pp. 89–95.
445. *See supra* paras 104–111.

Part VII. The Disabled Persons

637. The disabled persons and their problems have come to the order of legislator by Act No. 5378 on Disabled Persons which was adopted in 2005.[446] However, there still exist many problems on the implementation of that legislation. General Directorship for Disabled and Old Persons under the Ministry for Family and Social Politics is the main institution responsible for problems of disabled persons.

638. The main approach of the Turkish social security system to the security needs of disabled persons is disability targeting of transfers. The social inclusion of persons with disabilities is among the issues that Turkish social security continues to ignore.[447]

There exist special provisions which enable disabled persons to receive social insurance benefits fulfilling less heavy conditions. Insured persons suffering invalidity before starting work for the first time as an insurance holder are not entitled to receive benefits from invalidity insurance. Nevertheless, to be entitled to an old-age pension, they profit from better conditions.[448] However, the system does not provide many benefits to disabled persons who do not work under the cover of social insurances. Act No. 2022 grants financial allowances to those who have completed the age of 65 and who are indigents; it covers disabled persons also. If the disabled person is in need, limited financial assistance is provided under Act No. 2022. Otherwise, there exists no special legislation providing social assistance to disabled persons.

§1. Beneficiaries

639. There exist three different groups who receive benefits under Act No. 2022: Care-dependent disabled persons, disabled persons not recruited and caretaker relatives of disabled persons. Regulation on Granting Pensions to Persons over 65 and Indigents (RGPI)[449] determines the conditions for granting disability allowances.

446. OJ, 7 Jul. 2005, No. 25868.
447. C. Ünal, *Özürlülerin Sosyal Güvenlik Hakları*(Istanbul, 2012), pp. 87–88.
448. *See supra* para. 385.
449. OJ, 25 Jan. 2013, No. 28539.

640. It should be underlined that there exists a lack of coherence with regard to the definitions of disability and invalidity. Pursuant to Article 3 of Act No. 5378, disabled is the person who has difficulties in adapting to the social life and in meeting daily needs due to the loss of physical, mental, psychological, sensory and social capabilities at various levels by birth or by any reason thereafter and who therefore needs protection, care, rehabilitation, consultancy and support services. In addition, suffering a certain ratio of disability does not enable persons to get financial allowances. The disabled person must be in need and not have anybody who is under a duty to take care of him/her.

I. Care-Dependent Disabled Persons

641. The first group of disabled persons under cover of Act No. 2022 are those who are older than 18 and who cannot maintain his/her life without the assistance and care of others. A disabled person, whose loss of total body function is 70% or above, is deemed to be a care-dependent disabled person (Article 2/I, b of RGPI).[450] To get this allowance, the disabled person must have no spouse, ascendants or descendants who are legally obliged to support him/her. According to the Turkish Civil Code, spouses, both parents, children, brothers and sisters, only if they live in easy circumstances, have to provide the maintenance of each other.[451] Those who receive any benefit, whatever its nature, from social security institutions or who work in a job which requires a compulsory insurance holdership with respect to long-term insurance branches fall out of the scope of this Act. The indigence of care-dependent persons shall be confirmed by the Social Assistance and Solidarity Foundations.

II. Disabled Persons

642. The second group consists of disabled persons who are between 18 and 65 years. A total loss of 40% and 69% of physical, mental, psychological, sensory and social capabilities is required (Article 2/I, c of RGPI). They must not be placed on any job. In addition, there must be nobody who is under a duty to take care of the concerned person. However, disability allowance shall continue to be paid even if the beneficiary has completed the age of 65 under the condition that his/her poverty continues.

III. Caretakers

643. Since the institutional care facilities are not far from providing a satisfactory level of protection, the care of disabled persons are mainly maintained by families. Therefore, Act No. 2022 provides financial allowances to those who actively

450. C. Ünal, n. 492, p. 147.
451. C. Ünal, n. 492, pp. 152–153.

take care of disabled persons if they have Turkish nationality. Caretakers may only ask for allowances for disabled with whom they have a legal dependency and whose disability ratio is 40% or more. Since there is no family allowance, the system provides a limited benefit to families. The disabled person must be younger than the age of 18. An active care relation is required. The disabled person and caretakers must live in the same household (Article 2/ç and 7/IV of RGPI)

§2. Benefits

644. Act No. 2022 provides three kinds of benefits: care-dependent disability allowance, disability allowance and caretakers' allowance.

645. The amount of disability and caretakers' allowance equals the monthly amount to be achieved by multiplying the indicator figure (3.240)with the civil servant salary coefficient. The monthly amount in 2018 was about TRY 50,273, less than EUR 100. The Act provides a higher amount for care-dependent disabled persons. The monthly amount of care-dependent disability allowances is to be achieved by multiplying the indicator figure (4.860) with the civil servant salary coefficient. The monthly amount in 2018 was TRY 75,410, which is about EUR 100.

§3. Minimum Income Level

646. The main condition for these benefits is that the concerned beneficiary must be in needy circumstances. According to Act No. 2022, the domestic income per capita, a monthly average of all kinds of incomes under any name of the beneficiary, must be less than one-third of the amount of the minimum wage and the Social Assistance and Solidarity Foundation should decide on the indigence of the caretakers.

647. The Regulation enumerates certain groups who fall out of the scope of beneficiaries as below (Article 7/II):

- those receiving any income or pension from social security institutions or those who are working as subjected to Article 4/I, a (mainly employees), Article 4/I, b (mainly Self-Employed persons) and 4/I, c (mainly public civil servants) of Act No. 5510;
- those paying social security contributions voluntarily;
- those who have universal health insurance holdership according to Article 60/I, g of Act No. 5510;
- those who are eligible to be assigned maintenance allowance that the amount equals to or above the minimum required;
- those who are eligible to receive any kind of permanent income that the amount equals to or above the minimum required, which is one-third of the amount of the minimum wage;

– those who receive permanent care in public or private nurseries or institutions; and
– those who receive care in return for a transfer of his/her property to a real or legal person are not entitled to receive monthly allowances. Only caretakers who receive old-age pensions or disability allowances are entitled to receive caretakers' allowance if they have a disabled relative younger than the age of 18.

648. The Social Assistance and Solidarity Foundation shall investigate all incomes and expenditures of the household by a means test. In addition, each year, there is a social investigation which requires visits to the beneficiaries' household and surrounding.

§4. Procedure

649. The application must be addressed to the foundation founded in the place of residence of the beneficiary. The disabled persons are obliged to prove their disability by a health board report to be obtained from a fully equipped hospital. Allowances are allocated starting from the month, which follows the application to the Social Assistance and Solidarity Fund. The Fund pays allowances once every three months. If the income level or disability ratio of the beneficiary changes, the allowances will be terminated.

§5. Accumulation Rules

650. The beneficiary cannot receive any other benefits or income from the social security institution. If the beneficiary receives any income or pension from the social security system, the payment of financial allowances is terminated.

Part VIII. Right to Social Integration

651. Although the welfare state principle is guaranteed by the Constitution, a right to a minimum income for everyone is not recognized under the Turkish social security system. The struggle against poverty is maintained by a fragmentary and unsatisfactory system of social assistance and social services. The social inclusion of individuals is absent as a target of the actual social security system.

Part IX. Non-contributory Regime

652. The Non-contributory regime financed by tax revenues has a supplementary nature under Turkish Social Security Law. The Non-contributory regime is much more fragmented compared to the contributory regimes. Many different statutory regulations, some of which coincide with each other, ensure that this regime is far from being unified and coherent.

653. To provide a decent life for all citizens is one of the duties of the welfare state.[452]

Article 61 of the Constitution defines the general fundamentals of state responsibility as follows:

> The state shall protect the widows and orphans of those killed in a war and in the line of duty, together with the disabled and war veterans, and ensure that they enjoy a decent standard of living.
> The state shall take measures to protect the disabled and secure their integration into community life.
> The aged shall be protected by the state. State assistance to the aged, and other rights and benefits shall be regulated by law.
> The state shall take all necessary measures for social resettlement of children in need of protection.
> To achieve these aims, the state shall establish the necessary organizations or facilities, or arrange for their establishment by other bodies.

654. The Non-contributory regime consists of two main axes: social assistance and social services. Nevertheless, the lack of coordination and the difference of criteria and standards among the different organizations appear to be a serious deficiency.

655. The third axe of the reform project is the Non-contributory regime. The Draft Bill on Social Services and the Non-contributory Payments has been replaced by the Draft Bill on Social Services and Aids, which has not been enacted yet.[453] In lieu of the current system, instead of coordination and collaboration, an institutional

452. A.N. Sözer, *Sosyal Hukuk*, pp. 5 et seq.
453. For different drafts *see* E. Yuvalı, E. Yuvalı, *Türk Sosyal Güvenlik Hukukunda Merkezi (Kamusal) Sosyal Yardımlar*(Ankara, 2017), pp. 220–231.

restructuring is set up under the Social Security Institution, which would be the single organization responsible for providing services. However, in 2011, the Ministry of Family and Social Services took responsibility for an important part of social services and social assistance. Therefore, a two-headed administration with a lack of coherence continues.

§1. SOCIAL ASSISTANCE

I. Social Assistance Aiming to Protect Citizens Served to the Country

656. In order to protect citizens who have served the country both in peace and in wartime, many statutory regulations have been enacted at different times.[454]

Such legislated assistance is in the nature of compensation granted to individuals who suffered an injury while being in public service or working for the public interest:[455]

- Act No. 4109 provides help to soldiers' families in need.
- Act No. 1005 allocates a 'pension of honour' to those who have been granted the Independence Medal. In case of the death of the beneficiary, 75% of the salary is allocated to the widowed spouse.
- Act No. 3292 allocates a pension to those who have served the country with assiduity and success.
- Act No. 2330 grants compensation in grants and pensions to the survivors of those who lose their lives in service aiming to protect the safety and security in peacetime or to prevent or trace and investigate smuggling.
- Act No. 3713 includes provisions aiming to protect those struggling against terrorism. If they die or become disabled in the line of duty, they or their widows and orphans will receive benefits.
- Act No. 168 aims to provide social assistance to teachers of Turkish background but having foreign nationality if they perform services to Turkish culture abroad.
- Act No. 2629 provides a death or disability indemnity to holders of certain positions in the Turkish Armed Forces, such as pilots, parachutists, etc.
- Decree-Law No. 667 grants a pension to civilians who are veterans or to benefits' owners of civilians who lost their lives during the coup attempt on 15 July 2016 or following terrorist actions.

454. For further information, see A.N. Sözer, *Sosyal Hukuk*, pp. 35 et seq.; L. Akın, 'Sosyal Yardım ve Hizmetler', pp. 252 et seq.; A. Güzel/A.R. Okur/N. Caniklioğlu, n. 7, pp. 812–820; C. Tuncay/Ö. Ekmekçi, n. 7, pp. 742–745; F. Uşan, n. 28, pp. 64 et seq.; K. Arıcı, n. 7, pp. 514–522; E. Yuvalı, n. 499, pp. 143 et seq.

455. A.N. Sözer, *Sosyal Hukuk*, pp. 29–30; C. Tuncay/Ö. Ekmekçi, n. 7, p. 742; F. Uşan, n. 28, p. 64; E. Yuvalı, n. 499, p. 145.

II. Social Assistance Aiming to Protect Citizens in Need

657. Although no provision regarding minimum income benefit exists, there are certain regulations aiming to protect citizens in need.

658. Act No. 2022 grants a pension to those who have completed the age of 65 and who are indigents. The first condition for entitlement to these benefits is Turkish nationality. The person concerned must have completed the age of 65. There must be nobody who is under a duty to care for the concerned person. Furthermore, he/she must not be receiving a pension or income from the Social Security Institution. In addition, he/she must have no capacity to work and must be in need. According to Act No. 2022, the domestic income per capita, a monthly average of all kinds of incomes under his own name and the name of his/her spouse name must be less than one-third of the amount of the minimum wage. If the concerned person is married and his/her spouse possesses the same qualifications; the pension is increased by 50%. The Social Assistance and Solidarity Foundation is the institution which carries the social investigation and takes the decision on the entitlement.[456]

659. Disabled persons, who have not reached the age of 65 and who need the care of another person, as well as persons who have the duty to care for a disabled child also receive benefits under this Act.[457]

660. Pensions are allocated starting from the month, which follows the application to the Social Security Institution. The Institution pays pensions once every three months. If the income level of the beneficiary changes after pensions have been allocated, the pensions will be terminated.

661. Act No. 3294, Incentives for Social Assistance and Solidarity Fund, aims to help the poor and citizens in need and to take measures to strengthen social justice. Persons in need and who do not draw pensions or incomes from the Social Security Institutions, or persons who may become productive with a little support and education, fall under the scope of this Act. While determining whether the concerned person is in need or not, not only the person himself/ herself but also the family is taken into account.[458]

662. Besides citizens, those who have come to the country, in whatever manner, are covered. Therefore, foreigners, stateless persons and immigrants may also receive benefits. Immigrants come first in receiving the most benefits from certain foundations. Thus, the term 'citizen' in the Act must be understood as 'people residing in Turkey under the frame of this Act'.[459]

---

456. *See* E. Yuvalı, n. 499, pp. 179–188.
457. *See supra* Part VII.
458. T. Canbolat, 'Sosyal Yardımlaşma ve Dayanışmayı Teşvik Fonu', p. 7; A.N. Sözer, *Sosyal Hukuk*, p. 88.
459. S. Dilik, 'Sosyal Yardımlaema ve Dayanıemayı Teevik Kanunu', *Çimento İşv. Der.*(Mart, 1987), p.

663. Both benefits in cash and in-kind are provided. Benefits in cash may be paid on specific occasions, such as for medical expenses, or over a period of time, such as for food or heating costs. Permanent monetary benefits are also allocated to old persons or handicapped people suffering from poverty. However, the amount of income is not sufficient to lead a life suitable to human dignity. In addition, social assistance and solidarity foundations provide services such as serving food, care in rest homes, etc.

664. A special fund was established to provide financial support. The Social Assistance and Solidarity Fund is affiliated to the Ministry of Family and Social Policies.

§2. Social Services

665. Article 61 of the Constitution orders the protection of infants, disabled and aged persons. Furthermore, the state is under the obligation to regulate the central planning and functioning of health services (Article 56/III of Constitution). In addition, the state is to take the measures necessary to meet the need for housing (Article 57 of Constitution). Considering the Constitutional provisions, social services may be studied under three main axes: social services directed to indigents, infants and aged persons, healthcare and housing.[460]

666. At the institutional level, different public entities were responsible for social services. In 2011, the Ministry of Family and Social Policies undertook the Directorate-General for the Status of Women, the Social Services and Child Protection Institution, the Prime Ministry Administration for Disabled People, the General Directorship of Social Assistance and Solidarity.[461] Nevertheless, municipalities and some other institutions also continue to provide social services.[462]

I. Social Services Provided to Indigents, Infants and Aged Persons

667. These social services are provided by the Ministry for Family and Social Policies.

668. Act No. 2828 on Social Services aims to provide social services to families, infants, the disabled, the aged and to other persons in need of protection, care or help. The Act defines groups in need of protection, such as infants in need of protection are those who have lost either one or both parents, or whose parents are unknown and who have been abandoned or neglected; invalids, who are in need of

15; T. Canbolat, 'Sosyal Yardımlaşma ve Dayanışmayı Teşvik Fonu', p. 5; A.N. Sözer, *Sosyal Hukuk*, p. 90.

460. A. Güzel/A.R. Okur/N. Caniklioğlu, n. 7, pp. 828–833; C. Tuncay/Ö. Ekmekçi, n. 7, pp. 759–779.

461. Decree-Law/633 of 3 Jun. 2011, OJ, 8 Jun. 2011, No. 27958 (Mük.).

462. A.N. Sözer, *Sosyal Hukuk*, pp. 109 et seq.

care of someone else, aged persons. Although the Act covers every individual, the indigent, infants, disabled and aged persons are given priority. Also, rescue services, in case of national disasters, are considered under social services (Article 4/I, m of Act No. 2828).

669. In the reform project, the right to social benefits will be determined according to the minimum subsistence level criteria. The delay in the reform of Non-contributory social security regimes has postponed the implementation of the means test in Non-contributory regimes. However, by the entry into force of the universal health insurance as of 1 January 2012, those who were not covered by any social insurance regimes were under obligation to submit means test results by the end of 2012. But in terms of social services and social assistance, today, there is no clear means test. The proposed solution is that the minimum subsistence level would be determined according to the per capita expenditure and accepted as being one-third of the daily minimum wage.[463]

670. The nature of services depends on the person concerned. As regards children needing protection, in order to ensure corporal, mental or physiological development of the child, assistance in-kind or in cash may be directed to the family of the child. In addition, foster families or institutional care services (children's homes, orphanages, etc.) are other means of assistance. For women in need of protection, women's shelters have been established. Also for youths, rehabilitation services, dormitories or youth centres are to be established. Occupational rehabilitation is offered to the disabled in need. If neither occupational nor medical rehabilitation is possible, they will be taken under permanent care. As regards aged persons, old-age homes are set up.[464] It should be noted, despite the very detailed provisions of the Act, the quality of services is far from being satisfactory.

II. Housing and Other Social Services

671. Traditionally, foundations have played an important role in providing social services. The General Directorship of Foundations is affiliated to the ministry. Social assistance and social services are among the primary missions of foundations. Thus, the General Directorship has student dormitories, education and holiday facilities and soup kitchens. Monthly allowances are also allocated to disabled, children or unemployed persons in need.

672. The right to housing is recognized by the Constitution as a social right. Act No. 3320 was enacted with the aim of housing civil servants, employees and their survivors. That Act was abolished by Act No. 588. The Housing Development Administration of Turkey, founded by Act No. 2985, is responsible for housing services.

463. Proposal for the reform in the Social Security System, p. 22.
464. For further information, A.N. Sözer, *Sosyal Hukuk*, pp. 118 et seq.

Part X. Claims and Adjudication

§1. Claims

I. Introduction of Claims

673. Social Security Institution provides benefits to insurance holders, in principle, upon their written request. Only in certain cases, the Institution takes action on its own initiative.

674. The principal statute of limitation for long-term insurance branches is five years. The starting date of the statute of limitation varies in accordance with the benefits: Incomes and pensions, which should be granted in cases of industrial accident, occupational disease, duty invalidity and survivors insurances, should be requested within five years following the granting date of the right, which means the date of accident or decease of the insurance holder (Article 97/I of Act No. 5510). It should be underlined that other long-term insurance benefits, old-age pension and invalidity pension, are granted upon the written request of the beneficiary. Thus, there is no place for a statute of limitation. Nevertheless, only the amount of pensions or incomes, which have not been claimed by the expiry of the five-year period, shall be barred. The beneficiaries keep their rights for the future. The Act also enables individuals to prove justified grounds for the non-application to the Institute.

675. The Act sets another statute of limitation to collect granted incomes or pensions. Incomes and pensions, which have not been collected continuously for twelve months following the accrual dates, shall be suspended with an aim to control whether the conditions for granting income or pensions are still present (Article 97/IV of Act No. 5510).

676. Unlike permanent pensions and incomes, other benefits granted by short-term insurance branches, mainly temporary incapacity allowances, are lost by the expiry of the five-year period.

677. With respect to universal health insurance, claims of universal insurance holders and their dependants shall be barred if not requested within two years after the receipt of the information on the incident causing the right. In any event, those claims shall be terminated at the end of five years.

II. Protection Against Seizure and Transfer

678. Any kind of incomes, pensions and allowances allocated to insurance holders or their dependants cannot be transferred or alienated (Article 93/1 of Act No. 5510).

679. Unlike transferability, the Act adopts a more flexible approach to the seizure of allowances, incomes and pensions. The principle is the same as the transferability: all incomes, pensions and allowances granted according to Act No. 5510 cannot be seized. However, there exist two exceptions: First, the Social Security Institution is entitled to claim for the seizure of incomes, pensions or allowances because of non-paid contribution debts of the insurance holder. Therefore, the Social Security Institution is privileged among creditors. Second, there is no protection against alimony debts. In addition, by an amendment made in 2009,[465] the insurance holder or the beneficiary may give its permission to such a seizure. Therefore, the prohibition for seizure may be revealed by the clear consent of the insurance holder (Article 93 of Act No. 5510).

§2. Adjudication

680. Social security disputes are heard by labour courts, which are competent for labour law disputes also. Even before the reform, social security issues of wage earners and Self-Employed persons were held by labour courts. However, issues arising from Act No. 5434 on Pension Fund were held by administrative courts. By the unification of the system, unless otherwise specified, conflicts that may arise due to the execution of the Act No. 5510 shall be resolved in labour courts (Article 101 of Act No. 5510).[466] Therefore, claims related to social security of civil servants are brought before labour courts after the entry into force of Act No. 5510. Also, in certain cases, such as administrative fines, administration courts are competent.[467]

681. In addition, disputes arising from special acts, for example, Act No. 2022 on granting financial allowances to those who have completed the age of 65 and who are indigents are held by administrative courts.[468]

682. By an amendment made by Act No. 6652,[469] in all disputes related to Act No. 5510 or other legislation related to social security, it is compulsory to submit a request to the Social Security Institution before bringing an action. The only exception is the case aiming for the establishment of insured periods by court decisions. Unless otherwise specified, if the Institution does not respond within sixty days, the

465. Act No. 5838 dated of 18 Feb. 2009, OJ, 28 Feb. 2009, No. 27155 M.
466. *See* A.N. Sözer, 'Sosyal Güvenlik Hukukunda Yargı Yolu Uyuşmazlıkları', *İş Hukuku ve Sosyal Güvenlik Hukuku Akademik Formu*(Istanbul, 2014), pp. 573 et seq.
467. For different decisions and discussion A.N. Sözer, 'Sosyal Güvenlik Hukukunda Yargı Yolu Uyuşmazlıkları' pp. 584–595.
468. Court of Cass., 10th Ch., 5 May 2011, 201/10468, K. 2011/6782, www.kazanci.com.tr.
469. OJ, 11 Sep. 2014, No. 29116 (Mük.).

request is considered as refused. In order to bring an action against the Social Security Institution, it is mandatory that the applicant's request is refused or considered refused (Article 7/III of Act No. 5521 on Labour Courts). The time passed during the request and response to the Institution is not considered while calculating the statute of limitation or strict time limit.

683. Labour courts are composed of only professional judges. Suits may be brought before the courts in charge of the locality. Claims could be brought before the courts wherein the legal domicile of the defendant is located or wherein the establishment is situated. The Court of Cassation held that suits against the Social Security Institution might be brought either in Ankara, wherein the headquarters of the Institution is located, or in any town wherein a competent affiliation of the Institution is located.[470]

684. The appeal against the final judgment of labour courts is held by the Tenth and Twenty-First Chambers of Court of Cassation (Yargıtay), of administrative courts by the Council of State (Danıştay).

470. Court of Cass., 10th Ch., 11 Oct. 1984, 1984/4638, 1984/4642, M. Çenberci, n. 80, p. 703.

Selected Bibliography

Legislation

Kazancı Bilişim, Electronic Legislation and Jurisprudence Bank.
Hukuk Türk, Electronic Legislation and Jurisprudence Bank.
Legalbank, Electronic Legislation and Jurisprudence Bank.
Lexpera, Hukuk Veri Tabanı, Electronic Legislation and Jurisprudence Bank.

Reviews of Court Decisions and Commentaries

Aslanköylü, R., *Sosyal Sigortalar Kanunu Yorumu, Vol. 2*, Ankara, 2004.
Aslanköylü, R., *Sosyal Sigortalar ve Genel Sağlık SigortasıŞerhi (Bağ-Kur Kanunu ile Karşılaştırmalı)*, Ankara, 2015.
Çakmak, İ., *Şerhli 1479 Sayılı Bağ-Kur Kanunu ile 2926 Sayılı Tarım Bağ-Kur Kanunu*, Ankara, 2004.
Çenberci, M., *Sosyal Sigortalar Kanunu Şerhi*, Ankara, 1985.
Ekonomi, M./ Ulucan, D., *İş Hukuku Uygulaması (İHU), Kararlar ve İncelemeleri, SSK IV*, 1975–1989, loose-leaf.
Yelekçi, M., *Sosyal Sigortalar Kanunu Şerhi*, Ankara, 2001.
Tezel, A., *T.C. Emekli Sandığı Kanunu*, Ankara, 2004.
Tezel, A./Kurt, Resul, *Sosyal Güvenlik Reformu Yorum ve Açıklaması, 5510 Sayılı Sosyal Sigortalar ve Genel Sağlık Sigortası Kanunu*, Ankara, 2009.
Topçu, U., *Hizmet Tespit Davaları, Bilirkişi Raporları ve Yargıtay Uygulamaları Işığında,* 3. ed.,İstanbul, 2017.

Handbooks

Alper, Y. *Sosyal Sigortalar Hukuku*, 8. ed., Bursa, 2016.
Araslı, U. *Sosyal Güvenlik ve Sosyal Sigortalar,* Vol. II, Ankara, 2002.
Arıcı, K. *Türk Sosyal Güvenlik Hukuku,* Ankara, 2015.
Bal Bektaş, Ö., İşsizlik Sigortası, Ankara, 2016.
Dilik, S. *Sosyal Güvenlik,* Ankara, 1992.
Gerek, N. *Sosyal Güvenlik Hukuku,* Eskişehir, 2002.
Günay, C.İ. *İş ve Sosyal Güvenlik Hukuku Dersleri,* Ankara, 2008.
Güzel, A./A.R. Okur/N. Caniklioğlu, *Sosyal Güvenlik Hukuku*, 16. ed., İstanbul, 2016.
Karakaş, İ., *Emeklilik Uygulaması ve Davaları,* 4. Ed., Ankara, 2016.
Saymen, F.H./M. Ekonomi, *Sosyal Sigortalar Tatbikatı,* İstanbul, 1966.
Sözer, A.N., *Türk Sosyal Sigortalar Hukuku,* 2. ed.,İstanbul, 2015.

Selected Bibliography

Sözer, A.N., *Türk Genel Sağlık Sigortası,* İstanbul, 2014.
Şakar, M., *Sosyal Sigortalar Uygulaması.* 12. ed., İstanbul, 2017.
Talas, C., *Sosyal Güvenlik ve Türk İşçi Sigortaları,* Ankara, 1953.
Tuncay, C./Ekmekçi, Ö., *Sosyal Güvenlik Hukuku Dersleri.* 18. ed., İstanbul, 2012.
Tunçomağ, K., *Sosyal Güvenlik Kavramı ve Sosyal Sigortalar.* 5. ed., İstanbul, 1990.
Korkusuz, M. R./S. Uğur, *Sosyal Güvenlik Hukuku,* 4. ed., Bursa, 2015.
Yazgan, T., *Sosyal Sigorta,* İstanbul, 1977.

Monographs

Akin, E.P., *Türk Hukukunda Kadın İşçilerin Sosyal Güvenliği,* İstanbul, 2005.
Akın, L., *Bağ-Kur Sigorta Yardımları,* İstanbul, 1996.
Akın, L., *Sosyal Güvenlik Hukukunda BağımlıÇalışanların Maluliyeti,* Ankara, 2007.
Arıcı, K., *Avrupa Birliği Sosyal Güvenlik Hukuku,* Ankara, 1997.
Atabek, R., *İş Kazası ve Sigortası,* İstanbul, 1978.
Başterzi, S., *İşsizlik Sigortası,* Ankara, 1996.
Baycık, G., *İş ve Sosyal Güvenlik Açısından Maden İşçileri,* Yetkin, 2006.
Bulut, M., *Hizmet Tespit Davaları,* 2. ed., Ankara, 2016.Bulut, M., *İdari Para CezalarıItiraz ve Dava Yolları Tüm Yönleriyle Reform Sonrası Sosyal Güvenlik Uygulamalarında,*Ankara, 2010.
Bulut, M., *Sosyal Güvenlik Usul Hukuku Sosyal Parafiskal Yükümlülükler Yönüyle.* Ankara, 2010.
Bulut, M., *Sosyal Güvenlik Usul Hukuku.* Ankara, 2010.
Bulut, M., *Asgari İşçilik Uygulamaları Usul ve Esasları,* İstanbul, 2017.
Bulut, M., *Sosyal Güvenlik Uyuşmazlıkları ve Çözüm Yolları,* İstanbul, 2017.
Caniklioğlu, N.,*Sosyal Sigortalarda Prim Teşvikleri.* Beta, 2011.
Centel, T.,*Sosyal Güvenlikte Yapısal Değişim,*İstanbul, 1997.
Çelebi, D., *Türk Sosyal Sigortalar Hukukunda Yurt Dışı Hizmet Borçlanması,* İstanbul, 2017.
Demircioğlu, M./A. Güzel. *İşverenin Sosyal Sigorta Yükümlülükleri ve Sorumluluğu,*İstanbul, 2001.
Duman, B.,*506 Sayılı Sosyal Sigortalar Kanuna Göre Hizmetlerin Tespiti,* Ankara, 2002.
Ekin, N., *İşsizlik Sigortası,* Ankara, 1994.
Ergin, H.,*Türkiye'nin İmzaladığıİkili Sosyal Güvenlik Sözleşmeleri,* İstanbul, 2008.
Göktaş, M., E. Çakar/M. Özdamar., *Türk Sosyal Güvenlik Sisteminde Emeklilik ve Primsiz Rejim,* Ankara, 2011.
Güçlü, Y., *İş ve Sosyal Güvenlik Kanunlarında Yer Alan Süreler,* Ankara, 2010.
Güzel, A.,*95 Soru ve Cevapta İşsizlik Sigortası,*İstanbul, 2001.
Hacıoğlu, A., *Türk Sosyal Sigortalar Hukukunda Yersiz Ödemelerin Geri Alınması,* İstanbul, 2017.
Kandemir, M., *İş Hukuku ve Sosyal Güvenlik Hukuku Açısından Tele Çalışma,* İstanbul, 2011.
Karakaş, İ., *İş kazası ve Meslek Hastalığıİhtilafları ve Çözüm Yolları,* Ankara, 2012.
Karakaş, İ. *Uygulamada Meslek Hastalığı Davaları ve Tazminat Davaları Güncel Yargı Kararları Form Belge ve Dilekçe Örnekleriyle,* Ankara, 2012.
Karakaş, İ., *SGK İş Kazası Uygulamaları ve İş Kazası Davaları,* Ankara, 2011.

Kılıçoğlu, M., *Sosyal Güvenlik Hukukunda Borçlanma, İçtihatlı- Açıklamalı,* Ankara, 2002.
Mutlay, F.B., *Sosyal Sigorta Yardımlarına Hak Kazanma Koşulları ve Eşitlik İlkesi,* İstanbul 2014.
Olgaç C./M. Bulut, *1001 Soruda Sosyal Güvenlik Uygulamaları Son Değişikliklerle,* Ankara, 2012.
Olgaç C./M. Bulut, Tunçay, S., *Kısa Vadeli Sigorta Kolları Uygulamaları,* Ankara, 2011.
Orhan, C., *Türk Vatandaşlarının Yurt Dışında Geçen Sürelerinin Borçlanılması ve Türkiye'deki Emeklilik Hakları,* Ankara, 2007.
Bigat, Ş. G., *Beden Gücünün Azalmasından Kaynaklanan Tespit Davaları,* İstanbul, 2008.
Özdemir, C.S., *Sosyal Güvenlik Reformu,* Ankara, 2008.
Özdemir, D., *Bağ- Kur Sigortalılığı,* Ankara, 2001.
Özveri, M., *Yargı Kararları Işığında 506 Sayılı Yasa ve Sosyal Güvenlik,* İzmit, 2000.
Pınar, İ., Çalışkan, Ö., *Genel Sağlık Sigortası Sağlık ve Tedavi Yardımı,* Ankara, 2010.
Polat, G., *Yaşlılıkta Gelir Güvencesi,* İstanbul, 2011.
Savaş Kutsal, F. B., *Türk Sosyal Sigortalar Hukukunun Temel İlkeleri,* İstanbul, 2016.
Sözer, A.N., *Türkiye'de Sosyal Hukuk.* 2. ed., İzmir, 1998.
Sözer, A.N., *Sosyal Sigorta İlişkisi,* İzmir, 1991.
Şimşek, N., *SSK ve BAĞ-KUR'da Emeklilik En Son Değişiklikler ve Tüm Yönleriyle Açıklama, Yorum ve Örneklerle,* Ankara, 2012.
Topçu, U., *Hizmet Tespit Davaları Bilirkişi Raporları ve Yargıtay Kararları Işığında,* Ankara, 2012.
Uğur, S., *Sosyal Güvenlik Sistemlerinde Özel Emeklilik Programlarının Yeri ve Gelişimi,* Ankara, 2004.
Ünal, C., *Özürlülerin Sosyal Güvenlik Hakları,* İstanbul, 2012.
Ünan, S./A. Karayazgan, *Bireysel Emeklilik Hukuku,* İstanbul, 2009.
Yüksel, Ş., *İş Kazaları ve Meslek Hastalıkları,* İstanbul, 1985.

Periodicals

Çalışma ve Toplum, Ekonomi ve Hukuk Dergisi, Birleşik-Metal İş Yayını.
Çimento İşveren, Çimento Müstahsilleri İşverenleri Sendikası Yayını.
İş Hukuku Dergisi.
Legal İş Hukuku ve Sosyal Güvenlik Hukuku Dergisi (Legal- İSGHD).
Mercek, Türkiye Metal Sanayicileri Sendikası Yayını.
Sicil, Türkiye Metal Sanayicileri Sendikası Yayını.
Sosyal Güvenlik Dünyası Dergisi.
Kamu- İş, İş Hukuku ve İktisat Dergisi.
TİSK Akademi, Türkiye İşveren Sendikaları Yayını.
Tühis, İş Hukuku ve İktisat Dergisi.
Yaklaşım, Aylık Dergi.
Yargıtay Kararları Dergisi.

Selected Bibliography

Index

The numbers here refer to paragraph number.

Index

Made in the USA
Monee, IL
18 October 2026

66041404R10138